Beyond
the Beltway

THE AMERICAN ASSEMBLY was established by Dwight D. Eisenhower at Columbia University in 1950. Each year it holds at least two nonpartisan meetings that give rise to authoritative books that illuminate issues of United States policy.

An affiliate of Columbia, the Assembly is a national, educational institution incorporated in the state of New York.

The Assembly seeks to provide information, stimulate discussion, and evoke independent conclusions on matters of vital public interest.

CONTRIBUTORS

DANIEL F. BURTON, JR., Council on Competitiveness

I.M. DESTLER, University of Maryland

DAVID GERGEN, White House, Office of the President

JOHN IMMERWAHR, Villanova University

B.R. INMAN

ARNOLD KANTER, RAND Corporation

CATHERINE MCARDLE KELLEHER, The Brookings
Institution

DONALD F. MCHENRY, Georgetown University

NORMAN J. ORNSTEIN, American Enterprise Institute

WILLIAM A. REINSCH, Office of Senator Jay
Rockefeller

THOMAS B. STOEL, JR.

CYRUS R. VANCE

ERNEST J. WILSON III, National Security Council

DANIEL YANKELOVICH, DYG, Inc.

THE AMERICAN ASSEMBLY

Columbia University

Beyond the Beltway

Engaging the Public in U.S. Foreign Policy

DANIEL YANKELOVICH
and
I. M. DESTLER
Editors

W. W. NORTON & COMPANY
New York   London

First Edition

The text of this book is composed in Baskerville.
Composition and manufacturing by the Haddon Craftsmen, Inc.

Library of Congress Cataloging-in-Publication Data
Beyond the beltway : engaging the public in U.S. foreign policy /
Daniel Yankelovich and I.M. Destler, editors ; the American
Assembly, Columbia University.
p. cm.
Papers from the proceedings of a conference.
1. United States--Foreign relations--1993- --Citizen
participation--Congresses. I. Yankelovich, Daniel. II. Destler,
I. M. III. American Assembly.
E885.B49 1994
327.73--dc20   93-45536

ISBN 0-393-03598-0
ISBN 0-393-96468-X (pbk)

W. W. Norton & Company, Inc., 500 Fifth Avenue, New York, N.Y. 10110
W. W. Norton & Company Ltd., 10 Coptic Street, London WC1A 1PU

1 2 3 4 5 6 7 8 9 0

Contents

Beyond
the Beltway

Preface

CYRUS R. VANCE

Americans face today a two-pronged challenge in foreign policy. Abroad, we must respond to a sharply different world, with the cold war behind us but ethnic conflict and economic competition on the rise. At home, we must work with an intensely skeptical public to build consensus about the substance of that response.

This book addresses the second of these challenges. It is an exploration of the domestic processes involved in shaping foreign

---

CYRUS R. VANCE has a record of distinguished public service. He served the Kennedy administration as general counsel to the Department of Defense and as secretary of the Army. Under President Johnson, he served as deputy secretary of defense and as the president's special emissary in Cyprus, Korea, and at the Paris Peace Conference on Vietnam. He served as secretary of state under President Carter and was recently the United Nations secretary general's personal envoy in the former Yugoslavia, Nagorno-Karabakh, and South Africa. Mr. Vance is a founder and strong supporter of the goals of the Russian-American Bankers Forum. He is a partner of Simpson Thacher & Bartlett, a law firm in New York City.

policy. In particular, it focuses on how to address an unanticipated consequence of the end of the cold war, the need for our foreign policy leadership to build a new relationship with the American public.

It is growing ever clearer that foreign policy leaders can no longer take for granted the existence of a powerful national consensus on what the goals and priorities of our policy should be. For two generations, policy makers had the luxury of counting on firm, stable public support for the goal of containing Soviet power and expansion and for committing enormous resources to this goal. Today that consensus has diminished along with the threat that it addressed. In its place, we find a growing gap between our leadership's traditional emphasis on the military-political-ideological aspects of our foreign policy and the public's desire that our government give other concerns, both economic and humanitarian, a much higher priority. We find also a public much less trustful of its leaders, and hence demanding a larger role in the policy process.

These new circumstances demand new approaches by our foreign policy leaders. Secretary of State Warren Christopher has rightly argued that American foreign policy initiatives cannot succeed without strong public support. But that support is no longer available on leaders' terms. There will be occasional crises that will temporarily unite citizens behind their president, but for most issues the consensus-building process will necessarily evolve from a two-way dialogue. This American Assembly volume sets forth the problem and discusses how Americans can usefully respond.

Secretary Christopher has named four criteria for important foreign policy initiatives. The fourth criterion is that the policy enjoy strong public support. This volume is dedicated to clarifying how this objective can be met under radically new post–cold war conditions.

Preamble

DANIEL A. SHARP
President, The American Assembly

In 1987 The American Assembly initiated a series of Assemblies on the central theme of "U.S. Global Interests in the 1990s" in an effort to identify a long-term vision for United States international policy through the end of this decade. This sixth and final volume in the series focuses on the domestic process: *how* U.S. foreign policy is being formulated and ought to be formulated, *who* the new key players in this new process and environment are or ought to be, and *what* the new domestic and international forces are that will and or should influence that foreign policy. Given the end of the cold war and competing domestic pressures—economic, racial, ethnic, religious, political, and the impact of the media—it considers in particular the challenge of how to engage the public and mobilize a domestic constituency.

There is every indication of a new dynamic at work, one that redefines the relative roles of the public and leadership in the formulation of foreign policy, with the public assuming a larger role than some leaders may be comfortable with. In the years after World War II, international issues were the province of a small number of specialists and leaders, the so-called foreign policy establishment. But with the end of the cold war, the rise of economic and environmental concerns, and rising distrust of governmental institutions, genuine public participation in the setting of policy is becoming both a growing reality and an increasing necessity.

The Series

The International Series was designed to enable a significant number of leaders from the United States and around the world to make considered recommendations concerning the appropriate role for the United States as it moves from hegemonic power to a new role as one of several major powers. Throughout its development, this series has been guided by a distinguished steering committee of leading experts on each aspect of this theme. Its members are listed in an appendix to this book.

The first Assembly in this series was convened at Arden House, Harriman, New York, from November 17–20, 1988. Participants discussed overall U.S. international interests in the context of a global system that was changing substantially. Edward K. Hamilton edited the book of background papers, *America's Global Interests: A New Agenda*, which was published by W.W. Norton & Company, as were all books in this series.

"Managing the Global Economy," the second Assembly in this series, was held at Arden House from April 20–23, 1989. Senator William Brock and Robert D. Hormats were our coeditors and directors. Their book is entitled *The Global Economy: America's Role in the Decade Ahead*. C-SPAN broadcast the entire Assembly nationwide four times. In addition, we cosponsored two international regional meetings on this topic, in Tokyo (with The Japan Center on International Exchange) and in Brussels (with the European Community and Center for European Policy Studies).

The third Assembly in this series, "Preserving the Global Environment," was held at Arden House from April 19–22, 1990. It was jointly sponsored with the World Resources Institute, whose vice president, Jessica Tuchman Mathews, served as director and editor of *Preserving the Global Environment: The Challenge of Shared Leadership*. This program examined the increasing deterioration of the global environment, and the need for international action to deal with environmental problems. Participants from eighteen countries attended. An international regional Assembly, cosponsored by The Nature Conservancy and BIOMA, was convened March 7–10, 1991, in Caracas, Venezuela, with seventeen countries participating.

The fourth Assembly in the international series, "Rethinking America's Security," took place from May 30–June 2, 1991, at Arden House. The Assembly and the Council on Foreign Relations cosponsored this meeting, which examined comprehensively the global security issues in the 1990s, with particular emphasis on collective security, the lessons to be learned from the conflict in the Gulf, and the changed meaning of national security. Graham Allison and Gregory F. Treverton were codirectors and coeditors of the book, *Rethinking America's Security: Beyond Cold War to New World Order.*

The fifth Assembly, "After the Soviet Union," was held at Arden House from April 23–26, 1992, codirected by Professors Robert Legvold and Gregory F. Treverton. The volume of background readings, *After the Soviet Union: From Empire to Nations,* was coedited by Timothy Colton and Robert Legvold. It examined the impact of the unanticipated end of the Soviet Union. This program was added to the series by the steering committee because of the dramatic impact on U.S. policy of the collapse of communism.

This Sixth Volume in the Series

At the beginning, we designed Assemblies to focus on the major areas of foreign policy. In later steering committee meetings several of our advisers urged that we not stop with recommending policy but that we confront the domestic constraints on formulating that policy. Admiral Bobby Inman, our lead trustee for this program, properly described that approach as too negative and suggested that we consider instead the more positive challenge of how to mobilize a domestic constituency in support of foreign policy. Ultimately, we refocused this book and program to emphasize a much earlier and more significant stage in policy formulation, namely, how to engage the public in the formulation of foreign policy, and, only subsequently, how to mobilize a domestic constituency in support of that policy. This requires that we identify the emerging new players and forces in the United States on foreign policy and try to disaggregate "the public" into its newly dynamic components.

We were delighted to be able to engage two nationally known authorities as codirectors and coeditors: Daniel Yankelovich, chairman, DYG, Inc., and president, Public Agenda Foundation, with which we collaborated in this program, and one of this country's most prominent and thoughtful experts on public opinion and foreign policy; and I.M. (Mac) Destler, director, Center for International and Security Studies, School of Public Affairs, University of Maryland, and a leading expert on the domestic politics of foreign policy.

As Secretary of State Warren Christopher reminded us in his January 13, 1993, confirmation testimony:

> It's not enough . . . to articulate a new strategy. We must justify it to the American people. Today, foreign policy makers cannot afford to ignore the public or there is a real danger that then the public will ignore foreign policy. . . . We need to show that in this new era, foreign policy is no longer foreign. . . . I've long thought the State Department needs an American desk and this administration will have one, and I'll be sitting right behind it.

By stressing both policy's changing substance and the need for two-way dialogue, we believe that we can provide an important service for the Clinton administration. It faces a unique challenge: pursuing its commitment to domestic priorities while responding to urgent world problems, at a time when the domestic/foreign distinction has lost much of its meaning. We hope that the findings of this Assembly and the chapters in this book will be helpful not only to the government, but also to other key individuals and organizations in the United States whose voices need to be heard before foreign policy is determined and implemented.

We particularly wish to thank the Coca-Cola Foundation for its initial grant that assured the publication of this book, and we also gratefully acknowledge the support of the following other organizations that helped to fund this book and its related activities:

Major Funder
    The Ford Foundation
Funders
    Carnegie Corporation of New York
    ENI
    The William & Flora Hewlett Foundation
    Charles Stewart Mott Foundation
Supporters
    Xerox Corporation
    Bank of America
    U.S. West
    Volvo North America Corporation

These organizations, as well as The American Assembly, take no position on issues discussed in this volume.

Introduction and Overview

I. M. DESTLER AND
DANIEL YANKELOVICH

T his book develops a two-part thesis. First, American foreign policy is shifting—and will continue to shift—from the predominantly political-military focus of the cold war decades to a much greater emphasis on the nation's economic interests. Voters now favor such a shift. So do the nation's economic leaders as they struggle to overcome the damage done by lagging competitiveness to American living standards and world influence.

The second and closely related shift is toward greater public engagement in the foreign policy process. In the years after World War II, international issues were the province of a small number of specialists and leaders, the so-called foreign policy establishment. But after the Vietnam War, and especially after the cold war, the public has insisted upon having a greater say. Widespread mistrust of government, Congress, and the press reinforces this demand. While leaders would prefer to formulate policy without the public's help, they recognize that lack of public support can create policy gridlock, so they have begun to reconcile themselves to the new reality of greater public involvement.

The two shifts are independent, yet mutually reinforcing. During the cold war, national security decisions could be made and carried out by a handful of top leaders; economic decisions involve many other players: not only the Congress, but also multinational corporations, trade unions, financial institutions, and average Americans in their various roles as workers, savers, and voters. So the shift in policy substance broadens public engagement. This engagement, in turn, reinforces economic goals, since these are what the public cares most about.

Both these shifts are also linked to the administration in Washington. President Clinton was elected *both* for his priority to the economy and for his populist promise to connect better with average Americans. Yet if he were to look for in-print guidance of how he might jointly pursue these two goals, he would find the pickings very thin. For every thousand books and articles on U.S. international policies, there are barely ten or twenty that give sustained attention to the domestic political dimensions of these policies. Of these, only a handful give serious treatment to how the public can become engaged so the nation can develop policies that command broad understanding and support.

This book is an effort toward that end. It is the sixth and last in The American Assembly's International Series, aimed at broad reconsideration of U.S. foreign policy in the new global environment. Unlike the other volumes, which looked outward, this one looks primarily inward—at politics, processes, interests, and institutions within our borders. It builds on many of the conclusions of the earlier Assembly books, particularly their overriding judgment that to sustain political and economic leadership in the world, "the most urgent challenge for America is to get its own house in order."[1] The authors do not, however, define the domestic policymaking problem as simply winning popular support for expert prescriptions. Rather, the public's engagement will, in most cases, reshape the substance of what leaders propose and ultimately implement.

Neither of the elements we stress is new. From the earliest days of the republic, our foreign policy has had an economic component, and the United States led the postwar world in developing international rules and institutions for trade and finance. And public support for policy—if not deep public involvement—was recognized as essential by American leaders from Abraham Lincoln onward.

Nor does either imperative apply in all cases. Even in the 1990s there continue to be occasions when presidents engage the nation in noneconomic enterprises overseas without serious prior dialogue with the public. In his waning months in office, George Bush sent American forces to Somalia to enforce order and allow humanitarian relief. Under a modest United Nations umbrella, this move cast the United States squarely in the role of world police officer—a role the public vehemently rejects in the abstract. Yet the humanitarian action in Somalia won strong popular support.

Security issues cannot be avoided, as evidenced by President Clinton's troubles over Bosnia, which his secretary of state labeled "the problem from Hell." Yet at the same time, the elimination of the Soviet threat has accelerated a shift toward economic priorities that is altering our relations with our allies/competitors in the European Community and Japan, with the former Soviet empire, and with the world at large. The North American Free Trade Agreement (NAFTA) has become a first-order domestic issue, with Ross Perot's campaign against it rubbing the raw nerves of Americans worried about jobs flying south of the border.

The nation and the Clinton administration are in the early stages of a complex sorting-out process. There is the pull of continuity—to maintain a strong military and accept the burden of responsibility as the world's only superpower. But the superpower feels thin of wallet: the United States provided the leadership and firepower to expel Saddam Hussein from Kuwait, but needed others to pay for it. There is a new determination to strengthen economic competitiveness and deploy the tools of foreign policy to this end. But as a counterbalance, Americans also show growing concern about the global environment, and strong interest in the spread of democracy and human rights. All these shifts in substance are complicating the problem of setting priorities for the nation's foreign policy.

We are caught in a transition, and historical change is always murky for those living through it. Ambiguities and contradictions abound. Old ways persist as new ways are struggling to emerge; inertia and muddling through alternate with ad hoc lurching from issue to issue. The foreign policy debate is bound to be confusing as advocates of competing priorities rush to fill the vacuum left by the end of the cold war. But if durable new policies are to emerge, the American public must work its way through the current complexity and confusion: sorting out the pros and cons, addressing its own resistances and value conflicts, recognizing the necessity of hard choices, and coming to public judgment on priorities. Only this can give leaders a foundation to pursue policies that can be sustained.

The first two chapters of this volume, authored by the coeditors, develop the two central themes of this book. I. M. Destler examines the implications of the shift toward economics as the central U.S. international priority. He shows how and why serious pursuit of President Clinton's "domestic" economic goals spills over into American foreign policy and the process of making it. He then examines broader issues: the inherent divisiveness of economic issues, and the risk that U.S. leaders might seek to increase unity at home by trumpeting economic conflict abroad. He concludes by exploring whether consensus might be built around the more complicated, but ultimately more rewarding notion of international economic competition as a positive-sum, "win-win" game.

Daniel Yankelovich and John Immerwahr follow with their explanation of why American leaders need to develop a new strategy of public engagement. The widespread notion of "educating" the public or "selling" prepackaged policy solutions needs to be replaced, on important issues, with an approach that involves the public in the hard process of policy choice. To this end, they set forth "rules" and "stages" of public engagement aimed at replacing the old top-down communication model with effective two-way dialogue. Most day-to-day foreign policy issues will continue to be addressed outside of the public spotlight. But on critical issues whose impact on the public is sharp, a new deliberative form of leadership is needed.

The chapters that follow all focus on the politics and processes of foreign policy making within the United States, but they do so from a variety of angles. In an essay written just before his designation as counselor to President Clinton, David Gergen surveys the altered political environment faced by the chief executive: a balky Congress, an uncertain public, a wandering television eye. Today, leading on foreign policy means speaking effectively to multiple and competing audiences, addressing political-military issues in the absence of cold war consensus, and responding to growing links between the domestic and the global economy. Donald McHenry, whose distinguished public career includes service as U.S. ambassador to the United Nations, explores whether multilateralism can strengthen our policy's domestic base. Surveys indicate a public preference for foreign undertakings with UN sanction and other nations sharing the burden, he notes, but consensus will still be difficult to attain.

Chapters 5 and 6 examine governmental institutions in the light of the new substantive priorities and public engagement needs. Norman J. Ornstein, one of the nation's foremost authorities on American politics, draws upon his ongoing project on renewing Congress to explore how that much-maligned institution might play its *deliberative* role more effectively. His proposals range from reducing the proliferation of subcommittees to encouraging chamber-wide debates and committee roundtables, so that Congress is driven less by the short-term demands of 535 prima donnas and more by the need to strengthen the institution as a whole. Arnold Kanter then treats how the executive branch is coping with what he labels the "paradoxes of the post–cold war world." A foreign policy scholar-practitioner who served recently as under secretary of state for political affairs, Kanter describes institutional adaptation under Presidents Bush and Clinton and highlights a key dilemma: organizational innovations like President Clinton's National Economic Council, which integrate foreign and domestic policy within a particular substantive sphere, tend to have a *dis*integrating impact on overall foreign policy.

In Chapter 7, Ernest J. Wilson shifts the focus to changes within American society. Addressing what he labels "double diversity," Wilson examines how the upsurge of ethnic pluralism and multiculturalism at home intersects with the rising global impact of non-Western societies and cultures and the post–cold war outburst of ethnic conflicts. A University of Maryland scholar currently serving on the staff of the National Security Council, Wilson sharpens his inevitably speculative analysis by presenting utopian and dystopian views of double diversity's economic, political, and cultural effects on America's future.

The book's final four chapters address broad but discrete issue areas, selected for their intrinsic importance, but also because they are representative of the old and new faces of U.S. international engagement. Authors were asked to examine their particular topics with particular attention to:

Public attitudes—utilizing the Public Agenda Foundation's research and findings.

Conflicts within government—analyzing competition for jurisdiction and influence between and within executive agencies and congressional committees, and giving particular emphasis where appropriate to the roles of *state and local governments*.

Nongovernmental institutions—addressing the increased complexity of the policy process, involving political parties, media, business, labor, etc.

The impact of ideology—whether in the form of polarization (as in the cold war arms control debate) or widely shared views that hamper new approaches (like business attitudes toward government and vice versa).

Admiral B. R. Inman and Daniel F. Burton, Jr., apply their formidable experience and expertise in a lucid exploration of policy making and public attitudes affecting American competitiveness. (Inman has served government as a senior executive in three intelligence agencies, and has led two corporate high-technology enterprises; Burton is president of the private Council on Competitiveness.) After tracing the roots of the "adversarial tradition" between government and business, they ask whether changes in interests and public attitudes might form the basis for a new government-industry compact aimed at buttressing the global position of U.S. firms and workers. William A. Reinsch, one of the most respected congressional assistants on trade policy, looks at the issue many view as a key to U.S. competitiveness: the complex and fractious U.S. relationship with Japan. He examines both the ambivalence of public attitudes and the divergent perspectives within the policy community. He then explores the elements of a positive-sum strategy that might win broad support.

Our final two chapters serve to contrast "old" and "new" international issues. Catherine M. Kelleher, a Brookings Institution scholar and international authority on U.S.–European issues, analyzes policy making on the use of force. She begins with a look at how changing circumstances have reshaped old relationships: between president and Congress, and between civilian leaders and the Joint Chiefs of Staff. She then examines polling data about a broad range of issues, from the use of force generally to issues such as Bosnia and the role of gays in the military. She finds that while confidence in the military has risen, Americans remain reluctant supporters of the use of force. They are pragmatic in reviewing both past history and current prospects to judge specific cases. But they remain reactors to presidential proposals rather than initiators of action themselves. National security thus contrasts sharply with environmental policy, according to the author of the book's final chapter, Thomas B. Stoel, Jr., an attorney and consultant who previously directed the international program of the Natural Resources Defense Council. In the environmental sphere, it was citizen groups who put issues on the government agenda, focusing first on domestic matters like clean air and clean water but then broadening their attention to the ozone layer and global warming. Stoel traces how early consensus gave way to conflict as the antiregulation administration of Ronald Reagan came to power, and as environmental goals began being seen as threats to jobs and economic growth.

Each author has his or her particular emphases; none agrees with the editors in every respect, nor with one another. But together they supply powerful evidence of how and why Americans, in coping with a new world, must devise new means of policy making here at home. Central to these new means must be a better way of engaging citizens in two-way dialogue.

Never has this proposition been clearer than at this writing in mid-1993, as a new administration seeks to deliver on its promise of economic restructuring, and its promise to respond to a public fed up with top-down, elitist approaches on issues that affect people so deeply.

Notes

1 Allison and Treverton (1992), p. 446.

1

Foreign Policy Making
with the Economy
at Center Stage

I. M. DESTLER

I t seems so long ago, but it was in the fall of 1991 that George
Bush—the quintessential foreign policy president—planned an
old-style state visit to the Far East. In successive stops in the capi-
tals of long-standing allies, he would respond to regional complaints about "neglect of Asia" by reaffirming America's security
ties and its ongoing leadership role. The climax of the tour would
come in Tokyo, where Bush was to remain until the day before

I.M. "Mac" DESTLER is professor at the School of Public Affairs, University of Maryland, where he directs the Center for International and
Security Studies and the Maryland Seminar on U.S. Foreign Policy Making. Over the past twenty years, Professor Destler has published nine
books and scores of articles and papers on the interplay between U.S.
domestic politics and foreign policy making, including *Presidents, Bureau-
crats, and Foreign Policy, Managing An Alliance: The Politics of U.S.–Japanese
Relations* (coauthored), *Our Own Worst Enemy: The Unmaking of American
Foreign Policy* (coauthored), and the prize-winning *American Trade Politics.*
His previous positions include senior fellow at the Institute for International Economics, director of the Project on Executive-Congressional
Relations in Foreign Policy at the Carnegie Endowment for International
Peace, and consultant on government organization to the Office of Man-
agement and Budget and the Department of State.

Pearl Harbor's fiftieth anniversary. He would give a reassuring, forward-looking speech about how far the relationship had come since that grim event. Then, having lanced the boil of rising Japanese anxiety, he would fly to Honolulu for the ceremonies of December 7th.

The plan was very much in the mold of traditional presidential foreign policy leadership. East Asians had been unhappy when the Gulf War forced abandonment of plans for an earlier visit; the Japanese media were in a feeding frenzy, hyping national concern about what Americans might say and do once they re-remembered Pearl Harbor. So Bush would recoup with a grand gesture, allaying Japanese concerns, and stressing what presidents always stressed during state visits—the ongoing American commitment to international security.

But fate intervened, in the curious form of a political setback in the state of Pennsylvania. A tragic plane crash had taken the life of the incumbent senator, John Heinz, forcing a special election in November. The Republicans had a natural candidate, Attorney General (and former governor) Richard Thornburgh. The Democrats had difficulty fielding an opponent, finally settling on Harris Wofford, a state party official, former college president, and Kennedy-era civil rights activist. Wofford began over forty points behind in the polls. He won by more than ten, riding a wave of public frustration over lingering recession with the slogan, "It's time to take care of our own." Turning Bush's foreign triumphs into domestic liabilities, his campaign aides hawked T-shirts featuring "The George Bush Tour," in which the president would take people "anywhere but the USA."

Under attack for his foreign travels, the president panicked by calling off the East Asia trip. Before November 1991 was out, it had been rescheduled and recast as an economic mission: the goal now would be "jobs, jobs, jobs," and to underscore the point the president would be joined in Tokyo by twenty-one American business leaders. The trip was hastily planned and proved a political disaster, though some useful trade concessions were extracted from the put-upon but concerned Japanese. Bush's political slide continued, ending in his decisive election loss to Arkansas Governor Bill Clinton.

For the new president, economic policy was not just an election year act; it was central to what he wanted to accomplish. By mid-April 1993, his secretaries of state and the treasury were both in Tokyo underscoring the primacy of economic issues. Later that same week, Clinton himself was urging upon Prime Minister Kiichi Miyazawa the need for "the rebalancing of our relationship," through "an elevated attention to our economic relations," at their joint Washington press conference later that month.

Two incidents do not themselves constitute a decisive turnabout in presidential foreign policy priorities, and in the intervening period, the United States did not lack foreign policy engagements outside of the economic sphere. In his final months, Bush concluded an epochal arms reduction agreement with Russia, sent American troops on a humanitarian relief mission to Somalia, and bombed Iraq in support of United Nations resolutions. In his initial months, Clinton was active in supporting Boris Yeltsin in Russia, trying to bring democracy to Haiti, and wrestling with whether to engage American military force in Bosnia.

Yet President Clinton knew he would stand or fall with the success of his economic plan, and in mid-1993 he was struggling to keep it on center stage and maintain its public support. The end of the cold war had made it *possible* for an American president to extend the economic priority to our foreign relations; cumulative problems of debt, low productivity, and lagging competitiveness made it *important* for him to do so. There seemed every chance that he would. Moreover, public expectations were clearly pushing in that direction.

The end of the cold war thus meant changes not just in the *substance* of American foreign policy, but in the *politics* that shape it and in the *processes* by which it is made. This chapter explores one central feature of these changes, the apparent movement of economic issues to center stage. One must say "apparent" because the shift is recent, only partly realized, and plausibly subject to reversal. Moreover, buttressing American competitiveness is not the only contender for the role of central, defining, post–cold war U.S. goal. Millions of environmentalists will insist that urgent threats to our planet require that economic and geopolitical concerns be subordinated to campaigns like an all-out effort to reverse projected global warming. It is highly likely, in fact, that no single

focus will dominate U.S. international relations as did the U.S.–
Soviet rivalry of 1947–89.

This chapter, then, is inevitably exploratory rather than conclu-
sive. But if—as does seem likely—U.S. foreign relations gives top
priority to U.S. economic interests, it is useful first to explore how
different this will be from past patterns of postwar policy making,
when international economic policy was first subordinated to, and
then separated from, the dominant national security focus. After
suggesting that we may be entering a new "Phase Three" in the
relationship of economic issues to overall U.S. foreign policy, we
will then move to treatment of the Clinton program, considering
the domestic economic weaknesses that (by broad consensus) it is
designed to meet, and why every proposed remedy has a critical
international dimension. From there we will move to broader
questions of policy making, politics, and consensus building that
beset economic policy making in a fractious but interdependent
world.

How *would* priority to economic issues represent a change in
U.S. foreign policy making? There have been times in the past, of
course, when the United States has given priority to its economic
interests: these included, notably, the twenty years between the
two world wars. But for the last half-century, economic issues have
played a distinctly subordinate role.

Postwar Phase One:
Security Policy Dominant,
Economy Insulated

From the mid-forties through the late sixties, the United States
conducted a very active international economic policy. Washington led in creation of major international institutions and regimes:
the International Monetary Fund (IMF) to help maintain free exchange rates, the World Bank to support reconstruction and development, and the General Agreement on Tariffs and Trade
(GATT) to reduce national barriers to imports. Successive administrations provided assistance and incentives to help make
other nations strong economic players within these regimes, and in
the broader liberal order that they reinforced. In so doing, they

laid the foundation for the greatest period of prosperity and growth the world has ever known.

During these same years, however, the cold war came to dominate the international stage, and foreign economic policy was quickly subordinated to the demands of that ongoing struggle. Alliances with Europe and Japan were reinforced by asymmetrical trade concessions. Trade policy, the most politically sensitive of international issues, was led by the most politically insensitive of executive agencies, the Department of State. Foreign aid—controlled also by State and associated agencies—was a primary instrument for buttressing the free world coalition. Domestic interests affected the details of certain programs: food aid was particularly popular, for example, since it funded a significant share of U.S. grain exports. But the broad priorities reflected security policy goals.

As other nations recovered, this priority came to be challenged. In 1962 Congress insisted on taking from the State Department the responsibility for the forthcoming Kennedy Round of multilateral trade talks, though Foggy Bottom retained the lead role in most other international commercial negotiations. By decade's end, the United States was losing its trade surplus and its economy was running below capacity, its burdens exacerbated by the Bretton Woods requirement that Washington not devalue its currency. Finally, in August 1971 the United States broke free from this constraint, abandoning support of the dollar and thereafter of the fixed exchange rate system.

These moves responded to the inevitable decline of the U.S. economic position relative to Europe and Japan. They also reflected an increased exposure to the international economy. In the first twenty postwar years, Americans could and did treat their economy as self-contained. The high priority they gave to domestic prosperity did not much intrude on their foreign relations. Between 1950 and 1970, however, U.S. exports and imports each rose from 6 percent to 9 percent of total goods production. They would shoot up to around 20 percent by 1980. In 1973 sharp international inflation—first in food prices, then in oil prices—underscored how conditions in the United States had become hostage to world market developments.[1]

Phase Two:
Security and Economic Policy,
Separate but Unequal

This rise of economic issues twenty years ago did not bring a reversal of U.S. international priorities. The cold war did thaw in 1972-74, but tensions rose thereafter, and security issues continued to rank at the top of America's global agenda. This meant that when trade-offs reached the president, the security side typically won. As William Hyland has noted, with only modest exaggeration, during the cold war period "in almost every instance where there was a clash in priorities between economic policy and national security, the latter prevailed."[2] But the advocates of economic concerns were able to limit the number of occasions when their issues were "traded away" by developing parallel institutions and processes that provided insulation from the national security process. Increasingly, foreign economic issues were addressed separately, by a distinct set of institutions. U.S. foreign policy making in the seventies and eighties featured two semi-autonomous subgovernments, a *security complex* and an *economic complex.*

The security complex was centered in the Department of State and in the institutions inaugurated by the National Security Act of 1947—the Department of Defense, the Central Intelligence Agency (CIA), and the National Security Council (NSC) for overall coordination. In its first two decades foreign economic policy leadership was also typically centered there, in the hands of strong line officials like Under Secretary of State Douglas Dillon in the late Eisenhower administration, or NSC staff aides like Carl Kaysen and Francis Bator, who each served as deputy national security assistant under Presidents Kennedy and Johnson.

From Henry Kissinger onward, however, this all changed. The NSC staff gave less priority to economics: in the seventies and eighties, the number two NSC official was typically a general or an admiral. In the Reagan-Bush period, in fact, the number one NSC official was a career military officer more often than not.

Over this same period, foreign economic issues came to be managed by a separate set of institutions. The Office of the United States Trade Representative (USTR) extended its reach to cover the broad range of commercial negotiations, bilateral as well as multilateral, with Congress regularly acting to buttress its power and broaden its domain. The Department of the Treasury, working with the Federal Reserve Board, solidified its dominance over questions of international finance and exchange rates. Although fiscal and monetary policy increasingly spilled over into the international realm, they were still handled by the "domestic" institutions that had reigned since the Employment Act of 1946: the Treasury, the Office of Management and Budget, the President's Council of Economic Advisers, and the independent Federal Reserve Board.

Substantively, this separation made it possible to accommodate demands for "aggressive unilateralism" in trade policy and to link international economic policy more closely to domestic interests and priorities. But the free market convictions of most senior policy players acted as a brake on protectionist actions. While trade disputes grew sharper and more frequent with Japan, the European Community, and the newly industrializing countries of East Asia, ongoing security ties kept them from getting out of hand.

This economic complex was less centralized than the security complex. When international economic policy was coordinated, however, this was generally done not through the NSC but through parallel institutions like President Ford's Economic Policy Board, and above all by strong secretaries of the treasury like John Connally, George Shultz, and James Baker.

One key reason why international economic policy making was less centralized was that presidents typically played only a limited role. Ronald Reagan stressed his *domestic* economic program, but on trade and money matters he and his successor tended to ratify the priorities of their subordinates rather than exercise independent influence. Bush paid the price for such neglect when he suddenly took the initiative in transforming his Japan trip—he lacked any real feel for the economic and political nuances of U.S.–Japan trade issues, and he lacked close, day-to-day working relationships with subordinates like USTR Carla Hills who did have that feel. His resulting ineptness contrasted sharply with the cool professionalism he repeatedly exhibited in security policy.

Into Phase Three:
Economics as First among Equals?

During the Bush administration, the foreign enemy self-destructed—first the Warsaw Pact, then the Soviet Union itself. By 1990 and 1991 a broad range of security policy experts was arguing for a shift of priorities to the home front: Leslie H. Gelb of the *New York Times*, William Hyland of *Foreign Affairs*, and Steven Rosenfeld of the *Washington Post*. When The American Assembly brought foreign policy experts together in a 1992 study entitled *Rethinking America's Security*, they concluded that "the most urgent challenge for America is to get its own house in order."[3] A national commission sponsored by the Carnegie Endowment for International Peace declared later that same year that "America's first foreign policy priority is to strengthen our domestic economic performance."[4]

These voices joined others who had been calling for a shift in priorities long before the Communist collapse. Historian Paul Kennedy struck a national nerve with his warnings about "imperial overstretch" and consequent economic decline, and ex-official Clyde Prestowitz was arguing that it had already happened.[5] By campaign 1992 the erosion of U.S. economic strength had become *the* issue, turning Bush's international credits into debits. Though Clinton's policy interests were wide ranging, his campaign was built around "THE ECONOMY, STUPID," as highlighted by that famous sign hanging in his campaign headquarters. Charging his opponent with the worst presidential economic record since Herbert Hoover,[6] the Arkansas governor stressed both the current economic slump and the longer-term problem of sluggish growth in productivity and incomes. Bush had no choice but to accept the new priority, so he announced in the first 1992 presidential debate that he would invite James Baker to "do in domestic affairs what you've done in foreign affairs," to serve as "the economic coordinator."[7] Meanwhile, independent candidate Ross Perot was making the budget deficit his single, overriding issue.

When the votes were in, the result was a sharp repudiation of George Bush, and a clear signal of the primacy of the economy. More than 62 percent of the public cast their votes for economic change: 43 percent for Clinton, 19 percent for Perot. Clinton had a clear challenge if not exactly an overwhelming mandate. The fate of his presidency would ride on whether he could get the economy growing again, and renew Americans' hope in a brighter future.

It was clear by then, of course, that the end of the cold war had not brought peace and tranquility to the world: there was brutal Serbian aggression in Bosnia, continued confrontation with Iraq, and a deep political-economic crisis in the Russian Federation. But the collapse of the Soviet Union had removed the overriding threat to which Clinton's predecessors had to give top priority. Economic issues were moving to the center of the foreign policy stage. The new president was highlighting, in his inaugural, the "profound and powerful" economic and technological forces that "are shaking and remaking our world," and raising "the urgent question of our time . . . whether we can make change our friend and not our enemy."

With the president himself engaged in the details of international economic issues, the policy process seems to be entering a new phase. During the transition, Clinton's first major set of appointments was his economic team, and when he presented them to the public he also announced creation of a new White House coordinating body, a National Economic Council (NEC) parallel to the National Security Council. At first glance, this appeared to reinforce the separation of economics from security—a council for each complex! But priorities had clearly shifted. It was the economic group with which the new president worked most closely in his opening weeks in office. Economic officials, like Deputy Secretary of the Treasury Robert Altman, were assigned the lead on crosscutting economics-security issues like U.S. relations with Japan. International economic policy aides—like former Senate Finance Committee official Robert Kyle—were given joint appointments to both the NEC and the NSC. In the administration's early months, the two staffs and their heads—Robert Rubin and Anthony Lake—seemed to be cooperating well on international economic issues. And the president himself was personally engaged on many of these issues.

Clinton's Economic Plan—
and Its International Spillover

The most important initiative of Clinton's early presidency was the economic program he presented in February 1993 to a joint session of Congress. It contained a bolder-than-expected attack on the federal budget deficit, a modest, short-run economic stimulus package, and a range of medium-term steps aimed at addressing longer-term U.S. economic and social problems.[8]

By conventional wisdom, this was essentially a domestic initiative. Its basic goals were to improve conditions within the United States: providing more and better jobs, raising middle class living standards, increasing both public and private investment, improving the quality of the U.S. workforce, distributing income more equitably. The measures to be taken, moreover, were mainly actions within the United States: cutting and shifting expenditures, and raising taxes. This was consistent with most diagnoses of the economic and competitiveness problems facing the United States, including those quoted above. By mainstream analyses, our problems are, for the most part, "made in USA," and the key remedies are all "home remedies."[9]

If one translated these problems into economists' language, the home emphasis remained. The key question over time is increasing output per worker—if the aim is to improve average economic welfare, productivity is, in Paul Krugman's words, "almost everything."[10] One way to improve it is through more investment; one way to bring that about is to reduce interest rates; one way to do that is to reduce public demand in the credit markets—that budget deficit again. Another way is to encourage greater private saving, so there would be more funds available for investors to borrow. Productivity can also be raised by upgrading the workforce, or by supporting research and development, particularly that aimed at applying new technologies to production processes. It might not be easy to build public consensus to put aside money for these purposes—taxes would have to be raised, and private consumption curbed. But that, too, seems to be mainly a problem of ourselves and our political system.

Yet on further examination, every one of these "domestic"

problems has a critical international dimension.

In the short run, recovery from the prolonged economic slump requires strong demand for goods and services. Since 20 percent of our goods production is exported, strong *foreign* demand will help, and weak foreign demand will hurt. Yet as Clinton entered office, the economies of our major trading partners—Europe, Japan, Canada—were much weaker than our own. This drives us to press them to stimulate *their* economies, as Clinton and Secretary of the Treasury Lloyd Bentsen have in fact done.

In the medium term, we will depend more than usual on foreign demand because we want our production to grow while we are shifting our own resources from consumption to saving and investment. This makes export markets particularly important—they must take up the slack, as we move to restore our economic balance and stop consuming more than we produce. Again, this makes us want others to stimulate their economies, to ease their import barriers, and to allow their currencies to appreciate against the dollar.

Over the long term, raising our rate of productivity growth will depend, in important part, on learning from Germany about workforce training, from Japan about agile manufacturing, and from both about adapting cutting-edge technologies to production processes. It is private firms that must do this, of course; for too long in the postwar period, U.S. companies acted on the assumption that they had little to learn from overseas practices. But they are much more likely to learn if they are exposed to foreign competition at home and abroad. This means not just open trade, but the opportunity for U.S. firms to invest in Japan and for Japanese to invest here. Again, a "domestic" goal quickly brings us in touch with the realities of global economic interdependence.

In some cases, progress on the home front will help us internationally. For reasons discussed above, reducing our budget deficit will bring down our trade deficit by striking at the overconsumption that is its root cause. Furthermore, bringing down our trade deficit will mean less trade conflict with countries abroad, and less pressure for protection at home.

In other cases, however, steps to strengthen our competitiveness may increase international friction. There is much debate about how directly and actively government should support particular industries, but there is broad support for some priority to high-technology producers, and Silicon Valley was prominent in Bill Clinton's electoral coalition. Steps in this direction, however, may provoke greater policy controversy with Japanese and German competitors who see their futures tied to the strength of these industries in their countries.

By conventional wisdom, we are likely to do best if we keep our markets open. Exposure to world-class competition is the best path toward strengthening firms' performance: witness the GM Saturn, the Ford Taurus, and the new Chrysler models, and the recent rebounding of the U.S. market share of Big Three automobiles generally. But competition is disruptive. It spurs protectionism. Increasingly it will come, moreover, from China and Mexico and South America and (if reform succeeds) Eastern Europe and Russia. American workers will continue to suffer losses in jobs and income—*unless* they can upgrade their skills.

Their plight is part of the broader "middle class squeeze" that was a telling Clinton campaign theme. Earlier in this century, the rising living standards of manufacturing workers was viewed by many liberals as *the* preeminent economic accomplishment of twentieth century America, Marxism vanquished by Fordism. The present-day plight of this group casts doubt on the durability of that accomplishment. It is hard for those afflicted not to see some connection between international trade and the loss of their jobs or stagnation in their wages. Ross Perot has actively made this connection, suggesting that congressional approval of the North American Free Trade Agreement (NAFTA) would bring U.S. wages down to Mexican levels (or at least halfway). Objectively, this is absurd—while individual jobs will doubtless be affected, the Mexican economy is simply too small to have that sort of overall impact on the United States. Yet the more frustrated middle class Americans are with their current conditions and future prospects, the more they will harken to such messages.

The Inherent Divisiveness
of Economic Issues

As these examples suggest, economic issues not only blend the foreign with the domestic, but they typically find Americans on both sides of them. There is a broad, shared stake in the strength and growth of the economy as a whole, just as there is in the security of the nation as a whole. But in our politics, economic issues are much more likely to be explicitly distributional. They have typically been more subject to partisan conflict. While free trade is generally thought to bring benefits to the nation as a whole, issues involving particular products pit domestic producers against import users, industries impacted by imports against those who profit from exports.

Nor is the struggle limited to economic interests. A revolutionary feature of the NAFTA debate is the major challenge presented by environmentalists. Some pose a fundamental objection: trade is bad, they say, because it promotes growth, which increases the consumption of the world's finite resources, or spews more carbon gases into the atmosphere. Others worry about NAFTA's concrete effects: free trade with Mexico may create pressure to lower U.S. environmental standards to Mexican levels, or it may prohibit the use of trade sanctions for environmental purposes (like barring imports of tuna caught with nets that kill dolphins). But whatever their specific stands, environmentalists have brought their important but complicating perspective to the already difficult business of trade negotiations.

Economic Nationalism?

One way to mute divisions at home is to sharpen them with nations abroad. Exploiting widespread anxiety about the relative economic decline of the United States, scholars and politicians alike find a ready market for military metaphors: even presidential candidate Paul Tsongas labeled his economic plan "A Call to Economic Arms."[11] Much congressional trade initiative in recent years has been built on the premise that the United States hasn't been getting a square deal: we are more open to imports than most others; foreign firms "dump" products in our markets; we need to support our lead industries for international economic battle, as Europeans and Asians are supporting theirs. The result has been a plethora of legislation requiring the executive branch to identify foreign barriers to our products and demand their unilateral removal, under threat of retaliation. Symbolic of such measures is "Super-301," a mandate that the U.S. trade representative single out and denounce countries for "number and pervasiveness" of their "acts, policies, or practices" that impede U.S. exports. This requirement expired in 1990, but candidate Clinton supported its renewal, and it strikes a strong responsive chord in the public.

Up to a point, such measures are tactically useful. Their careful use by the executive has led to some lowering of foreign trade barriers. This, in turn, has demonstrated U.S. negotiators' "toughness," increasing their credibility with Congress and private industry and making it easier for them to win approval of trade-expanding agreements.[12] But suppose that they became not just a tactical means to internationally liberal market ends, and not just a supplement to policies whose main goal was reciprocal, cooperative international agreements, but the dominant element of U.S. commercial policy. In an exceptionally broad and lucid analysis, Theodore H. Moran sets forth elements of a "sophisticated neo-mercantilism" the United States might end up pursuing:[13]

Trade: Selective managed trade in high-tech industries; unilateral dictation of standards for unfair trade and national security exceptions (broadly and intuitively defined);
Foreign Acquisitions: Sweeping discretionary screening of foreign acquisitions, with acquisitions blocked in national security cases . . .
Technology Development: Large programs; U.S. firms only eligible . . .
Transborder Corporate Alliances: Supervision and restriction . . .

With such an agenda, the United States would give priority to its relative economic position, and "eschew mutual gains when relative gains were available." Economic nationalists might welcome such a strategy, and it might serve as a rationale for sacrifice and suffering at home, at least for a while. But it could end up making all nations worse off than they would be under a strategy that stressed multilateral cooperation and the encouragement of transnational ties. It would certainly render more elusive the sorts of foreign economic cooperation America needs to redress its imbalances. "The worst of all worlds," in Moran's words, "would be for neomercantilistic economic policies to take the place of (or even relieve the pressure for) progress in rebalancing America's own mix of savings, consumption, and investment. The result would be a deterioration of the United States' position . . . no matter how hard we twisted arms, accompanied by mounting tensions [with other nations] caught up in the cycle of reciprocal blaming and scapegoating."[14]

The alternative broad strategy is to build "win-win" relationships with other economic power centers, encouraging cooperation on economic policy and "transnational integration" in trade and crossinvestment, aiming at the internationalization of their economies as well as our own. This is fully consistent with a domestic strategy of economic rebuilding, but it would engage foreign firms in the process, offering them the same incentives for high-tech investment and worker training *within the United States* that we offer to U.S. owned firms.[15]

Such a strategy would place American economic revitalization within a broader view of economic competition as a positive-sum international game. The goal would be an explosion of global growth that would benefit all nations whose economies could respond. But this would in turn require trade and investment agreements that enforce openness at home and abroad, which bring the reality and appearance of "fairness." Americans would demand these; their leaders will need them to resist the many interests—here and abroad—who would restrict trade and investment for their special advantage. As economies become intertwined, negotiations will shift from traditional trade and investment issues to broader rules for regulating competition, new forms of government-business partnership, and national and international programs for technology development.

Pursuing such an approach would be a complicated political task. How does one mobilize desirable consensus to attack Japanese import and investment barriers, pursuing the good goal of a "level playing field" internationally, while at the same time defending (as good for *American* growth) those manifestations of Japanese economic strength most visible (and oft-discomfiting) to Americans here, Japanese subsidiaries producing in the United States? How does one engage what is still a *national* polity in developing a shared commitment to short-term sacrifice for long-term gain, without attacking those welfare-enhancing and economically robust but politically vulnerable transnational economic connections?

These are some of the policy and political dilemmas confronting Clinton's and future administrations. Without the easy consensus and constraint of cold war alliances, they must build an effective compact with U.S. business, whose performance will be the ultimate measure of success, as B.R. Inman and Daniel F. Burton, Jr. point out in chapter 8. They must find their way to a realistic but constructive relationship with Japan, as William A. Reinsch suggests in chapter 9. They must, above all, engage the public in a genuine dialogue about the realities of international interdependence and the problems and opportunities that this brings.

Clinton was elected to concentrate on the economy. He was also elected by a public increasingly distrustful of authorities of all kinds, and fed up with top-down elitist approaches to issues. He personally has shown exceptional ability to connect with the concerns of individual Americans. The need is for him and other executive and legislative leaders to engage seriously and systematically with the public, with the aim of *mutual* education and, eventually, consensus and commitment to constructive policies. In the chapter that follows, Daniel Yankelovich and John Immerwahr suggest how they might proceed.

Notes

[1] For sources of this data and the broader background, see Destler (1992), pp. 44–47.

[2] Hyland (1990), pp. 7–8.

[3] Allison and Treverton (1992), p. 448.

[4] Carnegie (1992a), p. 18.

[5] See Kennedy (1987) and Prestowitz (1988).

[6] Actually, the recessions of 1973–75 and 1980–82 had been deeper than the one on Bush's watch. But if one looked at average growth, adjusted for inflation, across a president's entire tenure, Bush's record was the worst—an average of .91 percent per year over 3.5 years. (Harry Truman's *first* term averaged negative real growth,

due to postwar readjustment, but the Korean War boom during his second term brought his overall average up to .925 percent per year.)

[7] Transcript of debate of October 11, 1992, *Washington Post*, October 12, 1992, p. A 17. Baker served as Bush's secretary of state until the summer of 1992, when the president reluctantly brought him into the White House as chief of staff to try to rescue his campaign and his administration.

[8] As this chapter was completed, the broad budget plan had won preliminary congressional endorsement, the short-term stimulus had fallen victim to a Republican filibuster in the Senate, and Congress was at work on the details of tax and spending legislation. The outcomes will be known to the reader by the time this book appears, so this chapter will not seek to provide "the latest" information. Instead, it will focus on the broad substance and politics of the program in terms of problems they pose for engaging the public and reshaping the policy process.

[9] See, for example, the March 1992 and March 1993 Annual Reports of the Competitiveness Policy Council, a body created in the Omnibus Trade and Competitiveness Act of 1988, appointed in Hoover Commission fashion by the president and congressional leaders, and including three members each from government, business, labor, and academia.

[10] Krugman (1992), p. 9.

[11] Even the GATT is built around a form of mercantilism: countries (not firms) negotiate over reciprocal market access for their exports, and easing an import barrier represents a "concession" to foreign interests, made in exchange for parallel concessions by others.

[12] Foreign governments went along in a number of cases, because they found U.S. threats credible, and/or because they wanted to liberalize anyway and found U.S. pressure helpful in bringing this about within their domestic political systems.

[13] Moran (1993), p. 77.

[14] Moran (1993), p. 81.

[15] The most prominent and comprehensive case for such an approach is found in Reich (1992).

2

The Rules of
Public Engagement

DANIEL YANKELOVICH
AND JOHN IMMERWAHR

E ven under ideal conditions, the relationship of the public to foreign policy is replete with difficulties. Compared to domestic issues, opinion polls show that average Americans know less

DANIEL YANKELOVICH is president of the Public Agenda Foundation and the author of numerous books and articles on social-political trends and public opinion. His book *Coming to Public Judgment* diagnoses today's policy gridlock. In a recent *Fortune* article, "The Seven Stages of Public Opinion," he discusses how policy makers can do a better job in building public support. He is also the author of the lead article in *Foreign Affairs* (Fall 1992), "Foreign Policy After the Election." Mr. Yankelovich is the founder of Yankelovich, Skelly and White and the Public Agenda Foundation (with Cyrus Vance), and is currently chair of the business research firm DYG, Inc. He is a director of various corporations and nonprofit organizations, including U.S. West, The Meredith Corporation, the Kettering Foundation, Educational Testing Service, Inc., and is a trustee emeritus of Brown University.
JOHN IMMERWAHR is a senior research fellow at the Public Agenda Foundation; he is also chair of the Philosophy Department of Villanova University. He is the author of a number of Public Agenda Reports, including *The Speaker and the Listener: Public Perspectives on Freedom of Expression; Crosstalk: The Public, the Experts and Competitiveness; Faulty Diagnosis: Pub-*

about foreign policy, care less, are more volatile in their views, and base their attitudes more on slogan-like generalizations (e.g., no-more-Vietnams) than on the specific merits of the issue. So, except when war threatens, the challenge of engaging the public in foreign policy is formidable.

Today's conditions are far from ideal, and engaging the public is particularly daunting in the present post–cold war climate of opinion. As former Senator Charles Mathias observed in a previous American Assembly volume, "The greatest problem that confronts American leadership with respect to future foreign policy is to achieve a new national . . . consensus in the absence of a powerful threat."[1]

For the past two generations our nation's adversarial relationship with the Soviet Union has been the framework within which all foreign policy initiatives were evaluated. Absent that framework, it is difficult for the public to know what criteria to bring to bear in making foreign policy judgments. For forty years, leaders and public alike were prepared to go to great lengths to contain a menacing Soviet power; today there is no consensus that the country should spend even a fraction of the "peace dividend" to ensure a peaceful, democratic Russia.

Ever since the troubles of the economy have come to preoccupy the public mind, voters have pushed foreign policy issues to the rear of the national agenda. Although for much of the postwar period foreign policy ranked near the top of the public's concerns, the combination of mounting concern for domestic issues and the collapse of the Soviet Union has greatly reduced public interest in international problems. On the Gallup/*USA Today* index of fifteen issues for discussion and debate in the 1992 presidential campaign, national defense ranked fourteenth out of fifteen, with only 43 percent feeling that it was a "very important issue" (Gallup/*USA*

---

lic Misconceptions about Health Care Reform; and (with Daniel Yankelovich) *Putting the Work Ethic to Work.* He has also written numerous other articles on philosophy and on public policy. This chapter is based on research conducted by the Public Agenda Foundation, with support from the Bohen Foundation.

Today, January 1992). When the goals of foreign policy are discussed, by two to one margins (62 percent to 31 percent), voters give greater priority to the pursuit of our economic interests than to more traditional political-military objectives. In brief, the gap between foreign policy leadership and the public—large under any circumstances—is particularly difficult to bridge under present conditions.

Traditionally, leadership has managed this gap by limiting the influence of the public in the foreign policy arena. Most foreign policy initiatives are taken without much public consultation. Even on issues that involve putting U.S. troops in harm's way, such as in Somalia, leadership sometimes does not even bother to consult or inform the public until after the fact.

Increasingly, however, despite its low level of interest in foreign affairs, the public insists upon being in the loop, especially when sacrifice and hard choices are involved. The public has come to feel that foreign policy competes with domestic problems for attention and resources. As a result, the public is no longer prepared to delegate critical foreign policy decisions to the judgment of experts; there is a concern that foreign policy leaders will distract the country from more pressing domestic issues. As the nation struggles to find solutions to both its domestic and foreign problems, leaders can expect a new aggressiveness and insistence on the part of the public that it be directly engaged in shaping the new post–cold war foreign policy.

Here we bump up against an unexpected obstacle. In the past, foreign policy leaders may have been reluctant to go to the trouble of engaging the public in complex foreign policy issues. But they never doubted their ability to do so. Yet the sad truth is that the foreign policy community has little or no idea how to go about engaging the public under these new post–cold war conditions.

"Selling" the Public

What foreign policy leaders do understand is the conventional top-down method for winning public support. In this approach, leaders first get together and hammer out policy positions among themselves. This process, which might take months or even years on complex policies, is often characterized by extensive, open, and thoughtful debate. But once a position is reached, the process of winning public support for it is usually far less thoughtful and open. It then becomes largely a matter of selling the public on decisions that leaders already have made.

The techniques for selling the public are familiar. Leaders make speeches, brief reporters, write op-ed pieces, and appear on talk shows to convey their thinking and to share a tiny fraction of their knowledge with the public. In effect, leaders present a simplified version of a lawyer's brief to the public, justifying their policy recommendations in a one-way process of communication.

Let us hasten to add that the top-down method is quite appropriate for many issues. It works well when public interest and concern are low, either because the issue is highly technical or because it does not touch people's lives directly. The decision of the National Aeronautics and Space Administration (NASA) to implement the shuttle program, for example, was intensely debated within the expert community but, appropriately, most of the public discussion was focused on selling the program to the public. The traditional method also works well on issues where no special sacrifices or actions are demanded of the public. Many foreign policy decisions have no immediate impact on the public. There is no special reason to engage the public in a lengthy debate about our policy toward Namibia, for example. Finally, this process works well when the goals of the policy are widely shared by the public and the leadership community, as in the cold war era.

But the top-down selling approach is surprisingly ineffective for other issues. It does not work well when the public has a real stake in the issue, such as military intervention in Bosnia or the North American Free Trade Agreement (NAFTA). It does not work well when the public does not share leadership's assumptions and priorities. It is especially ineffective on issues where demands will be made on the public, and where the public is expected to accept sacrifices. As a growing number of observers have noted, the top-down approach has not even worked well for domestic policies; it is hardly likely to do much better for foreign policy.

The Need for a New Approach

So we are confronted with a prickly dilemma: foreign policy issues have grown more elusive and less clear-cut. The public is eager to focus on urgent domestic concerns but is unwilling to delegate the shaping of foreign policy to experts who might give foreign policy too large a share of the resources needed to fix our domestic problems. Foreign policy leaders are (more or less) willing to engage the public to win its support, but don't know how to do so, and, worse yet, don't know that they don't know.

What is needed, then, is a new method for winning public support for vital foreign policy initiatives. Let us call this new method "engaging the public," to distinguish it from the top-down approach.

Engaging the public differs from top-down communication in a number of ways. Instead of selling the public on policy positions that leaders have prepackaged, the public is drawn into the process of deliberation and policy formation. Instead of one-way communication, there is dialogue between public and leaders. Instead of a public relations campaign, a more complex process of debate, discussion, and interaction between public and leaders is instituted.

Engaging the public is more difficult than selling or information sharing. It demands more time and energy from leaders, and greater sensitivity to the nuances of the public's thinking. Its difficulty should not be minimized. The price of winning public support for issues that require this approach is the adoption of a new set of rules for public engagement in foreign policy issues. These rules of engagement are the principal subject of this chapter.

The Stages of Public Opinion

The key differences between top-down communication and engaging the public reflect radically different theories of how public opinion actually works, theories that are almost never made explicit. It is only when we clarify the difference between two implicit theories of public opinion that a workable strategy for engaging the public becomes clear.

The top-down approach is based on the theory that public opinion is driven by information and persuasion. In this view, what prevents people from supporting a position is that they do not understand the issues and the reasons leaders support the positions they take. The appropriate role of leadership would appear obvious: leaders inform the public about the issues and present a cogent case for their preferred policy solution. The theory leads to the three-step model schematized in Figure 1.

FIGURE 1.
TOP-DOWN
COMMUNICATION MODEL

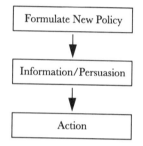

On the surface, this approach appears to make sense. Since leaders have much more information than the public, it is up to leaders to impart some of their information persuasively. Once the leaders' arguments are absorbed, the public is expected to reach the same conclusion.

The engagement approach is based on a more complex model of how public opinion works. Over the last several decades, together with colleagues at the Public Agenda Foundation (in collaboration with the Charles F. Kettering Foundation), we have been studying how public opinion develops on a series of policy issues, domestic and foreign. What we have learned is that public opinion moves through a multistage journey, starting from ignorant, volatile, impulsive, initial responses to issues (which we call "raw opinion") to firm, thoughtful, and responsible judgments (which we call "public judgment").[2] At certain stages the public does assimilate information, but the information component is often of secondary importance, as compared to people's values and moral convictions. The journey from raw opinion to public judgment is largely a matter of reconciling conflicting values and overcoming emotional resistances—a journey in which information plays a relatively minor role.

Sending foreign aid to the Russians, intervening militarily in Bosnia, lifting the ban on gays in the military, endorsing the export of jobs to Mexico, putting American troops under United Nations command, encouraging Japanese investment in American businesses—these are matters of deep concern that engage our prejudices, emotions, and values, as well as our minds. In the end, these kinds of policies cannot be effectively sold to the public in the traditional top-down manner.

Instead of seeking to inform and persuade as in the top-down model, leaders need to stimulate people to be more thoughtful, to confront their own prejudices and resistances, to embrace long-term goals as opposed to the impulses of the moment, to weigh the pros and cons of policy choices seriously and responsibly. They need to make it possible for the public to participate in the same deliberative process that they, the leaders, have shared. Average Americans are as capable of carrying out this difficult chore of citizenship as their leaders—if we cast the issues in their framework (not that of the experts) and if they are given the time to deliberate, the necessary incentives, and the right kind of communicative leadership.

Those leaders who are willing to go to the trouble of engaging the public in this kind of deliberative process need to ground themselves in a better understanding of how public opinion works when people's feelings, prejudices, and moral values are aroused. In the balance of this chapter, we will set forth the various stages of public deliberation and suggest what rules of engagement are appropriate at each stage.

Analysis of the public's response to hundreds of issues shows that the public moves through seven distinct deliberative stages in the journey from raw opinion to public judgment. These stages sometimes overlap, but they warrant being distinguished from one another for a very practical reason: the rules for engaging the public differ at every stage. Leaders defeat their own purposes when they take actions inappropriate for the stage the public has reached. The seven stages are schematized in Figure 2.

The Seven-Stage Journey from Raw Opinion to Public Judgment

In what follows we describe the seven stages of public opinion, and the rules of engagement appropriate to each.

FIGURE 2.
ENGAGEMENT
MODEL

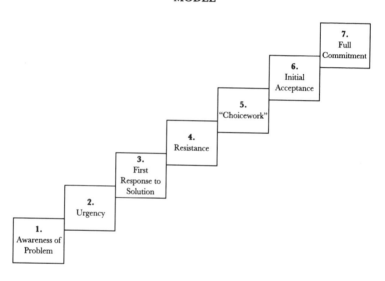

Stage One: Dawning Awareness

The first stage of the long journey to public judgment is the public's growing awareness that a problem is developing. What drives public awareness is a combination of events reported by the media and people's own responsiveness to the world around them.

At this initial stage of the journey the methods for creating public awareness are identical for both the top-down and engagement approaches. In both, it is the job of experts and the media to sound the "wake-up" call. Leaders traditionally have understood this as an important part of their role. Since this stage of the journey is well understood, it is not surprising that our culture has developed highly effective means for calling people's attention to an issue. Indeed, this stage calls for precisely the kind of one-way communication (with an active leadership and a passive public) that leaders are most comfortable with. It is only when we get into the later stages that new and less familiar communication approaches are called for.

Examples: Competitiveness and Developments in the Former Soviet Union

An excellent example of an issue that has grown gradually in public awareness is the competitiveness problem. One indicator is awareness of the trade deficit. In 1977 only a bare majority (53 percent) was aware of the trade deficit (Roper, September-October 1977). But as the trade deficit grew, as more and more attention was directed toward it by the media, and as people experienced the impact of stagnant economic growth on their own lives, consciousness of America's competitiveness problem grew accordingly. By the mid-1980s awareness of the trade deficit had reached the 75 percent level, and by the end of the decade awareness exceeded 80 percent (*Los Angeles Times*, 1985; Gallup/*Times Mirror*, January-February 1989). By now, awareness and concern about the competitiveness crisis are nearly universal. Seventy percent say that making the U.S. more competitive in world trade is one of the most important problems facing the country today (Yankelovich, Clancy, Shulman, September 1992), and 89 percent are concerned that U.S. industry is becoming less competitive in the global economy (Harris/*Business Week*, March 1992).

Turning to another issue—the future of the former Soviet Union—we can see that leaders have led a large majority of the public to at least this first stage of awareness. Sixty percent of the public says that it has been following political developments in the former Soviet Union (CBS News/*New York Times*, March 1993).

It is important to note that the growth of public awareness on issues is not always automatic; there have been spectacular examples where important issues failed to capture public attention. The key factor here is almost always the role of the press. (As political scientist Bernard Cohen observed a number of years ago, "The press may not be successful much of the time in telling people what to think, but it is stunningly successful in telling its readers what to think *about.* ")[3] When the media fall down on their job of bringing an issue to the attention of the public, public awareness is inevitably stalled. The savings and loan crisis, for example, developed gradually and was well known to many in the banking community, but the media paid relatively little attention to it until the problem reached an advanced state. Had the media been more alert, taxpayers might have been saved hundreds of billions of dollars.

Stage Two:
A Growing Sense of Urgency

To gain public support for a solution, it is not enough for people just to be aware of a problem. Before beginning the hard work of deliberating about it, people must be convinced that unless something is done about the problem soon, the consequences will be dire.

The shift from awareness to urgency is rarely automatic. The public can be aware of a serious problem for years without assigning urgency to it. For example, people have been aware of many environmental threats for decades without developing a sense of urgency. People were aware of rising health care costs and the growth of the federal budget deficit for many years before concluding that action was urgently needed.

Example: Aiding Russia

A good example of awareness without urgency in foreign policy is the issue of giving aid to Russia. For several years, the nation's leadership has been concerned about the dangers of potential instability in the former Soviet Union. As we have seen, leadership has succeeded in making the public aware of the issue. But attempts to give aid to Russia real urgency for the public have so far been less successful.

Survey results show that people are well aware of potential consequences:

- 79 percent express some degree of concern that if the former Soviet Union does not receive enough help from us, their nuclear weapons and technology will spread to other countries, and an equal number are concerned that if the former Soviet Union does not receive enough help there will be serious food shortages there (Gallup, April 1992).
- 67 percent express some concern that if the former Soviet Union does not receive enough aid from us, an unfriendly government may seize power there (Gallup, April 1992).

These concerns would suggest a certain amount of urgency regarding the need to help Russia. But there is actually little support for doing much more to help. The vast majority of the public (75 percent) thinks that we are already helping Russia to move toward capitalism and democracy (Gallup, March 1993). Fifty-four percent oppose giving more aid to encourage Russia to adopt a democratic government and a market economy; only 38 percent favor doing this (Yankelovich Partners/ *Time*/CNN, March 1993).

This example shows that while the public may play back concerns expressed by foreign policy experts, it obviously does not give them the same weight. Although these worries may be urgent for leaders, for the public they remain low-level concerns. The possible dire consequences required to give an issue real urgency remain remote and theoretical, rather than real and pressing. Soviet nuclear technology does not seem to be spreading, and places like Iraq seem to get what they need from other sources. While people may be waiting in longer lines than ever in Russia, the public is not deluged with daily pictures of starving stick-figure babies (as they see in the coverage from Africa).

In fact, for the vast majority of people, the real danger is that we will give so much aid to Russia that we will not have enough left for our own domestic needs. Three-quarters of the public says that what concerns them is that the United States will give *too much* financial aid to the former Soviet republics when we badly need it here at home; only 15 percent says that they are concerned that we may not provide enough aid (*Los Angeles Times*, January 1992). The dire consequence that people worry most about, in other words, is that the United States might sacrifice its own well-being for the Russians.

Focus group respondents, for example, express fear that if we help the Russian economy, the result will be a loss of U.S. jobs. People are worried that goods produced by low-wage workers in the former Soviet republics will undercut U.S. products. For many people, the idea of helping the Soviet Union evokes memories of helping other former enemies such as Japan and Germany, countries that are now seen as taking away American jobs.

Rules of Engagement

At this stage, the top-down and the engagement approaches begin to diverge from one another. Leaders often assume that if the public does not see the urgency of a problem, it is because people do not have enough information about it. But, as we see from the example above, people are aware of at least some of the consequences of failing to come to Russia's aid, and they still are not convinced of its urgency—or even its desirability.

How should leaders go about the task of imparting a sense of urgency to the public on issues such as this? We propose that they keep in mind two rules of engagement that will make the dire consequences of inaction real for the public. While there is no guarantee that these will work every time (even under the best of circumstances, the public may simply not share leadership's priorities), following these two rules will give leaders a much better chance than will the top-down approach.

Rule: Identify the reasons for the urgency gap. There are many possible reasons why, on any particular issue, the public may not share leadership's sense of urgency. One reason is different priorities. With respect to aid to Russia, for example, the foreign policy community is still mainly focused on the military and political threat (e.g., the failure of democracy leading to authoritarianism), while the public is much more concerned with the economic threat. This difference in emphasis is not surprising. It is difficult for foreign policy experts to shed habits of thought ingrained over several generations. The reality is that the public has probably made the transition from the cold war era faster than the experts have. In any event, the experts and the public are in different stages of the transition, and consequently do not see things in the same light.

Another reason the public may not share the experts' sense of urgency is that the threat may be too abstract and, therefore, not real enough to rouse people to action. For decades people felt no urgency about rising health care costs, because the costs were paid by others through the third-party payment system. It was only when employers began to require higher co-payments for fewer services that people demanded action.

A third reason for the urgency gap is more subtle. Most people feel excluded from foreign policy decisions. Looking in from the outside, they adopt the stance of critics rather than participants. The attitude is, "It is their problem, not ours." When people feel excluded, it is difficult to stir up feelings of urgency.

These are only a few of the causes of an urgency gap, but perhaps they are enough to indicate why it is imprudent to guess at the public's frame of mind. The likelihood is that the guess will be wrong, since the public and the foreign policy community rarely think alike. There is a variety of research techniques available for revealing the public's mindset, but policy makers should be wary about relying on "quickie" media sponsored polls. They are rarely subtle enough to dig beneath the surface, nor are they usually concerned with the reasons that public urgency is lacking. Once leaders understand why the public does not share their own sense of urgency, they will be in a better position to connect the dire consequences of inaction concretely to the public's deepest concerns.

Rule: Stimulate grassroots demand for action. Ideally the demand for action should well up from below rather than be imposed from above. When the demand for action comes directly from the public, people feel ownership in the issue and engage it as participants rather than as critics.

What would make aid to Russia assume greater urgency for the public? The best solution would be for leaders to credibly attack the public's zero-sum assumption: "aid helps them, hurts us." This assumption may be unfounded but it has to be understood and responded to sympathetically, even to the point of acknowledging that, at first glance, it seems plausible. The argument that we might, putatively, save defense dollars in the future will not be persuasive.

The case can be made persuasively only if the policy itself can be broadened so that it results in direct economic benefit to the United States. Can Russian oil make us less dependent on the Middle East? Can American jobs be created by helping Russia to build a new infrastructure? Can access to vast new markets help to simulate our own economy, as happened in Western Europe after the war? A positive answer to these questions would transform what appears in the mind of the public to be a zero-sum strategy into a win-win strategy.

In brief, if the policy justification of aid to Russia were shifted from a military-political one to an economic one, and if this shift were both real and credible (and not merely spin control), then thoughtful segments of the public would begin to demand action rather than brush aid to Russia aside as a deflection from the nation's real priorities.

Stage Three:
First Response to Solutions

As an issue becomes more urgent, there is a growing desire for action. At this stage, people start to look for solutions. Sometimes ideas for solutions rise up from the grassroots, such as the nuclear freeze movement of the 1970s. But typically solutions are shaped and presented by leadership.

Characteristically at this stage people begin to grope for an answer to a problem they are starting to take seriously. Not surprisingly, they may initially overreact to proposals for solutions without having thought through the complexities of the issue and the consequences of their views. At this stage of public opinion, people's responses are unstable and given to rapid fluctuation.

What makes both this stage and the following one difficult to grasp is that the public's deliberative process diverges from the more systematic process that leaders seek to adhere to in their formal analysis of issues. When leaders in the military, government, business, or think tanks deal with a problem formally, they follow a systematic approach that starts with the analysis of a problem and concludes with choosing among an array of options for dealing with it.

In the hurly-burly of political life, however, decision making is much less systematic, and much more based on trial and error. Culturally, Americans react to problems by rushing to action, giving short shrift to lengthy and laborious analysis: people leap to solutions without pausing to formulate alternatives and without deliberating at length on which solution would be optimal. Instead, people focus on one solution at a time, moving on to alternatives only when serious doubts develop. This may not be the ideal way to approach a problem, but it is the way the American political process works.

Example: NAFTA

One example of this trial-and-error style of thinking is the public's reaction to NAFTA. People have reached the stage of urgency both about the problem of immigration and the potential threat to American jobs. Over the past several years, as leaders tossed out ideas about how to deal with this issue, the public initially reacted favorably, eagerly seeking a solution to the problem.

The early reactions to a North American Free Trade Agreement thus tended to be more emphatic than what developed later.

- A March 1991 question found that an overwhelming majority (72 percent) thought that a North American Free Trade Agreement would be good for this country (Gallup, March 1991).
- In more recent surveys, however, people are saying that they have not heard enough about the agreement—49 percent felt this way in early 1993 (ABC News/*Washington Post*, March 1993).

In other words, people seemed surer—and more positive—about their position in 1991 *before* they had really had a chance to think about the subject. Two years later, in 1993, after the issue had been ventilated in the 1992 presidential election, people were saying that they had not heard enough about it. Rather than starting with a need for more information and gradually moving toward a solution, people started with a proposed solution, and only gradually came to realize that they needed more thinking *and* information about the problem.

Rules of Engagement

An understanding of how public opinion works at this stage suggests two rules for engaging the public in the deliberative process.

Rule: Assume that poll results about solutions are soft. It is at this third stage that public opinion polls are most misleading. Policy makers need to learn that opinion polls conducted before solutions have been fully absorbed are merely initial—and highly tentative—reactions rather than either final support or ultimate rejection.

When people are first reacting to a solution, their opinions are highly unstable, and poll results can and do shift dramatically based on small changes in the wording or order of questions. In some of the early opinion polls on NAFTA, for example, support for the agreement changed by large margins based on small changes in question wording. The reason for this is clear: sometimes people are saying yes to a solution when all they really mean is that they want someone to deal with the problem; they are not yet focusing on the drawbacks of that particular solution. At other times, the public reacts violently against a proposal, because it has not yet realized that its unattractive implications may be necessary. In both cases, what it is registering is an initial reaction, rather than a firm judgment one way or the other.

The danger is that policy makers will overreact in two different ways. If the poll results show that the public opposes a promising solution, policy makers may throw up their hands in disgust and assume that the public is completely hopeless (rather than working to facilitate the public's movement through this stage). In other cases, leaders make the opposite mistake: they seize upon favorable early opinion polls as a mandate and rush ahead, only to find that public support evaporates when the implications of the choices become clearer.

Rule: Use policy proposals as "trial balloons." Leaders can sometimes accelerate the public's deliberative journey through the use of trial balloons. If leaders know that a policy will encounter serious public resistance (for example, military intervention in Bosnia) the sooner resistances can be brought into the open, the sooner they can be confronted and dealt with. This is the subject of stage four, which follows below.

Stage Four: Resistance

When people start to consider new policies seriously, the journey to public judgment hits its most serious obstacle. Most foreign policy initiatives encounter some resistance. The question is, how much, how serious is it, and how can it be confronted.

Sometimes resistance is mild; other times it is fierce and unyielding. The key point is that resistance always indicates the presence of strong feelings. People don't resist new proposals simply because they don't have the facts. They resist either because the proposal conflicts with established values and beliefs, or because it collides with their interests (raising their taxes, threatening their jobs, causing them inconvenience). These perceptions may be erroneous or exaggerated. If so, factual information can help to dispel the misconceptions. But when strong feelings are involved, simply giving people the facts can be an ineffective and alienating tactic for those whose feelings are being ignored.

During the presidential campaign of 1992, for example, there was some discussion about lifting the ban on gays in the military. But it wasn't until after the election, when the proposal to lift the ban began to loom as a real possibility, that serious resistance started to emerge; only then did the conflict come to the surface. On the one hand, there is in the culture a general movement toward acceptance of alternative life styles. Majorities of the public are comfortable, for example, with the idea of a gay person serving in the president's cabinet (Gallup, June 1992). (Indeed, only a minority of the public says that being gay would disqualify someone as a presidential candidate.) But, on the other hand, many people still harbor a deep-seated emotional antipathy toward homosexuality and a lingering conviction that it violates moral values. Their emotional resistance is triggered when they imagine themselves sharing close quarters with a gay or lesbian person. When the proposal to lift the ban on gays in the military is taken seriously, it causes these conflicts to come to the surface.

In politics, we are most familiar with conflicts between groups of people, such as the bitter and irreconcilable conflict between pro-choice and pro-life groups on the abortion issue. But most conflicts on public policy issues take place within the individual psyche. These kinds of inner conflicts usually lie dormant until events force them to surface. (For example, in good economic times an individual might support both affirmative action *and* a seniority system; economic cutbacks cause a conflict between these values as society makes hard choices about who will be laid off first.)

People find it difficult enough to deal with emotional conflict in their personal lives. When it comes to public policy, they are under less pressure to resolve the conflict. If they can avoid doing so, they will.

Example: United States as the World's Police Officer

One good example of inner conflict is the public's view of the proper role of the United States in world affairs. On the one hand, people say that they want the United States to assume a lower profile in world affairs, but on the other hand, they are not quite ready to relinquish or share American power with our allies or with international organizations such as the UN. What is at stake here are two conflicting value systems that people wish to embrace simultaneously. On the one hand, voters want to focus on the domestic economy and limit our commitments abroad. At the same time, the appeal of a special leadership role in world affairs—moral, political, military—is deeply embedded in our national identity. There is a deep suspicion of our allies and a sense that, when the chips are down, the United States must ultimately act on its own.

Survey findings document this conflict. Some of the most interesting findings focus on the concept of the United States as the world's police officer. Only a small minority of Americans (21 percent) endorses this concept in principle, while 75 percent opposes it (Yankelovich, Clancy, Shulman/*Time*/CNN, March 1991).

On specific issues, however, there is strong support for the United States playing the role of world police officer. Some examples:

- Eighty percent supports U.S. air strikes inside Iraq, because of Saddam Hussein's violations of UN resolutions (Harris, January 1993). Nearly six out of ten (59 percent) think that we should continue military actions until Saddam Hussein is removed from power (Gallup, January 1993).
- Fifty-seven percent says they favor using U.S. ground forces to restore peace and humanitarian aid in Bosnia (Gallup/*Newsweek*, January 1993), and 54 percent says they think the United States has an obligation to use military force in Bosnia if there is no other way to get humanitarian aid to civilians and prevent atrocities (*Los Angeles Times*, August 1992).
- As many as 70 percent supports the general principle that "the U.S. and the United Nations should take clear actions" against dictators such as General Rodriguez in Paraguay to stop all sorts of human rights violations (Market Strategies/Americans Talk Security, November 1991).

The conflict crystalizes when people are asked about relations between the United States, the UN, and our traditional allies. One side of the public's thinking resonates with the idea that the United States should not attempt to "go it alone" in foreign policy:

- Eighty-seven percent believes that the United States should commit its troops only as part of a UN operation (Gallup, December 1992).
- Seventy-three percent believes that the United States should commit troops only in concert with allies (Gallup, December 1992).

But when people are asked questions that evoke the other side of the conflict (namely that the United States must stand up for its own interests), large majorities support the notion of unilateral U.S. action. For example, almost two-thirds of the public (63 percent) believes that the United States should be willing to commit troops on its own in some cases (Gallup, December 1992).

When both values are directly pitted against each other, the result is a kind of stalemate, as we can see in the following question:

Now that the Soviet Union no longer exists, do you think the United States should share world power with other nations, or should we use our power to ensure that no other nation can challenge our dominance in world affairs? (Yankelovich, Clancy, Shulman, March 1992.)
Responses:
Share world power	46%
Ensure no one can challenge us	43%
Not sure	11%

This example helps to illuminate the nature of what we mean by resistance: the presence within the same individual of two conflicting values. In this instance the two values are a belief in the "special mission" of the United States to act unilaterally to protect its own interests and to impose its own moral standards, coexisting with a belief in the need to act in concert with allies and to delegate the world police officer role to international bodies such as the UN so that we can pay more attention to urgent domestic concerns.

People are reluctant to give up either value. This reluctance gives rise to a variety of forms of resistance: wishful thinking ("Surely we can do both if we put our mind to it"), avoidance ("Why can't we just ignore the conflict?"), contradictory thinking (support of mutually exclusive policy options), and procrastination ("Maybe if we are lucky it will just go away").

Rules of Engagement

This stage and the next highlight the most important differences between the two models. The greatest limitation of the top-down model is that it is often ineffective in dealing with resistance caused by conflicts in values because it either ignores them or rides roughshod over them. The reason it does so is because the top-down theory of public opinion assumes that the public's thinking process is driven by information and persuasion. Most resistance, however, cannot be overcome by giving people more information or even by providing a more persuasive argument. Rarely do the arguments of policy makers address the fundamental value conflicts that are at the root of resistance.

By contrast, the engagement model takes seriously the emotional resistance caused by conflicts in values. Three rules of engagement are important here.

Rule: Allocate time and attention to countering resistance. The first principle is simply that foreign policy leaders take into account that such conflicts exist and cannot be ignored. Acknowledgment of this reality can take several forms. Leaders can give people more time to "work through" these conflicts. Leaders can also make sure they understand the public's inner conflicts and how these differ from their own concerns. The foreign policy community has its own subculture and value system. It is sufficiently removed from the general culture that leaders should never assume that their own value conflicts (or lack thereof) are shared by the general public. It is always worth making the extra effort to learn the precise nature of the public's inner conflicts when resistance makes itself felt.

Rule: Bring the conflict into the open. Leaders must be prepared to bring the conflict into the open where it can be confronted and discussed. One reason the race problem continues to fester in the United States is that the real nature of racial conflicts is rarely made explicit. As long as white Americans are reluctant to discuss the sources of tension with black Americans as openly as they do among themselves in private, then the processes of reconciliation, compromise, and resolution cannot proceed. Making conflicts explicit and giving both sides of the conflict their proper weight and dignity are important leadership functions without which procrastination and resistance can persist indefinitely.

Rule: Create the conditions for public resolution to occur. Finally, leaders must recognize that the public has to do the heavy lifting here. Leaders alone cannot overcome these resistances. Leadership needs to provide a format for people to work through the conflicts themselves. But if an issue has real urgency, and leadership has successfully identified the resistance that stands in the way of facing the issue squarely, then the public itself can do the hard work of resolving its own value conflicts. And, with some leadership support, it will do so. If people can get together (literally or figuratively) and deliberate, they will almost always gravitate toward balance and compromise.

It is this deliberative process that is almost totally absent from today's American life, due partly to the dominance of the top-down model.

Stage Five: Choicework

Once people have worked through their resistances to dealing with an issue, they are ready for the hard work of sorting out choices, weighing their pros and cons, and beginning to make the difficult trade-offs. We call this stage "choicework," to connote both the process of wrestling with choices and the fact that this is a very arduous task for the public.

This stage is an easy one for policy makers to understand. This is how leaders themselves come to grips with an issue when they are being systematic: an array of options is developed, their costs and consequences are thought through and discussed, and a choice is made. What is new and different about the engagement model is the idea that—at least on certain issues—the public must take part in a similar process.

One of the advantages of involving the public in the choicework process is that it is an excellent way to transfer a sense of ownership. If foreign policy leaders want people to make a real commitment to policies so that they stand behind them even when they involve hard choices or sacrifices, leaders need to find a way to help people become invested in those decisions. Obviously, many foreign policy issues do not require this level of public ownership. But for the few that do, there is no better way to bring the public toward a stable and responsible position.

In practice, this stage and the preceding one often overlap. Weighing alternative choices is a good way to bring people's resistances to the surface to work them through. But while these stages may overlap in time sequence, the business of seriously weighing alternatives usually does not begin until people's emotional resistances have been confronted and reduced.

In other words, there are two analytically distinct tasks the public must accomplish once an issue has been fully engaged. One involves resolving value conflicts that arouse emotional resistance—a task for the heart as well as the mind. The other is a more purely cognitive task (weighing pros and cons). The relationship between the two is often complex. Deciding among competing alternatives is hard work intellectually, especially when choices involve difficult-to-assess trade-offs. Decisions become even harder when there are deep-seated conflicts of interests and moral values to be worked out.

Rules of Engagement

The engagement model and the top-down approach differ strikingly at this stage. The essential contrast is between including the public in the deliberative process versus simply giving people information or selling them on a previously decided option.

For the public to share fully in the deliberative process, a number of conditions must obtain. All of them revolve around the concept of "choicework"—the empirically grounded discovery that the single best mechanism for advancing public deliberation is to give people real choices to mull over.

Research on public thinking about scores of public policy issues shows that presenting choices is a far better method for advancing deliberation than merely laying out the arguments for a single solution: presenting choices gives people a systematic way to consider the consequences of alternative solutions so that they can be weighed against each other thoughtfully and judiciously. Examination of choices is the essence of the deliberative process; it is the one that leaders themselves follow when they are serious about solving a difficult problem.

The message to foreign policy leaders is this: a solid public consensus for new policies is most likely to flow from including the public in the consideration of choices. This means that leaders must give up their double standard, which has traditionally meant presenting options to each other but single solutions to the public.

The rules of engagement for this stage dictate that special effort is required in preparing the conditions for public choicework.

Rule: Provide enough choices. The choices have to be the right ones, and there must be enough of them. It is not enough to present choices if all are inadequate.

In some cases choices can be confined to two alternatives. In the national debate about the response to the Iraqi invasion of Kuwait in 1991, the country eventually focused on two fairly clear choices: direct military intervention or continued sanctions. In most cases, however, such as improving trade relations with Japan, the issues are tremendously complex and the choices manifold. Unless the choices presented to the public include at least one credible solution to a problem that people feel is urgent, the deliberative process will be aborted.

Rule: Use the public's framework, not the experts'. The choices must be defined in the public's terms rather than in the terms experts favor. Frequently experts use terms that mean something very different to the public. During the cold war, for example, there were countless discussions of arms control. By arms control, most experts meant achieving a balance of arms, usually at a high level. To the public, however, the idea of arms control meant arms *reduction.* In effect, the two groups were talking past each other, thinking that they were speaking to each other but not really communicating. In fact, the public's conception of arms reduction was not employed until the very last years before the collapse of the Soviet Union.

Rule: Allocate sufficient time. Deliberation takes time. It is not enough to present choices, do an instant poll, and expect that the process has been completed. It takes an irreducible minimum amount of time to work through difficult choices, especially if strong feelings are involved. Even when an issue does not stir emotional conflicts, it takes time to grasp and absorb all of its implications. It often takes leaders themselves months or even years to come to a consensus or compromise; it is hardly reasonable to expect the public to do it overnight.

Rule: Give the public an incentive. Because deliberation is hard work, people must be motivated to do it. One of the most effective incentives is to convince people that leaders will actually listen to them and take their thoughts seriously after they have gone to the trouble to debate and work their way through an issue.

A national election forces leaders to listen. In a presidential election, a debate on foreign policy will draw 70 to 80 million viewers. This same debate, in a nonelection context, might have only 1 or 2 million viewers. The main reason people follow debates in presidential elections more closely than debates at other times is that an election offers them an incentive; at some future date they will vote, and their vote may make a difference.

Elections on specific issues, however, are neither practical nor even desirable. People must have an incentive, but it need not be as tangible as an election. Any sign that leaders are heeding the public's concerns will serve as an incentive. Informally, through their speeches and interviews with media, leaders may invite the public to debate various choices. More formally, other mechanisms can be invented to give the public a sense that leaders are really listening. The Public Agenda Foundation, for example, has experimented with what it calls "public choice campaigns," where leaders and the media work together at the city or state level to present a range of choices on a controversial issue. The final step of the process is a mail-in "ballot" where citizens register their final opinion, with some assurance that leaders will take what they say seriously. The public is hungry for any sign that leaders are responsive to their views. A great deal has been said about public apathy, but our experience has been that as soon as the public comes to feel that leadership is genuinely interested in what it has to say, the apathy melts away as if by magic.

Rule: Make leadership debates meaningful to the public. Our research suggests that indirect and vicarious methods of expediting the public's choicework can also be used to great effect, if done well. For example, congressional debates carried by the media will sometimes directly engage the public. When they do, people feel that they are participating in the debate themselves.

Unfortunately, most congressional debates are remote from the public's concerns and do little to advance the public's choicework. Debates fail to engage the public when they are pursued in either a lawyer-like or a partisan manner—the usual style of congressional debates since most people in Congress are lawyers and partisans.

On rare occasions, however, leadership debates do speak directly to the public. Here again, the national debate in 1991 over the proper response to the Iraqi invasion of Kuwait provides an excellent example of how the public can become vicariously involved in the deliberative process. The debate in Congress over military intervention or continuing nonmilitary sanctions was strikingly different from the usual partisan, lawyer-like format.

The voters appreciated the difference and were helped by it. In this case their elected representatives were seen to be seriously deliberating and searching for an answer to a very difficult problem. The legislators agonized over the issue and were honest in expressing their own doubts and reservations. Rather than advancing interest group positions or offering lawyers' briefs, they drew on their own personal experiences and values, and the public was able to identify with them.

This form of public deliberation (which was widely covered by the media) creates a climate where the public feels it is participating in an extended process of debate and deliberation. The public nature of the debate helped people to do the choicework associated with stage five. As a result, Operation Desert Storm developed strong public support.

Stages Six and Seven:
Initial Acceptance and Full Commitment

In the final stages of the process, people sign on, having worked through both their emotional resistances and the weighing of pros and cons. Full resolution moves through two distinct stages, as people advance from intellectual assent to a full commitment of both heart and mind. Empirical research shows that the cognitive aspects come first, while the moral and emotional aspects lag behind. People form a resolution first in their heads; it takes a while for their hearts and consciences to catch up.

Example of Initial Acceptance:
Women in the Military

One area where people have come to at least an intellectual resolution is on the question of women assuming combat missions in the military. The public has thought this issue through and is ready to accept the concept on an intellectual level. In this connection it is interesting to contrast attitudes today with attitudes a decade ago.

• In a 1981 survey, for example, the clear majority (59 percent) opposed the idea of women serving in combat positions. Only

36 percent favored this concept (NBC/Associated Press, July 1981).

• Today the numbers have completely reversed. In one survey, 74 percent said that "qualified women" should be allowed to serve in combat positions (Gallup, April 1992).

Once again, there is a striking contrast between attitudes toward women in the military and attitudes toward gays in the military. (The issue of gays in the military remains stuck in stage four—resistance.) A January 1993 survey showed that people oppose lifting the ban on gays in the military by margins of 48 percent opposed to 43 percent in favor (Yankelovich Partners, *Time*/CNN, January 1993).

Although Americans have intellectually accepted combat roles for women in the military, it is far from clear that they have emotionally accepted its full consequences. The American public remains uncomfortable with the idea of women in the front line. It will take time for this new reality to be emotionally internalized.

Example of Full Commitment: Support for a Strong Defense

One area where Americans have made a full stage seven commitment is to the maintenance of a strong defense. Given the concern that people have with the economy, one might expect that deep cuts in the defense budget would be enormously popular. But there is strong support for only moderate cuts. People have thought this issue through, and support intellectually, emotionally, and morally the concept that America must remain strong, even though the cold war has ended and domestic issues cry out for greater resources.

Rules of Engagement

Here are the rules of engagement that are useful to observe in these last stages of resolution.

Rule: Synthesize conflicting values. When two conflicting values are both important to the public, resolution can be enhanced by com-

promises that preserve at least some elements of each of the conflicting values. Political leaders are usually comfortable with reaching compromises among themselves, but some inspired tinkering
has to be carried out with the public as well.

Cutting the defense budget is a good demonstration of this principle. People want to devote all available resources to the domestic
economy, but they also value a strong America. If the country
were to pursue either radical cuts in the defense budget or no cuts
at all, one or the other value would be flatly rejected. The idea of
moderate cuts preserves elements of each conflicting value.

Rule: Make the broader context explicit. To ensure final resolution,
leaders must relate policies to a broader vision. Whether it be
working with the UN to achieve the world police officer role, or
U.S.–Japan trade, or support for European unity, policies must be
articulated in a way that stresses their place in the larger context of
America's interests and ideals. The issue of a strong defense has
such powerful support precisely because it has been attached to a
broader vision of America's role in the world.

In foreign policy more than domestic policy, people think in
terms of general principles (often encapsulated in slogans and code
words). People easily forget the specific pros and cons of an argument, but they remember the general principles (e.g., "protect
American jobs," "create a level playing field," "keep America
strong") and relate policies to them. The key here is to find and
articulate the general principle that will reinforce resolution.

Rule: Celebrate the result. Finally, leadership needs to find occasions
to pause to recognize and celebrate a genuine accomplishment of
democracy. Reaching public judgment on an important issue is no
small task, and everyone deserves—and needs—to be con-
gratulated on achieving it. This includes leaders, experts, and the
public alike.

Implications for Leaders

We have presented our framework for reaching public judgment analytically, separating out seven conceptually distinct
stages. To give a sense of how it can be applied in practice, it may
be helpful to focus on a single policy issue, and ask how leaders

who want to invite the public to participate in the process might use this framework as a way of understanding what needs to be done.

Let us take as our example competitive relations with Japan. We can assume, as William Reinsch argues in his chapter in this volume, that the United States has yet to find a consistent and effective response to Japanese economic competition.

The first question for leaders is whether this is an issue where public judgment is required. It is neither practical nor desirable to engage the public on all foreign policy issues; indeed the public can focus only on a small number of central issues at any given time. But there is no question that U.S.–Japan relations is an area where public judgment is needed. The Japanese economic challenge affects the lives and financial well-being of every American. More to the point, the public has, in effect, a veto over any far-reaching solution it does not accept. Effective responses to Japanese economic competition demand an active level of commitment from the public—as voters, as jobholders, and perhaps as taxpayers. Finding a sound response to Japanese competition is thus a prime candidate for applying the seven-stage framework.

The first point to be observed is that there is no problem with stage one, "building awareness." Americans are aware of the issue and have been for a number of years, if for no other reason than that they are constantly reminded of it by the universal presence of Japanese consumer products.

Leaders will find, however, that there *is* a need for action on stage two—the public's perception of the urgency of the problem. At this writing, the Japanese economic threat (which has had a high degree of urgency in the public's mind for quite some time) has lost some of its intensity. In the 1992 presidential campaign, candidate Ross Perot shifted the public's attention to the federal budget deficit, giving the public a new economic villain and diverting attention from competitiveness with Japan. (There is, of course, a relationship between the two issues, but it is indirect because the federal deficit problem focuses more on rising health care costs and other entitlements than on competitiveness.) Also, for a variety of reasons, including their own economic difficulties, attention grabbing Japanese investments in U.S. real estate—such as the purchase of Rockefeller Center—have come to a halt.

The task for leaders is not to *create* an entirely new sense of urgency, but to reinvigorate one that lies just beneath the surface of public attention. This involves stressing the connections between foreign trade and American jobs, the standard of living, and the nation's future economic well-being. The public senses these links but needs to have them reinforced.

The most serious obstacles to engaging the public on this issue arise when we move to the next three stages. As we will discuss in more detail below, Americans have not been offered an adequate range of options to engage their thinking (stage three: "first response to solutions"), leaving unraised and unresolved the deep-seated resistances and value conflicts that must be confronted (stage four: "resistance"). The institutions that will ultimately allow the public to debate and discuss choices and to weigh their pros and cons (stage five: "choicework") are not yet equipped or ready to do so. In the rough and tumble of political life, these stages need to be addressed in an overlapping fashion, but it clarifies the process to think of them seriatim.

So far, the main choices of policies toward Japan offered to the public fall along the continuum of what Reinsch calls "managing the relationship," characterized by a wearying series of disputes and resolutions of specific problems (baseball bats, leather, rice, etc.). We share Reinsch's view that such an approach "requires no vision and little leadership, [and] . . . does not by its very nature address . . . larger developments."

The public is not engaged by this approach for several reasons. The first is so obvious that it is easy to overlook. No one has invited the public to participate—not the president, nor the Congress, nor the media. And on issues of this sort it requires a deliberate effort to formulate options the public can understand, and to invite people to consider them. Secondly, this approach is designed to contain the problem, not solve it. By definition it focuses only on the short term and on narrow tactics, but so much energy is devoted to it that none is left over for addressing the fundamental terms of the relationship. From the public's point of view, all that it offers is the prospect of continuing an unattractive status quo. Third, the policy of managing the relationship does not address what the public takes to be the real issue, namely that the problem does not lie so much with Japan as with our own economy. Indeed, more than two-thirds of the public believes that we are blaming the Japanese for problems of our own making. In the absence of other choices (which might have a better chance of engaging the public), people's thinking becomes blocked, further dulling the urgency of the issue.

The most appropriate step at this point would be for leaders to invite the public to move into stage three ("first response to solutions") by presenting a wider range of choices, both to underscore the urgency of the issue and also to give some concrete choices to chew upon.

Fortunately, as Reinsch implies, there are credible choices that fall outside of the narrow range of managing the relationship. At one end of the spectrum are those choices that regard Japan as a unique adversary in world economic competition, calling upon the nation to "fight fire with fire." This might include strategies such as a serious industrial policy, where, as in Japan, government supports R&D, provides special preferences for competitive industries, and carries out an aggressive managed trade policy. At the other end of the spectrum, leaders might propose a cooperative, win-win relationship where the two countries seek out areas of mutual economic benefit, engage in much wider technological cooperation and initiate joint efforts to develop new markets in Eastern Europe and other areas where the world economy can benefit. In between these two ends of the spectrum are a variety of possible options, featuring both competition and cooperation (these options are the most realistic and promising).

If the public were presented with a much wider array of proposals, the journey to public judgment would move rapidly into stage four, "resistance." We can predict that proposals such as the ones we have just mentioned will provoke strong emotional reactions and deep value conflicts. On the industrial policy choice, for example, the public clearly is sick of conflict between government and business and wants them to cooperate to improve our national competitiveness. At the same time, however, people are deeply suspicious of attempts to help business. Many are afraid that steps such as tax cuts to stimulate investment will translate into greater corporate profits and higher CEO salaries, rather than more jobs for Americans. People are equally apprehensive about greater efforts to cooperate with Japan. The general perception is that cooperation with Japan, both after World War II and in the race to commercialize new technologies, has invariably left the U.S. poorer and Japan richer. Nonetheless, the goal is not to avoid these sources of resistance, but to surface them and let people finally wrestle with them.

With an array of new options the process of "choicework" (stage five) can begin. Leaders should present these choices (or others) to the public, and then create mechanisms for average Americans and leaders to engage in dialogue about them. The goal, at least initially, is not to sell the public on any one choice, but to advance the deliberative process. This is the area where the most new institutional thinking is required. American society is only beginning to experiment with institutions that are necessary to permit millions of people to participate in genuine dialogue about issues. One mechanism is to institute city-wide or regional campaigns (such as those that have been developed by the Public Agenda Foundation and the Kettering Foundation) that integrate news media, discussion groups, town meetings, and citizen balloting. New interactive technologies may also be promising, although so far they have mostly been used in precisely the wrong way, emphasizing superficial "instant" reactions, rather than deliberation on complex problems.

To move into stages six and seven ("resolution"), decisive leadership is required. After a period of national discussion and dialogue, it would be appropriate for a president (who, it is assumed, has participated actively in the dialogue) to recommend one of the options with strong conviction. His or her choice will undoubtedly have been modified by the national dialogue (if it is a real one and not a phony form of "spin-meistering"). In advancing a recommendation, the president would spell out all of the reasons why that particular choice serves the national interest better than the alternatives. If the public has been actively engaged in the dialogue up to that point, it will be ready to hear president, press, Congress, and interest groups debate the choices and to give genuine support to their resolution.

Conclusion

The top-down model grows out of a conception of political leadership implicit in the theory of representative democracy where leaders take responsibility for solutions, and the electorate holds leaders accountable for results. Taking their case to the public may help leaders to inform people and win their support, but the main avenue of public accountability in the top-down model is at election time when leaders who have not done a good job can be replaced ("Throw the rascals out"). The division of tasks is clear: the leaders do the thinking, the public judges the results.

This concept has great strengths, but time has shown that it also has serious limitations. In today's world, accountability only at election time is frustrating to the electorate. For one thing, our governance system has evolved ingenious ways to insulate itself from the public, and the public, excluded from the process, fights back by blocking solutions that require it to make sacrifices. As a result, the country is increasingly trapped in a far more serious gridlock than that between the legislative and the executive branches, much discussed in the 1992 presidential election.

The adequacy of the top-down model of leadership is now being questioned in many quarters, not just in government. Nowhere has the top-down model been more deeply entrenched than in large corporations. Traditionally in the corporate world the boss makes the decisions; employees are informed of them and expected to carry them out. But some corporations have discovered that under today's conditions of brutal global competition, there are serious limits to the old style of top-down communication with employees. In virtually all major business corporations today, the management styles of the mass production era are being transformed to fit the new age of information.

The old management methods work well enough when employee obedience and conformity will do the job; they don't work well when what are needed are employee initiative and dedication—not just better compliance with the rules but genuine commitment. Companies are discovering that if they are required to reinvent the company so that it can prosper in today's world, they must shift from the top-down form of management to one where people are empowered rather than ordered around, and where a vision of the future is shared by all rather than being the exclusive concern of senior management.

The result is a form of business leadership essentially political in nature. Instead of the boss barking orders, managers have to find ways to make people think for themselves and internalize the goals of the institution. There is still a boss; indeed the CEO function becomes more important than ever, because at the end of the deliberative process it is up to the boss to articulate its results and draw inferences from it about the future direction of the company.

In the world of theory, scholars (including philosophers such as Germany's Jurgen Habermas and American social thinkers such as Jane Mansfield, Amitai Etzioni, and James Fishkin) have also been exploring the concept of deliberative democracy based on new principles of communication and leadership. A number of research institutions and foundations such as the Public Agenda, the Kettering Foundation, the Markle Foundation, and more recently The American Assembly, are also exploring these concepts.[4]

This way of thinking has yet to penetrate the world of foreign policy. In the cold war era, it was not needed. The foreign policy community was entrusted with carrying out a goal—contain Communist expansion—which virtually all Americans accepted. Today there is no comparable single threat and no widely shared goal. There is, in fact, a disparity in emphasis, with the leadership continuing to stress America's political-military-moral objectives, while the public has shifted its emphasis to the economic domain.

As a result, foreign policy leaders need to find new ways to work with the public. What is called for is not just new communication techniques, but a new concept of leadership, one that shifts from the traditional "we do the thinking" style to one that encourages a more deliberative public. This will not be required all the time, or for every issue. On most decisions, foreign policy leadership can continue as usual, with most of the decisions made outside of the spotlight of the public. But on a few critical issues where real public commitment is required, a new deliberative form of leadership is needed. The seven-stage theory of public opinion presented here should give leaders a practical method for seizing upon it and making it work.

Notes

[1] Mathias (1992), p. 77.
[2] For a more detailed discussion of this concept, see Yankelovich (1991).
[3] Quoted in McCombs and Shaw (1976), p. 13.
[4] For more elaboration, see Yankelovich (1991).

3

Adapting U.S. Foreign Policy Making to Changing Domestic Circumstances

DAVID GERGEN

Toward the end of the Gorbachev era, Georgy Arbatov wryly warned his friends in the West that the Soviet Union was going to do something very dangerous to us: "We're going to deny

DAVID GERGEN wrote this chapter prior to joining the Clinton White House in June 1993 as counselor to the president. It represents his personal views, not those of the administration. He previously served as editor-at-large for *U.S. News & World Report*, writing editorials and columns for the weekly news magazine. His frequent commentary on television and radio included his weekly joint Friday night political analysis with columnist Mark Shields on the *MacNeil/Lehrer Newshour* and his reflections on National Public Radio's "All Things Considered." Mr. Gergen entered journalism in the mid-1980s after serving eight years in the White House under Presidents Nixon, Ford, and Reagan. From 1981 to early 1984, he was the first communications director for the Reagan White House. He has served on advisory boards of several nonprofit organizations, including the National Committee on U.S.–China Relations, the Center for Strategic and International Studies, the Smithsonian Institution, Congressional Fellows, the International Media Fund, and the American Committee for Aid to Poland. He is a trustee of The American Assembly.

you an enemy." While Arbatov was of course wrong in a fundamental sense—the collapse of the Soviet empire has left the world a good deal safer from fear of a nuclear holocaust—he was prescient in another: the demise of its archrival has also made the conduct of U.S. foreign policy a great deal more complicated than in the past.

During most of the cold war, the marshaling of support for foreign policy initiatives was relatively straightforward for a president. Most Americans agreed that the Soviets posed a deadly threat and that the United States must "pay any price, bear any burden" in the defense of freedom around the world. In Congress, Democrats and Republicans alike willingly voted during the Kennedy years for defense budgets that were more than twice the size of today's, measured as a share of the gross domestic product (GDP). The public, if anything, tended to be more hawkish. The press was generally supportive. And allies overseas quickly fell into line behind U.S. policies. To the extent that economic conflicts arose among the industrialized nations, they were downplayed in the interest of political harmony.

The Vietnam War obviously splintered some of that bipartisan, domestic consensus on foreign policy, at least on the matter of using force to settle disputes on the periphery of the Soviet empire. But on the central issue of matching the direct threat of the Soviet military, the United States remained firmly united. Indeed, by the end of the 1970s, the perception that the country might be slipping led to a strong public desire for beefing up the armed forces and gave Ronald Reagan the impetus to undertake the biggest defense build-up in peacetime history. How long ago that all seems now.

Today the United States has neither a recognized enemy nor a strategy for shaping the world's future. During the early months of confrontation with Iraq, George Bush often spoke about creating a "new world order" and even planned to give a series of four commencement addresses after the war, outlining his vision; in the event, he gave only one of the speeches and the phrase dropped from his lexicon. Bill Clinton spoke broadly about foreign policy during his campaign, but in his opening months his primary preoccupations have been domestic.

Just as importantly, the world has turned out to be much mes-

sier in the post–cold war era than most had expected. Indeed, the
euphoria that greeted the liberation of Eastern Europe and the fall
of the Soviet Union has given way to a sober, rather pessimistic
view that the world is sliding toward disequilibrium as smaller
conflicts break out, tensions rise, and the industrialized nations
dither on the sidelines. History has not ended, it is said; it had
merely been frozen, and the old ethnic and nationalistic hatreds
are now thawing. Despite its preeminence as the world's single
superpower—first in military, political, economic, and cultural influence—the United States seems unable to imprint its own sense
of order. Observers such as James Schlesinger, Zbigniew Brzezinski, and Daniel Patrick Moynihan all write rather darkly about
prospects ahead. No wonder some foreign policy buffs grow nos-
talgic for the simplicities of the cold war.

Lining Up Support for
Military Engagements

Just how complicated and difficult the conduct of foreign policy
has become in the new era is best illustrated by the imposing array
of forces a president must now align in his favor in order to undertake a military engagement by U.S. troops. Sending in forces for a
brief, police-type action, as in Panama, does not require much
advance effort, but something more dangerous, as in Kuwait and
the former Yugoslavia, is incredibly demanding. Consider the
players the president must corral in his corner:

Competing advisers: The question of when and how to commit the
United States to an overseas venture seems to arouse conflicts
among presidential advisers far more than in the cold war period.
During the Reagan years, for example, Secretary of State George
Shultz was more hawkish than Defense Secretary Caspar Wein-
berger, and the latter could usually count on help from the Joint
Chiefs of Staff (JCS). In the Bush years, Defense Secretary Dick
Cheney was often more willing to use force than was Secretary of
State James Baker, but again the Joint Chiefs could be lukewarm.
In both administrations, the national security adviser could be a
swing vote, especially in the case of Brent Scowcroft, in whom
Bush invested a great deal of trust. The line-up is less clear, so far,

among Clinton's advisers. Again, in the absence of a clear, definable mission, the Joint Chiefs tend to be the most reluctant to use force, as shown during early discussions on Bosnia.

For a president, the bottom line is that divisions among his own ranks can be troublesome. Clinton, for example, is the first president since World War II who has never worn a military uniform. Before he took office, some worried that he would be too trigger-happy, anxious to prove that he was macho enough for the job. In fact, judging from the outside, the lack of enthusiasm by military advisers for military air strikes in Bosnia apparently made Clinton more reluctant to proceed there.

A balky Congress: Since Vietnam and passage of the War Powers Act in 1973, Congress has insisted that it have a large voice in any decision to send troops into combat. The executive branch has long disagreed with leaders on the Hill about the extent of congressional approval required by the Constitution, but as a political matter, the fact that Bush sought authorization from both chambers prior to launching an attack against Saddam Hussein's forces will probably make it imperative that future presidents obtain similar support before starting major missions.

The problem for the executive is that Congress wants to share authority but won't share equal responsibility. In early debates on Bosnia, for example, members took to the floor demanding a chance to vote and, in the same breath, demanded that before they voted yea, the president—not they—must muster support among voters back home. In the case of Kuwait, members wanted advance support of both the voters and the United Nations Security Council. Few are the members who are willing to step forward in a dicey situation and help the president take his case to the country (Senators Richard Lugar, Joseph Lieberman, and Robert Dole are among the exceptions). It's mostly, "After you, Alphonse."

Moreover, the disappearance of the Soviet threat has also scrambled the old coalitions that were for and against military action. Now a president must start afresh in every conflict, seeing whom he can line up. One irony of the new era, it has been said, is that some liberals have become extremely enthusiastic about using force everywhere, even as they work to dismantle the defense establishment, while some conservatives never want to use force any more, even as they work to preserve the biggest military in the world. With so little help from Congress, a president is almost on his own in convincing the country that the United States must take action.

An uncertain public: With no obvious enemy lurking over the horizon, the public is paying even less attention to international affairs than in the past. That's hardly encouraging for a president who must look to the public for guidance: after all, a poll by ABC and the *Washington Post* in the early 1980s found that when people were asked which of two countries, the United States or the Soviet Union, was a member of NATO, only 47 percent could identify the United States (a flip of the coin, it was noted, would have produced more right answers).

In today's context, the lack of public attention often means that polls probing opinion on overseas conflicts are often haunted by "mushiness," a phrase Daniel Yankelovich introduced a few years ago to describe the vast uncertainties and volatility of opinion when people have only the vaguest idea of what's at stake. One week in spring 1993, polls said, for example, that Americans were prepared to use force to stop the Serbs in Bosnia; the next week, polls showed just the reverse. For a president, such uncertainty makes all the more challenging the task of building stable public support for a military engagement. He knows that as soon as he sends troops, Americans will automatically "rally 'round," but if something goes wrong or conflict turns into "quagmire," support will melt away. And a president knows that the public won't take its cues just from him; people will also pay a great deal of attention to what they see on their television screens. Yet another player enters the game.

A wandering television eye: As James Schlesinger writes:

In the absence of established guideposts our policies will be determined by impulse and image. . . . National policy is determined by the plight of the Kurds or starvation in Somalia, as it appears on the screen; "If a tree falls in the forest"—or a catastrophe occurs, but is unrecorded on tape— it is unseen. Starvation continues in the Sudan or Mozambique, suppression in East Timor or India, ethnic wars in parts of the former Soviet Union, but it is Somalia or Bosnia that draw the attention, because the cameras are there.[1]

For a president, the degree to which the modern media—print as well as television—can shape the public's foreign policy agenda is a mixed blessing, indeed. In some cases, the fact that the media ignore a problem of serious interest to the government makes it more difficult to generate support for action there; more often, the media may goad a president to action, even when no large U.S. interest is at stake. And as many presidents have found, the press can be notoriously fickle, helping to build public attention in a potential conflict and then on the eve of potential military action, as in Kuwait and Bosnia, nearly frightening the public out of a military response because of all the horrible consequences that may flow. Every contemporary White House thus finds the modern media both unpredictable and difficult to master as it tries to marshal public support for its international initiatives.

Weak allies: In an earlier American Assembly session in this series, participants agreed upon a central recommendation: in the post–cold war era, the United States must learn to share responsibility with its allies far more than it has in the past. Unilateralism is out; multinationalism is in. Right? But what if the allies aren't willing to play? What if their governments are in so much trouble at home that their leaders aren't willing to take risks, or they roll out arguments that because of history and legal constraints at home, they can't help? Is the West to be paralyzed? How far should the United States go in bullying others to follow its lead? Should it resort to unilateral action? Or should it shrug and walk away, taking the view that it cannot and should not be the world's keeper? Those questions are certainly on the table after the long, agonizing failure of the industrialized nations in addressing the slaughter in Yugoslavia. They also underline just how tricky it can be for an American president to serve as leader of a coalition, especially as leaders such as Margaret Thatcher and Brian Mulroney pass from the scene.

A wavering Security Council: The issue of allied support is important not only in and of itself—NATO is vitally affected, of course—but is also tied to prospects for support in the United Nations Security Council. The Security Council is in turn linked to support in Congress: in the cases of both Kuwait and Bosnia, Congress wanted the Security Council to give its blessing before it would vote in favor of committing U.S. troops. These linkages are all rather novel but seem destined to become a fixture of the new era.

Again, however, the challenges grow ever bigger for a president. Assuming the White House can line up the British and French through alliance talks, it faces separate and thorny considerations at the United Nations in lining up the Russians and Chinese. Boris Yeltsin showed that the Russians still have their own interests to pursue, independent of his patrons in the West, in his approach to the Serbs. China could become even more problematic in years ahead. Their economy is bounding ahead so rapidly that Chinese leaders may wish to exercise more muscle at the UN than in the past; and the pressures arising from within the Democratic party for Clinton to toughen U.S. policies toward Beijing could easily complicate efforts to win Chinese cooperation at the United Nations.

In short, it won't be easy for Clinton—and probably for his successors—to ride high in the saddle, solving the world's problems. A president's horse has so many hurdles to clear—his own advisers, Congress, public opinion, the press, allies, the Security Council—and any one of them could trip him up.

Steering a Straight
Course in Economic Policy

Just as security policy is buffeted by more forces, so is international economic policy. Throughout most of the cold war period, of course, the United States set the rules of economic engagement. In the aftermath of World War II, it took the lead in establishing the General Agreement on Tariffs and Trade (GATT), the World Bank, and the International Monetary Fund (IMF), and because its economy represented half of the world's GNP, it was successful in pushing the world toward a more open trading system. For the most part, that new system was an extraordinary success, as the world's GNP grew from $2 trillion in 1950 to over $8 trillion by 1980. At home, the disaster of Smoot-Hawley in the 1930s had led Congress to cede to the president a rather free hand in shaping trade relations overseas. On many an occasion, the executive branch looked the other way if another nation such as Japan seemed to take occasional advantage of its economic relationship with the United States. After all, the United States needed Japan as a strong partner in order to solve a larger problem, containment of the Soviet Union. Nor did the public seem to mind very much, since the U.S. economy was growing so rapidly that in the quarter century after World War II, national income doubled, creating a vast middle class. Looking back, that quarter century may well be remembered as the golden era when all seemed right with the world.

With the end of the cold war, the rise of Japan and Europe as economic competitors, falling incomes among unskilled workers, a scarcity of good jobs, and a growing sense that America's best days are behind us, the conduct of international economic policy is much more perilous. Many of the same domestic players who are so balky when a president must pull them together before dispatching troops overseas are equally difficult when a president wants a unified national policy toward the world economy. Within his own government, a president can no longer count on his secretary of state and secretary of defense to reign preeminent on international economic matters. In the past, a Secretary Henry Kissinger could tell a Commerce Secretary Peter Peterson that international economics was "low policy," compared to geostrategic affairs; no longer. Power has shifted within the executive branch so that when President Bush went to Japan late in his term, the secretary of state wasn't even on the trip. The journey, ill-fated as it was, was organized by the commerce secretary and the trade representative and invited along was a squadron of private business executives. Early on, it appeared that Clinton's economic advisers were divided on trade policy: in this case, the Treasury Department leaned toward a free trade policy while the trade representative and the Council of Economic Advisers chairperson were seen as flirting with notions of managed trade. Nations from Japan to Mexico to Europe expressed anxiety at confusing signals coming from the administration; fortunately, Clinton had achieved more order in his team, and his trade policy was gaining respect at home and abroad.

Outside the executive branch, a president also encounters more fractious parties. Congress continues to grant presidents "fast track" authority to negotiate international trade agreements, but it threatens to upend agreements not fully to its liking. Rising congressional opposition now casts a serious shadow over the NAFTA agreement with Mexico and Canada, so that Clinton will probably have to expend a good deal of political capital to obtain passage in both chambers. Congress is also pressing him to gain better access to markets in Japan and China. Thus the congressional voice in trade policy—just as in security policy—is much louder than in the cold war years. At the same time, the public is also more vexed about economic affairs. For years, polls have shown a streak of protectionism and economic nationalism within the populace, but the public has left policy making to Washington. No more. Now voters flood their congressional offices with hot letters, protesting one action or another with overseas trading partners. The rise of economic nationalism should not be overstated: in the past two presidential campaigns, the most protectionist oriented candidates fell by the wayside in primary season (e.g., Richard Gephardt in the 1988 Democratic primaries, Patrick Buchanan in the 1992 GOP primaries). Nonetheless, adverse public attitudes toward free trade have become significant and can now bedevil policy makers. In spring 1993, for example, pollsters found grassroots opinion shifting away from the NAFTA treaty, whipped up in part by the protest of Ross Perot, and that stiffened opposition in Congress.

As if his hands weren't full enough, a president in the 1990s finds that the economic arena contains several other major actors who aren't part of the security picture. Each demands serious attention by the executive branch. Among them:

Private interests: Trade is not yet as large a proportion of the U.S. economy as of European economies, but it is playing an increasingly critical role. It is thought, for example, that the growth of exports in the late 1980s prevented the United States from falling into a much deeper recession: without the export surge, the drop in GDP would have been twice as large. On the flip side, the cooling off of exports in 1992–93 dampened the size of the recovery. Not surprisingly, a large number of major U.S. corporations now have a keen interest in shaping U.S. trade policy, and they are increasingly aggressive in seeking to influence policy makers in Washington, as well as in overseas markets. At the same time, other nations have hired a small army of lobbyists in Washington and elsewhere around the country to represent their interests (while stirring up a strong populist reaction). The net result is that the executive branch must entertain a steady stream of CEOs, and those winds blow heavily through the Oval Office. Their force is considerable. As noted in the *New York Times,* a study by the United Nations estimates that the total annual sales of the world's 350 biggest multinational companies are equal to one-third of the combined GNP of the industrial world.

Just as large manufacturing companies are pressuring the executive to complete a NAFTA accord with Mexico and Canada (along with a revised GATT agreement), organized labor is pushing in the opposite direction. Environmental groups have also jumped into the fray (their nongovernmental organizations or NGOs have become a powerful player in environmental negotiations as well, as witnessed by their unprecedented influence at the Rio conference). For a Democratic president in particular, the entry of labor and environmental lobbies in opposition to large corporations turns trade into a political minefield.

States and cities are in the game, too: The spring 1993 issue of *Foreign Affairs* featured an article on the foreign policy of California.[2] It recognized that states have now jumped into the international game, too. Indeed, state governments in recent years have maintained more offices in Tokyo than in Washington, D.C. A growing number of cities, such as Dallas, have also sent representatives abroad on economic missions. Their purpose, of course, is to attract more investment and jobs. Fortunately for a president, governors tend to be more supportive of free trade than Congress (e.g., Republican Governor Pete Wilson of California will give Clinton much more support on NAFTA than will many Democrats in California's congressional delegation). Even so, a White House soon learns that trying to formulate and carry out a smooth, coherent economic policy is almost impossible: long before the executive branch has figured out what it thinks, governors, mayors, and CEOs have been busily cutting a series of private deals with parties overseas. Washington has to scramble just to keep up with an ever-changing, growing web of connections spun by other players. In the new global economy, the private marketplace is so powerful and shifts so quickly that it will inevitably shape public policy. The primary goal of policy makers should be the removal of impediments so that the global marketplace can grow as rapidly as possible, creating more jobs and prosperity.

No Easy Answers

How can a president make sense of this kaleidoscope? How can he exercise leadership and ensure that others will march behind him, whether it is his desire to dispatch troops or negotiate a trade agreement with Mexico and Canada? There are no simple, easy answers. Each case demands imagination and effort—and often a lot of political courage—from the White House. But there are some steps that President Clinton and his successors can take that would enhance prospects for their success. Presidents Reagan and Bush started down some of these paths, but they spent most of their time bringing the cold war to a successful conclusion and then cleaning up its debris. It is up to Clinton and others who follow to fashion the new world. Among the steps most obviously needed:

(1) *A clear, concise framework for foreign policy.* As the dust settled after World War II, President Truman directed his advisers to prepare an internal document outlining the challenges that the nation faced overseas and a framework for meeting them. What emerged, of course, was NSC 68, the document that not only sealed a place in history for Paul Nitze, but became the foundation of U.S. policy for another four decades. It drew heavily upon the work of several others such as George Kennan and, some argue, did not break much new ground, but in helping to forge a bipartisan consensus on foreign policy, it served an extraordinarily useful purpose.

No such document now exists for American policy in the 1990s and beyond. The closest that has been written so far was drafted by a bipartisan commission sponsored by the Carnegie Endowment for Peace and headed by Winston Lord (this writer was a member). Now is an appropriate time for an updated version of NSC 68, building upon the Carnegie recommendations as well as others. After its development within the executive branch, it could be published—in the spirit of the times—so that it would stimulate a national dialogue. The president might then issue a revised statement that would serve as a foundation piece for his own administration.

The point is that the nation needs to build a new, bipartisan consensus about the goals of international policy in the new world, as well as the means that it intends to use in pursuing them. Some will argue in opposition that the new world is still unfolding and until the pieces fall into place, it is impossible to say what America's role should be. But that wait-and-see approach may let several of the pieces fall out of place, contrary to America's own interests. The United States would miss an opportunity to shape a new world that is more consistent with its own values. Without a framework, U.S. policy may also become a jumble of ad hoc decisions, confusing everyone and ceding U.S. leadership to the winds.

We have tasted the fruits of adhocracy already, and they are hardly sweet. In the absence of a strategic framework for a U.S.–Japan partnership, for example, relations have been buffeted hither and thither by every new irritant between them, no matter how trivial. It is small wonder that relations deteriorated in recent years. Similarly, U.S. policy toward ex-Yugoslavia would not have drifted so long, nor would Clinton have faced such a difficult struggle, had the Bush administration developed a sound, long-term approach to the region.

(2) *Better multinational structures for resolving conflicts.* The aftermath of World War II not only led to a reformulation of U.S. policy but, with the United States acting as chief catalyst, also spawned a whole set of international structures—the United Nations, GATT, World Bank, IMF, and so on—that were consistent with the kind of world Americans wanted. A similar effort at institution building is needed today.

Two institutions in particular deserve early scrutiny. The first is the United Nations. Professor Richard Gardner of Columbia University along with others has for several years been advancing the notion of a rapid deployment force at the United Nations, composed of troops donated by several nations and under UN command. The Clinton administration has expressed interest, but U.S. military leaders are generally opposed. There are some obvious shortcomings in such an idea, but in view of the paralysis that gripped the industrialized nations for so long in the case of ex-

Yugoslavia, the idea needs more serious examination. If it is workable, it would obviate the need for a U.S. president to round up
reluctant allies for every expedition, with all the risks of failure and
vacillation. Polls suggest that the American public would also be
much more supportive of a UN led military response, even if it
included U.S. volunteers and U.S. support teams, than unilateral
intervention by U.S. troops. After the success of Desert Storm, the
public greatly prefers multinational efforts. Whether models can
be developed that would meet the objections of the U.S. military
is, of course, an important question to answer. In a similar vein,
the Clinton administration could work with other nations to put
UN peacekeeping operations on surer financial footing. In recent
years, the United Nations has undertaken an unprecedented number of such missions, but it continues to live hand-to-mouth. Since
those missions often relieve pressure upon the United States to
take the lead, the U.S. government has a strong interest in
strengthening them. One other reform is also needed at the United
Nations: an expansion of the Security Council so that it includes
Germany and Japan, as proposed by the administration, and possibly Brazil and India. Olara Otunnu, an active force in international affairs, has suggested some innovative, two-tier approaches
to voting within an expanded Security Council that might help to
preserve U.S. leadership there.

The second institution that should be tuned up is the GATT. So
many American parties complain about the dispute resolution
mechanism there—too cumbersome, too slow, too ineffective—
that the U.S. government has resorted more and more often to
bilateral or even unilateral means to settle conflicts. The result is a
patchwork that has weakened GATT and left other nations steam-
ing. Assuming that a free trade framework for world trade remains
in America's best interest (as this writer does), GATT needs to be
strengthened, not shuttled to the sidelines.

No structure can guarantee a successful outcome to an international dispute, but a renewal of the United Nations and of GATT
should mean that a higher percentage of conflicts can be resolved
there—and not dumped on the doorstep of an American president. It would also strengthen the rule of international law, a desirable goal in itself. And it would create greater confidence among

the American people that they can entrust knotty problems to international institutions and not see American interests sold out.

(3) *Revamping America's own institutions.* Shortly after taking office, Secretary of State Warren Christopher observed that one of his first missions at the State Department should be the creation of an "American desk." Since then, he has said on many occasions that his first goal as secretary is to ensure economic renewal at home. Those sentiments are novel for the seventh floor. Yet they also capture an important point: citizens want to see all of their governmental institutions, including those in foreign policy, work more effectively to serve the nation's own needs. Christopher is right to take the lead.

Public cynicism about government has been rising for years and, at the moment, is at an all-time high. People are especially dubious about foreign aid, seeing it as a vast give-away of scarce dollars sorely needed at home. Even though Clinton asked for relatively small amounts of aid for Boris Yeltsin's Russia, he ran into roadblocks on Capitol Hill because voters back home are so lukewarm. After turning down money to create jobs at home, Congress faced scalding opposition to creation of jobs in Moscow.

To overcome such obstacles, it makes eminent sense for the Clinton administration to convince voters that in its international policies, it is working harder to advance American interests. For example, U.S. diplomats have usually avoided helping U.S. companies trying to sell their products overseas. Some companies complain that U.S. embassies have in the past been one of their biggest stumbling blocks. In the Bush years, Vice President Dan Quayle started touting U.S. products on his overseas trips and drew some criticism. Quayle was right, and the Clinton administration, led by Commerce Secretary Ron Brown, has been even more aggressive. The practice does not violate international trade customs; in fact, leaders such as Thatcher and Mitterrand relentlessly promoted their national products. More to the point, helping out U.S. companies will not only assist in prying open markets, but will also deepen public support for U.S. foreign policy makers. The populist notion of a "striped pants set" trying to set up a world government, dominated by elitists on Wall Street, runs deep in the culture; U.S. policy makers should take clear, well-publicized steps to build confidence that their first interest is America.

(4) *Serious salesmanship.* After Clinton swept Bush out of the White
House, it was widely assumed that he should focus almost exclusively on domestic affairs. Early in his presidency, Clinton even
apologized to an audience for taking his eye off a domestic problem: he had had to "take time off," he said, to work on international issues.

There is no doubt that in order to maintain its international
leadership, the United States must concentrate first and foremost
on domestic renewal. Continued decline in personal wages, for
example, will pave a sure path to protectionism. Even so, a president can ignore overseas trends only at his peril. Ideally, he needs
to take the lead in developing a coherent, internal framework for
foreign policy, work to reform institutions as noted above, and
then take his views forcefully to the country. The best means of
ensuring that public support will be there in the future for an
international challenge, whether Bosnia or NAFTA, is to educate
people in advance about America's interests in the new world.
Otherwise, opinion can drift rapidly in the other direction. During
the 1992 political campaign, for example, supporters of the emerging NAFTA agreement sat on their hands, afraid to stir up the
issue. In retrospect, that was a terrible mistake. While they were
lying low, opponents worked hard at the grassroots and persuaded
many new candidates for Congress to oppose NAFTA. The result
is that the 1993 congressional class, which represents about a
fourth of the House of Representatives, is heavily tilted against the
agreement. NAFTA could possibly fail in Congress because a public education campaign in its favor has been so long in coming.
The clear message for the White House is that it is better to undertake a continued process of public education about international
affairs than to wait until the last minute: by then, it may be too late.

In the introduction to its report, *Changing Our Ways,* the national
commission set up by the Carnegie Endowment pointed out that
we have now reached the third great watershed of the twentieth
century. The first came after World War I, and the United States
blew it. "Despite Woodrow Wilson's good intentions, our response
was too idealistically conceived, too rigidly presented." The sec-

ond came after World War II, and America succeeded beyond its best dreams. "There were moments (during the cold war) when we were not true to our ideals at home or abroad. But the policies put into play starting in 1947 ultimately succeeded in their fundamental objective four decades later—the containment and defeat of Soviet Communism." The end of the cold war brings us to a third watershed. The Carnegie group summed it up:

Now America once again faces a rare opportunity, an open but fleeting moment in world history. We must seize it now. This is our chance to ensure that recent enemies become future friends and that present allies do not become new antagonists. This is our chance to shape new forms of leadership before the fluid trends of the moment harden into something not to our liking.

Well said.

Notes

[1] Schlesinger (1993), p. 18.
[2] Goldsborough (1993), pp. 88–96.

4

Post–Cold War
Foreign Policy:
Toward Shared Responsibility

DONALD F. McHENRY

There are few times in history when the old order ends as abruptly and as decisively as did the cold war. Except in the case of some dominating individual or cataclysmic event, the end of an era seems to ebb or wane. Almost imperceptibly, one era gives way to another. The task of deciding when and why the change occurs is left to historians. In the case of the cold war,

DONALD F. McHENRY is university research professor of diplomacy and international affairs at Georgetown University. He was with the Department of State for ten years beginning in 1963. From 1971–73 Ambassador McHenry was a guest scholar at the Brookings Institution and was an international affairs fellow at the Council on Foreign Relations. He then became the project director at the Carnegie Endowment for International Peace. From 1977–79 he was U.S. deputy representative to the UN Security Council and from 1979–81 served as the U.S. ambassador to the United Nations. He is on the board of directors of several not-for-profit and for-profit organizations, including AT&T, International Paper Corporation, Coca-Cola Co., Bank of Boston, Smith Kline Beecham Corp., and First National Boston Corporation, as well as the Institute for International Economy and the Ditchley Foundation. He is a trustee of the Brookings Institution and the Ford Foundation.

though historians may eventually conclude otherwise, the end came with an abruptness that has proven to be both welcome and unsettling. Welcome because the threat of mutual destruction casts a less ominous shadow over humankind; but unsettling because the veil of tidiness and predictability of international affairs has been lifted, revealing a messy, complicated political structure whose fundamental aspects had been studiously avoided during the cold war.

Instead of a struggle to the death with an ideological, political, and military enemy with awesome destructive power, the post–cold war foreign policy landscape is littered with the debris of the disintegration of the Soviet Union. The components of the old Soviet Union are faced with far-reaching economic and social problems with only shaky governmental structures in place to handle them. In the developing world, ethnic, religious, and regional problems, which a short time ago would have constituted unwelcome or challenging moves on the cold war chess board must now be dealt with on their own merits.

There has been a great deal of talk in the United States about having won the cold war. This debate too might best be answered by historians. It is true that the United States emerged preeminent from the cold war. But it emerged to face post–cold war problems of enormous proportions. Some of the problems concerned the disintegration of the Soviet Union such as what to do about nuclear weapon stockpiles and how to avoid economic and political chaos among the ranks of the old enemy. Still other problems had been aggravated by but postponed during the cold war. Among these is the economic strength of the United States, particularly in relation with Japan and Europe.

At the height of the cold war, a general consensus existed on foreign and defense policy. The Soviet threat and the Soviet effort to spread communism were a recognizable threat. The public was largely willing to leave foreign policy decisions to national leaders and to make almost any sacrifice in the interest of national security. This is not to say that there was no debate on tactics or that various interest groups did not exercise decisive influence on American foreign policy at various points, as indeed they have throughout American history. The Vietnam War resulted in a new and intense level of questioning of the necessity for military actions and, probably more importantly, increased skepticism about the veracity of government. It was not simply that the Vietnam War resulted in high casualties, it was also the effect of the conflict on other public agendas. The war pushed the civil rights agenda aside; it diverted human and fiscal resources just as the government was embarking upon broad and costly social reforms; the level of destruction in a far away place against a small determined people and the association of the United States with despots and inhumane actions in the pursuit of security put moral values and perceived security in conflict. And, of course, deep differences on Vietnam divided the generations, and, though one can argue about the depth, profoundly affected the approach of political and military leaders toward future conflict.

Contemporaneous with the Vietnam War and the cold war, but not necessarily directly related to them, has been an increase in the number, range, and effectiveness of public interest groups. Groups, organized along substantive, ethnic, political, and economic lines, have acted alone or in alliance to greatly influence foreign policy. Greek-Americans, Black Americans, and other groups have followed the precedent of Jewish groups in influencing American foreign policy, sometimes in ways strongly opposed by the federal government. Human rights and labor groups have succeeded in attaching amendments to legislation governing policy, sometimes robbing the government of flexibility that might be needed to achieve the same policy results mandated as a result of the group's influence.

What is significant about American public opinion in the 1970s and 1980s is not that there was decreased support for strong opposition to communism and whatever sacrifice that entailed, for in the final analysis, even when American intervention in Grenada or Panama strained credulity, the majority of the American public tended to support the action. It is that the level of sacrifice, among other factors, rose at precisely the same time as other policy priorities became more important. These new areas of concern are clearly outlined in the five previous assemblies in The American Assembly International Series. These assemblies brought out concern for human rights and democratic values; global issues such as the environment, population growth, and resource conservation; burden sharing; multilateral problem solving; deficit reduction; and free trade. In addition, there was a considerable emphasis on domestic aspects of policy, including education. Some policy areas such as human rights and population got a bureaucratic toe-hold in the 1970s, only to suffer setbacks in the single-minded ideological policies of the Reagan administration.

Not only has the central tenet of post–World War II American foreign policy disappeared and new concerns arisen, it is highly unlikely that in the near future a new single issue will command the fervent and united support of the American public. Such an issue is not currently on the horizon. Moreover, even during the cold war the American decision-making process became progressively fragmented between and within the executive and legislative branches. Only the occasional perceived threat brought factions together, and even then it is likely that some suppressed their true positions in the light of the political necessity to rally around the flag.

In the absence of a new world order, the task before the United States and the international community is to find or develop a new order and to determine their respective roles. In the meantime, there is the need to discover how to get there from here and how to conduct the world's business in the interim—an interim that is untidy and complex and that will not postpone problems while awaiting a new consensus.

For the United States, there is a special responsibility and a special difficulty. It must make the transition to the new order, where economic and global issues are of greater concern than ever, while meeting its responsibilities for leadership, but at a level and pace that the American public will support. It must also be seen to be turning to and delivering on the dividend that the American public invested in defense. Ironically, the task is probably more difficult than that faced by any president since Franklin Roosevelt cautiously tried to build a constituency for American participation in World War II. Even Roosevelt might have failed had not Germany and Japan attacked and, in the view of the American public, donned black hats. In the same vein, it was relatively easy to build support for policy against communism after

World War II, or for President Bush to rally the public against Saddam Hussein.

However, as Bosnia has shown, it is more difficult to develop support for an activist American foreign policy. (It is also worth noting that Europeans have become more rancorous among themselves and with the United States now that cooperation is not mandated by the threat of war.) In the absence of a clearly perceived threat to their security, Americans are reluctant to participate, and even more reluctant to act unilaterally, in post–cold war ethnic and regional conflicts. Bosnia, for example, is seen as a problem for Europeans to handle. To the extent that there is a willingness to do so, Americans prefer a multilateral effort, although Somalia proves that Americans are responsive to large-scale human suffering. In general, one gets the impression that Americans feel that they have made their sacrifice. It is time for others to bear some of the burden and for America to spend time on problems at home. In fact, the belief is that American security depends on building America's economic security.

The Clinton campaign slogan, "It's the economy, stupid," is borne out not just by the election results. Election year surveys highlighted the public's concern that too much time was being spent on foreign affairs.[1] Surveys taken for this American Assembly show that 65 percent of the public believes that the best way to improve the United States economy is to "pay less attention to world affairs than in the past, and focus on the things here in the United States," while only 35 percent would improve the U.S. economy by continuing a foreign affairs concentration but focusing on those "things abroad which affect the U.S."[2] Moreover, respondents in the same survey thought the United States could be of some help in relieving famine and hunger abroad but had serious doubts about the ability of the United States to promote democracy in the former Soviet Union, or to promote peace in the Middle East or in areas of ethnic unrest like the former Yugoslavia.

It is frequently said that the United States does not wish to play the role of the world's police officer. The survey data tend to support this view. In response to several questions, the respondents tended to support the view that the United States should act only in concert with the United Nations, particularly when it comes to sending military forces.[3] Consistent with a later survey already cited, the American public appears more open to use of American military forces for humanitarian purposes, though the preference is as a part of United Nations operations, and there is concern the other nations might not bear their fair share.[4]

Although looking to the United Nations to perform a stronger role in the maintenance of peace, the American public is ambivalent about the capability of the United Nations[5], and the respondents are split when asked whether the United States should make forces available to the United Nations on the basis of a standing commitment (42 percent) or on a case-by-case basis (45 percent). In the economic area, the ambivalence is also pronounced. Respondents were split when asked if the United Nations should have responsibility for making trading rules, and preferred (49 percent to 34 percent) that the United States and other countries rely on their own actions against competitors in trade disputes.[6]

For the United States, adapting to the changed political climate will not be easy or without cost. The so-called military-industrial complex, already under pressure to change because of excessive expansion in the Reagan years, suddenly finds it necessary to downsize at a far more rapid rate than it could ever have imagined. Downsizing of the military-industrial complex, coming as it does in the midst of the adjustment of the United States economy to global economic forces, causes some who otherwise might welcome military downsizing to argue for a less hurried pace or, significantly, to support the closing of military installations in someone else's neighborhood. And during a period of budget stringency in the United States, those who would assist the old enemy in order to prevent chaos are pitted against those who oppose aid for ideological reasons joined in an uncomfortable alliance with those who argue the time has come to devote resources to problems at home.

The abrupt end of the cold war has had a profound influence on the making and content of American foreign policy. Within the immediate future no aspect of government will escape review, including the intelligence community. However, the participants in the foreign policy decision-making process, the process itself, and the substance of foreign policy have been changing for some time.

Congress, which reasserted its role in foreign policy during the Vietnam War, continues to insist on a stronger role. However, it is at a general level of oversight. Membership on the committees on foreign affairs, for example, are no longer prized assignments as members seek committee assignments of more direct benefit to their constituents.

By the end of the cold war, the Department of State, which had escaped dominance by the Ivy League early in the cold war, had lost its dominance in foreign policy. (It is doubtful, however, that the public perceives the changed role of the Department of State.) The Council on Foreign Relations, although more diverse in its membership, is no longer dominant in foreign policy influence. Economic issues have attained an importance equal to political questions and are challenging the dominance of security considerations. The public, through nongovernmental organizations, multinational corporations, and various interest groups have claimed pivotal roles in both the formulation and implementation of foreign policy. Finally, the so-called CNN factor has placed an informed public in a position to reach its own conclusions on substantially the same knowledge base as the government.

Moreover, in part due to the very success of the United States in helping other nations recover from the devastation of World War II, in part due to technological advancement, and in part due to neglect of its own affairs, the position of the United States in the world economy has changed profoundly. Under the American nuclear umbrella, the European Community and Japan have emerged to play central roles in economic and political affairs. The United States, correspondingly, is less dominant and no longer has the world market or even its own market to itself. Indeed, the public perception is of a United States unfairly attacked by its own allies and getting weaker.

Finally, the distinction between foreign and domestic policy is now blurred at best. The result is that foreign policy is no longer the preserve of the Department of State within the executive branch of the national government. Almost every department of the federal government now has some interest in foreign policy decision making. Similar changes have taken place in the legislative branch of the government.

Similarly, more than ever, foreign policy is influenced by the actions of state and local governments. In their quest for investment, trade, and tourism, state and local governments have dispatched missions, established offices abroad, and offered lucrative concessions in their efforts to attract foreign money. Inevitably, therefore, both state and local governments have become interest groups to be reckoned with in decisions that might affect their promotional efforts. Nor is state and local influence limited to trade and investment. For example, states have been known to reject representatives seen as too involved in foreign affairs. In the Nicaragua conflict, several states sought, albeit unsuccessfully, to restrict the use of their national guard units because the state (or governor) opposed Nicaragua policy. In the campaign against apartheid in South Africa more than 150 states and localities endorsed sanctions in their local commerce before and more stringently than did the federal government. Even after the federal government had lifted its sanctions, many of the state and local sanctions continued in force. Indeed, long after Namibia had been independent, the removal of state and local restrictions was a problem for the federal government.

Toward Shared Responsibility

There is a convergence of factors that makes this a propitious time for the United States to formulate a post–cold war foreign policy with a decided multilateral bent. Such an approach would allow others to share routine burdens while the United States continues to fulfill the strategic security role that it cannot relinquish. And, of course, attention to domestic economic affairs and neglected domestic problems is necessary for the nation's strength and to avoid further disenchantment with foreign affairs. Finally, the public prefers a multilateral approach at precisely the time when the international climate makes it possible to make further advancement in the directions stalled by the cold war.

While the provisions of the United Nations Charter for the maintenance of international peace and security were almost frozen in place at the beginning of the cold war, that was not entirely true for those provisions of the charter that promoted cooperation in social, economic, and cultural fields. Indeed, it was work in the latter fields and its work in peacekeeping that advocates of the United Nations usually cited in describing the positive accomplishments and the potential of the organization. In spite of the autonomous nature of the specialized agencies they are an integral part of the United Nations system and have played a key role in demonstrating the value of multilateral approaches to problems that cut across national lines and that cannot be resolved or even managed within the authority of a single state.

Working cooperatively with the specialized agencies or independently are numerous nongovernmental organizations and such regional and international governmental organizations as the European Community, NATO, the General Agreement on Tariffs and Trade, the Gulf Cooperation Council, the Organization of African Unity, the Association of Southeast Asian Nations, and the Organization of American States. The perceived need for and the relative success of these organizations undoubtedly spur additional efforts along the same lines. However, the major impetus for multilateral organizations is increased interdependence. Long a cliche, interdependence has been given a major boost by such cross-boundary problems as the environment, AIDS, and the flow of refugees. Indeed, while massive oil spills at sea played a role, it was probably the disastrous consequences of Chernobyl, a product of the cold war, that may have been the final demonstration of interdependence.

Technology and trade and commerce have also played key roles in encouraging interdependence. Telecommunications and transportation have made it possible for multinational corporations to operate efficiently in various parts of the world. Manufacturing processes are integrated in ways that allow parts of a final product to be fabricated in various parts of the world. Telecommunications make it possible to conduct transactions instantly. Indeed, currency transactions by multinational corporations and banks have greatly lessened the control that countries have on the value of their own currency, a fact that can affect economic conditions, and therefore political conditions, in the country.

In a very real sense, therefore, the end of the cold war allows interdependence in the security aspects of international affairs to catch up with developments that are well on their way in the social and economic realms. Catching up does not simply involve dusting off the unused provisions of the United Nations Charter. The momentum of World War II might have been sufficient to persuade nations to fulfill obligations to provide military forces to the United Nations, but more than forty-five years have intervened and the United Nations is a far more heterogeneous institution, making consensus more difficult to reach. Nor is it possible to simply use the institutions that grew out of the cold war. NATO, for example, besides being a regional alliance with political baggage of its own, is restricted to a defined area. The Conference on Security and Cooperation in Europe, once thought of as a possible player in resolving the Yugoslav conflict, has no experience in peacekeeping. Similarly, the Organization of African Unity does not have the resources to handle problems in Africa; and the European Community demonstrated during the Yugoslav situation that the Community was without experience, and worse, was not sufficiently distant from the problem. Clearly it will be necessary to strengthen and adapt the machinery of the United Nations.

Catching up also means recognizing that the nature of the problem before the international community has significantly changed. The United Nations of 1945 envisioned collective responsibility for preserving peace between nations. While interstate conflict will probably always remain a serious problem, the international community of the 1990s and for the foreseeable future must also handle the problem of intrastate conflict. Disputes within states, between ethnic, religious, and political groups, disputes labeled civil wars in an earlier stage of history and later caught in superpower maneuvering, are today's problems. So are total breakdowns in government (e.g., Uganda and Somalia) as fragile governments in post–World War II independent countries face difficulty in governing. The United Nations has become a 911 service for the world.

In a very real sense there is a convergence between the end of the cold war, the desire of the American public to avoid being the world's police officer and to pay more attention to problems at home, and the renewed ability of the international community to act together in international crises. The United States cannot avoid a leadership role in international affairs nor the responsibility to act, alone if necessary, in those instances when no other alternative to peace or chaos is present. However, more than ever before there is an opportunity for shared responsibility and with it the further advancement of international cooperation in the maintenance of peace and security.

Shared responsibility is neither immediate nor without costs. In important respects the American public will have to be persuaded to buy into it. Shared responsibility is not immediate because it will be some time before the international community will have developed the necessary multinational military forces. It may not be possible to move immediately to national forces placed at the disposal of the United Nations under agreement as called for in Article 43 of the United Nations Charter. On the other hand, the practice of voluntary forces placed at the disposal of the United Nations as each situation arose is clearly inadequate. Valuable time was lost during the period required to persuade countries to volunteer forces; financing remains a serious problem; and forces deployed have no common training, equipment, or communications capability. Command and control is difficult at best and even more so given the lean and primitive staffing that the United Nations is accustomed to using. The only thing they have in common is their blue helmet. Limited weapons and armament were sufficient during peacekeeping ventures during the cold war where the parties to conflict had already largely agreed to cease fire or peace terms. However, the peace enforcement or peacemaking ventures that face the international community require more firepower and sophisticated transport, something heretofore available only to larger countries.

In order to ensure United Nations capability and to reduce its role as the world's police officer, the United States will have to take a lead role in helping improve the capability of the United Nations to respond to crisis situations. Member states could be asked to participate in a United Nations force that with improved staffing, improved command and control, a system of predesignated units consisting of volunteers, with common training and common equipment, pre-positioned where necessary, and financed by a sufficiently large reserve fund would go a long way toward enabling the international community to respond rapidly to crises.

While the American role in such a force inevitably would be larger initially and would remain relatively large consistent with the size and capability of the United States, it could in time be placed in the same perspective as in the whole of the United Nations, that is, important, essential, but not dominant. The same can be said for the one element of a United Nations force that seems to concern the American military and American politicians. That is concern that American forces in international service remain under command and control of the United States. That is a problem that is larger in theory than in practice. In the first place no American forces could be used without American agreement in the Security Council where the United States has a veto. Moreover, at its root, the American concern should be over the safety of American forces, not who commands. As in NATO, common training should allay American concern about safety and objectivity. This has already been demonstrated in Somalia where initial concern about placing American troops under the command of the United Nations was overcome by the assignment of a Turkish commander with whom the United States was thoroughly familiar through NATO. As a practical matter, however, given the financial and military dominance of the United States and its allies, there is no reason to believe that the United States could not be satisfied about the command of American forces under United Nations command.

Development of an international force is not simply an intellectual or desirable objective; it is a necessity. Twice in the early 1990s, just after the end of the cold war, the United States bore most of the physical burden in responding to aggression in Kuwait and chaos in Somalia. In both instances, President Bush argued that the United States was the only country that could project the necessary force. Of course, it helped that other countries helped bear the financial cost of Kuwait. However, it is precisely the police officer's role that the American public wishes to avoid and that accounted for the refusal of the United States to dispatch troops to Bosnia in the absence of a settlement. Yet the United States will repeatedly find itself in the position of being the only country capable of projecting the necessary military force unless it assists and insists upon the development of a United Nations force.

Implicit in the above discussion is the firm conclusion that the United States cannot push foreign policy to the back burner as was done in the 1992 presidential campaign. It is very likely that the effort to concentrate on domestic affairs will be subject to constant distractions and, particularly where domestic and international economic concerns intersect, will complicate foreign policy. The task is to find a foreign policy mechanism that will more reflect a reordering of American priorities. Shared responsibility has the added advantage of promoting international institutions as a way of resolving problems and promoting international cooperation.

Notes

[1] Gallup/CNN/*USA Today*, January 1992.

[2] Gallup/CNN/*USA Today*, January 1992.

[3] Gallup poll, December 4, 1962. See also *Los Angeles Times*, January 26, 1993; Gallup poll, December 3, 1992; *Time*/CNN/Yankelovich, Clancy, and Shulman, September 10, 1992; Roper Organization for the United Nations Association in *American Public Opinion and the United Nations*, March 1992.

[4] Gallup poll, July 31, 1992. See also *Los Angeles Times*, January 26, 1993; Gallup poll, December 4, 1992.

[5] Roper Organization for the United Nations Association in *American Public Opinion and the United Nations*, March 1992.

[6] Roper Organization for the United Nations Association in *American Public Opinion and the United Nations*, March 1992.

5

Congress in the Post–Cold War World

NORMAN J. ORNSTEIN

A s the 1992 election approached, the U.S. Congress found itself embattled, uneasy, and off-balance. Bruised by press and public reaction to issues like a congressional pay raise and congressional "perks," reports of scandals like the Keating Five and the House bank, and public unhappiness with policy "grid-

NORMAN J. ORNSTEIN is a resident scholar at the American Enterprise Institute for Public Policy Research, political contributor to the *MacNeil/Lehrer Newshour,* and election analyst for CBS News. In addition, Mr. Ornstein works with Al Franken as a commentator and pollster for the Comedy Central Television Network's political coverage, and is a senior adviser to the *Times Mirror* Center for the People and the Press. He was a founding member, serving on the board of directors, of the National Commission on the Public Service, chaired by Paul Volcker. Mr. Ornstein has worked at different times on Capitol Hill, starting in 1969–70 as an American Political Science Association congressional fellow. Currently, with Tom Mann of the Brookings Institution, he is codirecting the Renewing Congress Project, a major, comprehensive examination of the changes likely to occur with the 103rd Congress. He is the author of several books and numerous articles and reviews and lectures frequently in the United States and abroad.

lock," and frustrated by their own sense of inability to act on important policy priorities, members of Congress found themselves scrambling to regain some measure of public acceptance, if not approval. The public antipathy toward politics and politicians extended beyond Congress, of course, and underscored a mood for change—one reinforced by the Perot phenomenon.

The image was defined clearly and in stark terms by Perot and his adherents. Trapped by their solicitude to special interests and their high-powered lobbyists, seduced by the perks and privileges of pampered power in Washington, controlled by their overriding desire to get reelected, members of Congress were caught "inside the beltway," simultaneously out of touch with real America and too willing to pander to public opinion to stay in office. The result, went the Perotian vision, was a combination of corrupt public policy and policy gridlock—the inability to get anything of importance done. As a consequence, Perot posited, America drifted, with an economy in disarray, while politicians made sure first to enhance their own status and benefits.

The election itself reflected the desire for change and the high level of voter hostility toward the political status quo. George Bush received only 38 percent of the popular vote in a three-way race— the lowest support for an incumbent president since 1912. Nineteen incumbent members of the House of Representatives were defeated in primaries, a modern record; another twenty-four were ousted on November 3, 1992. At the same time, the average margin of victory for incumbent winners declined sharply for a second consecutive election. There was no significant partisan shift in the election; the desire for change cut clearly across party lines.

The 103rd Congress that convened on January 3, 1993, contained 110 new members of the House, reflecting the largest turnover since 1948. The Democratic majority was jubilant that it was returned to serve with a Democratic president, creating united government, under their party's control, for the first time in twelve years. But it was extremely sensitive both to continuing public antipathy toward Washington and especially toward Congress, and to the Perot driven move for sweeping governmental reform.

There was striking irony in the fact that public antipathy toward politics and governmental institutions and a strong desire for change, including sweeping reform, were central components of American government and politics in the early 1990s. In other ways, after all, the early 1990s represented one of the greatest policy triumphs in history.

When the cold war ended with the collapse of the Soviet Union and international communism, it represented an unprecedented victory for American values, policies, and institutions—including Congress. Rarely does a society have a singular goal, sought over decades at enormous cost in money and lives, that is achieved quickly and clearly, without a costly military battle or a tactical retreat and ambiguous results.

The collapse of the Soviet empire and philosophy did not bring with it, however, an American celebration of the policies and institutions that contributed to the result. Rather, the end of the cold war was, and continues to be, accompanied by deep-seated unhappiness by American voters with politics and political institutions. Public confidence in Congress reached new lows in 1991 and 1992, moving out of the depths only briefly with the triumph of the Gulf War only to sink again with the House bank scandal.

To be sure, the public reaction to the political status quo in 1992 was far from unique. Societies often opt for major political change following a great military triumph. Britain unceremoniously dumped the Conservative party and Winston Churchill following World War II, even as U.S. voters threw out the Democratic majority in both houses of Congress in 1946. The Democrats and Woodrow Wilson had suffered the same fate in 1918. Gratitude is rarely a lasting sentiment among voters; when wars, with their massive sacrifice and dislocation end, voters want change.

Reform, too, often is precipitated by the end of a major war, moved both by the overall desire for change and by the recognition that the world has changed, and institutions need to respond to the new environment. The Budget and Accounting Act of 1921, creating the modern budget system that gave the president a major role for the first time, followed the First World War. The end of the Second World War brought the sweeping Legislative Reorganization Act of 1946, the Employment Act of 1946 (creating the precursor to the Office of Management and Budget), and the National Security Act of 1947, creating the National Security

Council. The Budget and Impoundment Control Act, the War Powers Act, campaign finance reform, and internal congressional reform all followed the Vietnam War.

The cold war was not conducted in the same way as other wars, and it did not end in the same way. But the desire for change and reform is obviously there, as is the clear reality that the world is fundamentally different now. How will Congress respond to the altered world order—and to the new politics accompanying it? How will Congress relate to the American public in this environment? How will it—and how should it—alter its institutional framework?

That the world—and America's role in it—has changed in fundamental ways in the past few years is indisputable. The end of the cold war, precipitated by the increasingly rapid globalization of the economy, has brought and will continue to bring profound changes in the way nations interact, in the way the United States views itself, and in the way it relates to the rest of the world. These changes cannot help but affect American politics, American political institutions, and American voters.

The New Policy Environment

How will the end of the cold war change Congress and its role in the American foreign policy process? To answer that question means looking not just at Congress internally, but at its relationships with other institutions, its overall role in American politics and policy making, and the broader dynamics of all these forces.

The role and behavior of Congress can be affected by many forces. *Structures and rules* can change; that may mean changes in the Constitution, or in laws affecting constitutional roles and responsibilities, such as the War Powers Act; or it may mean internal changes in rules, committee jurisdictions, or internal powers via reform. *Events*, such as a war or a scandal, can precipitate change. *Political alignments* can change, as the presidency, the House, the Senate, or some combination of the three shift partisan control. *Personalities* can change, as a new president, new congressional leaders, or a new class of members alter the relationships within and among the branches. *The public* can change its basic attitudes toward governing institutions, toward foreign policy, or toward the relationship between domestic and foreign affairs, in turn altering Congress's perceptions of the same areas or policies. Many forces can, of course, move in combination, reinforcing the dynamics of change.

The Constitution has not changed foreign policy decision-making power, but all the external forces that shape U.S. governing institutions have—and so have the internal dynamics of Congress. This chapter will try to sort out what is fundamental and enduring change from situational change, and to look ahead to see what might occur through the rest of the decade.

As I noted above, the end of the cold war brought with it an election of change; one important by-product was the end of twelve consecutive years of divided government, supplanted by at least two, probably four, and perhaps more of one-party control of the reins of government in Washington. Of course, divided government has actually been the dominant framework for American politics for a much longer period of time; before 1993 it was present for twenty-six of the previous thirty-eight years.

Divided government per se does not mean policy gridlock or unremitting hostility and distrust between the branches of government. Yale political scientist David Mayhew has made a persuasive case that in the postwar era, both significant legislation and investigations have been as prevalent in periods of divided government as united government.[1]

Neither does divided government mean automatic tension and disagreement over foreign policy—or the reverse. United government in 1940 did not prevent bitter struggles between Franklin Roosevelt and his Democratic Congress over lend-lease to Britain and the extension of the draft. Divided government in the 1950s did not block Republican President Dwight Eisenhower and a Democratic Congress from basic harmony over foreign policy. The "credibility gap" was defined during an era of united government, under Lyndon Johnson and the Democrats.

But the Nixon-Congress relationship soured over Vietnam, Cambodia, and impoundment politics long before Watergate, and the lack of trust between the branches expanded into even more areas in the Reagan/Bush era. In the latter period, twelve consecutive years of divided government clearly exacerbated tensions and hostilities between the executive and legislative branches. For Democrats, accustomed to holding majorities in Congress but increasingly removed from power (and responsibility) in the executive, efforts to weaken executive control over foreign policy and maintain more aggressive oversight of executive actions abroad, all within a climate of skepticism and distrust, became major focal points. For Republicans, facing more than three consecutive decades of minority status in the House of Representatives but blessed with a series of landslide victories for the White House, finding ways to hamstring Congress and reduce its power and prerogatives, or at least to bypass it, became a basic driving goal. The Iran/Contra affair showed both sides of this attitudinal struggle.

To be sure, hostility driven by divided government did not prevent presidents from acting decisively when they wanted to, or when conditions warranted. Ronald Reagan successfully completed his Grenadan and Libyan operations, received a congressional go-ahead to station and—via the War Powers Act—keep Marines in Lebanon, got the defense budget increases he wanted, and achieved major arms control treaties with the Soviet Union that were ratified by the Senate. George Bush had success in Panama unhampered by Congress, and of course was given authorization by Congress to take military action in the Gulf.

But even with these examples of legislative-executive cooperation, there was still little basic trust between the branches. Now at least one root cause of that lack of trust has been removed. Congressional Democrats have long-time friends and colleagues in top positions in the Clinton White House, including one of their own, Les Aspin, as secretary of defense. They have a deep desire to restore cooperation with the executive, and a president who appears genuinely to believe in communication and consultation with Congress.

It is not clear, however, that the sudden return of united government will itself make any fundamental difference. The long pattern of divided government, in an era of investigative journalism, with a Congress that has beefed up its own institutional capability to deal with foreign, national security, and intelligence policy and that is not readily responsive to strong centralized leadership, has created other dynamics that will make instant cooperation unlikely.

Even before Bill Clinton had been inaugurated, he was embroiled in a tough dispute with his fellow southern Democrat, Senate Armed Services Committee Chair Sam Nunn, over gays in the military. Within his first few months in office, Democrats were critical of his aid plan for Russia, outraged over base closings, and unhappy over his defense budget. Long-dominant patterns of distrust of executive power will not change readily; the old-time executive pattern of settling foreign policy arguments by saying, "We have more information than you do" is simply no longer possible when a legislative branch is loaded with experts in every regional, technical, and policy area who can match their own expertise with ready access to sources in the executive, and who can supplement their information with networks of contacts in academia and industry.

At the same time, other important dynamics have changed. Most of the partisan and institutional divisions of the past several decades revolved around the struggle against international communism and the Soviet Union—including Vietnam, aid to the Contras, Grenada, and Cuba. For three decades, anticommunism was the major institutional wedge between the parties, and it shaped the institutional conflicts between president and Congress. Now that anticommunism is no longer a factor, partisan tensions may in fact decline—but new tensions, some fueled by isolationist versus internationalist impulses, others by protectionism versus free trade sentiments, yet others perhaps by budgetary considerations, are likely to emerge—all cutting across party *and* ideological lines.

Some of these tensions are related to traditional geopolitical considerations, of course, but most have a strong economic tenor. The end of the cold war has meant a sharp change in the international policy agenda. The timing of the collapse of the Soviet Union and its satellites is related to the rapid change in the world in the 1980s and 1990s toward economic globalization, fueled in part by changes in information technology and transportation.

For the Soviet Union, the need to open up its previously closed economy and currency to the outside world meant that it lost its ability to declare inflation and employment to be nonexistent; the outside economic forces acted like a virus, accelerating the economic collapse of the system. For the United States, the globalization of the economy led to a decade of leveraged buyouts, mergers, bankruptcies, and corporate restructurings that contributed mightily to the public unease about the economy and unhappiness with the country's governing elites, which set the stage for the election in 1992.

More generally, in the post–cold war era, geoeconomics increasingly drives geopolitics, compared to a cold war agenda where geopolitics drove geoeconomics. For Congress, this means that the fuzzy line between domestic and foreign policies and politics grows even fuzzier; the number of members of Congress who assert their role in foreign policy increases, as does the number of interested groups.

As a consequence, members of Congress can exert greater influence over foreign policy from the vantage points of committees like Ways and Means, Banking, Energy and Commerce, and Agriculture. In turn, the relative prestige and attractiveness of the House Foreign Affairs and Senate Foreign Relations Committees is likely to decline; unless reform or restructuring changes things, the relative locus of foreign policy decision making will move toward committees and chairs whose basic orientation is inward and domestic.

The context for Congress is thus one of paradox and uncertainty. A time of triumph is accompanied by widespread vilification of the institutions that presided over the triumph. One result has been to create a fertile climate for institutional reform, which in turn has left lawmakers grappling with alternative reform ideas, and uneasy about what might result.

A new period of united government leaves both parties uncertain of their role and future, and the institutions of government, Congress and the executive, groping to develop new styles of decision making and comfortable roles in the policy-making process. A new world order means a new climate for policy and the need to build a new framework for foreign policy—one that will not come easily, will not be easy to define in black-and-white terms, and will upset previous power relationships and change the importance of areas of expertise on the Hill.

The Congressional Response

Congress is in the process of responding to this climate, and to all the changes around it. Some of the responses will be reactive, de facto adjustments to events or pressures; some will be proactive—reforms or changes that anticipate the new political and policy world and try to craft an appropriate and constructive role for the legislative branch. In the remainder of this chapter, I will try to suggest some of the ways Congress is likely to react, and, perhaps more important, some of the ways it should.

For Congress, the challenges are multiple. The institution and its members need to respond to public unhappiness, both to keep the individuals from being swept out on a wave of voter disgust, and to keep destructive "reforms," such as term limits, from doing deep and permanent damage to congressional power and capacity. But the response needs to be a real response to institutional shortcomings and failures in performance, not simply a cynical or knee-jerk response to the surface reasons for public unhappiness, such as eliminating minor congressional perks.[2]

That is only one set of goals for Congress. Congress also has to devise a better way to coordinate or develop foreign policy with the executive branch, using the opportunity of united party government to get beyond the institutional distrust that has typified the process for many years. Improving executive-legislative communications may mean internal changes, including structural ways to facilitate consultation and communication between the branches; it may also mean revising laws like the War Powers Act.

Congress further has to respond to the challenges of the new world order. If the world indeed is driven more by geoeconomics and less by geopolitics, and if geopolitics has changed from a dominant focus on superpower conflict, the ways in which Congress considers issues should change to reflect these new realities—including perhaps alterations in the jurisdictions and focuses of committees and subcommittees.

At the same time, as the United States moves to develop a vision of its role in a redefined, post–cold war world, and as it deals with examples, events, and crises that will help to define such a role, Congress must play a constructive part, educating the public about the policy choices available to the country, and helping convert public opinion into broader public judgment.

In this new and challenging environment, the most important thing for Congress to do is to step back and define its main missions as an institution. Congress is a policy-making body, but it was not set up simply to reflect public opinion. The Framers designed Congress to be a *deliberative* body. The job of Congress, James Madison noted in *Federalist 10*, is to "refine and enlarge public views." To refine and enlarge public views meant creating processes for debating and considering the range of viewpoints and positions, gathering and taking into account public opinions, and, through a process of give-and-take, argumentation, and persuasion, creating a judgment that was a level above the initial views themselves.

Translating public views into public judgment has two components: the translation and the action. Congress was also designed to have the capacity to act when the society and its needs demanded it, whether it be creating policy to respond to domestic need, or responding to a foreign challenge with action that might range from new tariffs to a declaration of war.

Setting Its Agenda

The capacity to act requires Congress to have both a mechanism to set priorities and an agenda, and the ability to carry out action on that agenda. Congress is inherently a reactive body, operating most comfortably when a president leads the way and it responds. But the political system works best when Congress can set a reasonable set of priorities, and can move on them when circumstances and politics require. A president's agenda must inevitably be negotiated with Congress; that is most effectively done if the president has a specific group of lawmakers, ceded authority by their colleagues, to negotiate with. But Congress must then have the capacity to carry out its part of the bargain.

The House of Representatives took the first important step toward a better agenda-setting capability in December 1992, when its majority Democratic Caucus created a Speaker's Working Group on Policy Development, explicitly designed to meet before each new Congress to set a yearly agenda. The Democratic Caucus also pledged to organize each Congress early, and to get off to a swifter beginning, both prerequisites for an effective action agenda.

It also strengthened the power of the leadership, and the speaker particularly, to work the majority's will with committee chairs by giving the leadership oriented Steering and Policy Committee more control over the fate of chairs. The steps were salutary, but more steps are necessary—and every action taken in the House should be matched by comparable actions in the Senate.

One need is a more effective mechanism to act on wide-ranging national policy issues that cut across the lines of several committees. The House has a rule permitting the creation of ad hoc committees, temporary panels with members drawn from a variety of committees, to expedite action on an important bill. In 1977, at the outset of the Carter administration, Speaker Thomas P. O'Neill used this authority to create an ad hoc committee on energy to pass successfully and expeditiously the president's comprehensive energy bill. But the power has atrophied since; it is time to revive it, and to create a similar mechanism in the Senate.

The Senate needs some additional specific attention. In foreign policy, of course, the Senate has some unique powers that signal its special role, particularly the sole power to ratify treaties and to confirm executive nominees. Senate rules do provide special status for privileged consideration of a treaty—within the context of a body designed to protect and enhance the role and views of minorities, to make it easier not to act than to act.

It would go against the basic design of the American political system to do violence to the Senate's special place in the great design. But the fact is that the Senate's special concern for minority viewpoints, expressed through the deference given to its individual members, has turned in recent years to a simple indulgence for the whims and predilections of 100 prima donnas. Routine debate drags on for unnecessary hours and days to accommodate senators' speaking schedules and outside commitments. Filibusters, once limited to issues of great national moment and invoked by one or more senators who felt intensely about them, now are invoked routinely on trivial matters by individual senators who use the threat of a filibuster as a bargaining tool.

Furthermore, the "hold," the unwritten practice of allowing any senator to delay action on a bill or nomination to give him or her a chance to marshall arguments and evidence to make a case, has degenerated into regular, anonymous, and indefinite delays to kill nominations or to gain leverage on entirely extraneous matters. For example, several major State Department nominations were put on hold, apparently by Senator Jesse Helms, in March and April 1993, putting key areas of the Clinton foreign policy in limbo, so that he could block a $50 million aid package to Nicaragua.[3]

Changing the rules of the Senate may not be enough here; it is the *culture* of rampant individualism in the Senate that has taken a practice like the hold—which is not in any rule—and turned it into a weapon unanticipated by its creators. But changing the rules may help to change the culture, and in the process strike a better balance between delay and action, and between minority views and majority rights.

One possibility might be to alter the routine aspect of the filibuster, by creating two classes of filibusters: Class I would be for those issues of great national moment, but it would require senators, as in the old era, to take the floor and keep it continuously, perhaps around-the-clock, à la *Mr. Smith Goes to Washington*. The other, for more routine matters, would be harder to begin, requiring ten signatures on a petition, and would be easier to end; as with the current practice under Senate Rule XXII, cloture (an end to debate) would require sixty votes to invoke—but only on the first cloture petition. A second cloture vote, taken at least a week after the first, would require only fifty-five votes, and a third, another week or more later, only a majority vote.

This change would elevate the filibuster as it was originally envisioned, while diminishing the modern version, which itself denigrates the concept of unlimited debate to protect minority viewpoints, and which has been frequently misused in recent years.

Another would be to create procedures, such as a Committee of the Whole in the Senate, to expedite routine business by imposing more disciplined time and amendment procedures. A third would be to bring holds into the rules, banning anonymity and putting a time limit, say two weeks, on them.

Of course, these kinds of changes are not aimed specifically at the Senate's ability to act on a foreign policy agenda. But, by tilting slightly away from individualism to collective action, they would have a positive impact on foreign policy and a more direct impact on executive nominations for foreign policy and diplomatic posts.

Dealing with the Executive

General changes to create more flexibility for Congress to respond to outside forces, and to act in a rapidly changing world, are one forum for movement. Another area Congress must address in the post-cold war world is its relations with the executive—both generally, and in specific relation to foreign and national security policy.[4] The major source of conflict—widespread disagreement over policy choices, made especially tough during nasty budgetary times—remains a prime factor, unified government or not. A slightly more centralized system of party leadership in Congress might help here, by giving leaders more ability to negotiate with the president on behalf of their chambers, and to keep compromises they achieve. But other factors besides fundamental disagreements over policy have exacerbated interbranch friction, and can be addressed directly.

One problem is "micromanagement." From the Civil War roughly through Vietnam, the opposite occurred; the norm was broad delegations of discretionary authority by Congress to the executive branch. But since the early 1970s, steadily increasing reassertions of congressional authority have led to executive branch unhappiness over congressional meddling, which executives commonly refer to as micromanagement.

These charges cannot easily be dismissed as simple interbranch or partisan rivalry. In fact, committee reports and legislation are regularly filled with legislative demands, from reporting requirements and administrative directions to regulations, usually with little regard for the real managerial or substantive concerns of agency administrators.

Of course, the problem does not stem simply from unilateral

congressional aggressiveness or highhandedness. In the Bush White House, at the direction of White House Counsel C. Boyden Gray, the executive frequently deliberately ignored or defied congressional intent, exercising a kind of executive veto of legislative provisions they did not like or deemed excessive.

If unified government does not magically change the attitudes or behavior of actors in both branches, it does provide an opportunity to take steps to reduce the climate of distrust, and to change the incentives for overreaching. Clearly, a goal is to make sure that the players no longer see executive-legislative relations in zero-sum terms. It is in the interests of both sides to strengthen each branch's comparative advantages. For the system to work best, Congress should deliberate about the major legislative policy options and the president must provide leadership.

Structural reforms themselves cannot provide an atmosphere of mutual respect, or alter patterns of behavior that have become ingrained. But some changes can help provide better communication when policies are formulated and priorities set, which in turn can help ensure that legislative delegation and executive action can be appropriately coordinated. At the same time, some changes might be able to redefine consultation to fit the prerogatives and goals of both branches.

An important area for action is *legislative intent.* One of the main zones of friction between the branches is conflicting interpretations of what Congress means in its statutes; consider, for example, the various Boland Amendments that were designed to prevent forms of unilateral executive support for the Contras in Nicaragua, which were at the root of the Iran/Contra conflict between the Reagan White House and Congress.

Congress needs first to develop a clearer definition of what counts as legislative intent, including the language of a statute, along with committee reports that are explicitly approved by a committee and ratified in some formal way by Congress. Where Congress can make its intent clear directly in the language of a statute, it should, but that is not always practical or desirable. Writing even more detail into law can mean more rigid micromanagement than leaving statutes as concise as possible. The lawmaking process is unavoidably fluid and messy, but Congress needs to make a major effort to work out new ground rules, with the executive, on legislative intent and administrative interpretation, to avoid future Iran/Contras if for no other reason.

Another area to address is *executive branch testimony*. Top executive officials, especially cabinet officers, have spent an increasing share of their time and energy testifying in front of a growing array of congressional committees and subcommittees. The regular presence of top executive officials before Congress is a requirement for making laws and overseeing their implementation, but that presence should be limited to those committees and subcommittees that have official jurisdiction over the departments, or those where there is a compelling justification for requiring a top executive official to appear.

In recent years, though, more and more panels, for extraneous, often ego-driven reasons, have demanded appearances by the secretary of state and other officials, creating an increasingly inefficient use of executive officials' time. Congress could use majority party organs, like the Speaker's Working Group on Policy Development in the House and the Democratic Policy Committee in the Senate, to act as arbiters in this process. Where cabinet officers and other top executive officials feel that an appearance is unnecessary or superfluous, they would be able to appeal to these panels to defer or cancel a committee or subcommittee demand to testify.

This may seem like a small, even trivial issue and reform. But it would be a significant step toward a more productive relationship between the branches.

Third is *consultation*. The level of communication between president and Congress depends primarily on the willingness of the president and congressional leaders to meet together and be open with one another. No structural reform can create that willingness if it does not exist. But creating a mechanism to bring officials of both branches together on a regular basis can increase the possibility that the branches will be aware of what the other is doing, and cut back on the level of misunderstanding.

In the national security area, specifically, a joint consultative group on national security policy should be formed, consisting of top members of the congressional party and policy leadership and executive counterparts; this group would be consulted first in the event of a national emergency, but more important, it would meet regularly to build a congressional role in setting broad policy goals, explicitly trying to avoid the recent reliance on detailed, restrictive, and frequently punitive measures passed after the fact.

In addition, it would be wise to amend the War Powers Act by substituting an explicit consultation mechanism for the existing requirement that troops be withdrawn if Congress doesn't act to extend their stay in a potential war zone. Consultation should also be the norm for a president before he uses force, except in the rare event that requires immediate response to repel an attack.

Even though these recommendations may be especially timely now, most would have been relevant in the cold war era too. It may also be true that a careful look at the committee system in Congress would have been in order during the cold war (indeed, both houses did just that in the mid-1970s). But the dramatic change in the international arena, including both America's role as a superpower and the growing primacy of geoeconomics, makes a post-cold war look at the committee system particularly necessary.

Realigning Committee Jurisdictions

As I note above, the centers of power in the committee system are changing as the world changes, even without a realignment in committee jurisdictions. As international issues have changed, committees with an economic focus—Banking, Budget, Energy and Commerce, Ways and Means, just to take the House of Representatives—have become more significant players. Even panels like Agriculture or Science and Technology have increased their focus on international issues, and become players of sorts. As other foreign policy issues have emerged, so too have such panels as Governmental Affairs in the Senate, which has taken up the issue of nuclear nonproliferation. In the meantime, the committees with a more traditional focus, especially House Foreign Affairs and Senate Foreign Relations, have become less central than they were. Through the 1980s, these panels tended to be overshadowed by the more assertive and representative Armed Services Committees, which, led by their bright and energetic chairs, Senator Sam Nunn and Representative Les Aspin, redefined foreign policy into national security terms. But the relentless budget pressures on defense, combined with the departure of Aspin, leave the Armed Services panels with some identity crisis as well.

Lacking any meaningful array of substantive jurisdictional responsibilities, the House Foreign Affairs Committee has been plagued in recent years with a dearth of members seeking assignment to it; it has faced the embarrassment of as many as eight or nine vacancies each Congress. The Senate Foreign Relations Committee, with its historic prestige and role, has fared better, but has its own problems, including a bland and unassertive chair, Claiborne Pell.

It has also had its membership difficulties. In an open, decentralized, and democratized Congress, legislators can assert an individual viewpoint or role in foreign policy from any vantage point their individual entrepreneurial talents allow—membership on the core panels is not a requirement to claim expertise or garner attention. In fact, given the poor electoral record of Foreign Relations Committee members in recent years, it may be more advantageous for senators with some interest in foreign policy to pursue their interests outside the committee. While the Foreign Relations Committee does have some highly respected and visible foreign policy experts, such as Richard Lugar and Daniel P. Moynihan, many of the most important and assertive voices, including Bill Bradley, Joe Lieberman, and David Boren, have not been committee members.

The impetus to realign the jurisdictions of committees in Congress comes from more than just a realization that the world has dramatically changed. The drive for reform is broader than that, and reform of the committee system is a natural concomitant of the overall push for reform. Jurisdictions are the subject of scrutiny and realignment periodically, for several reasons. The world changes; areas of vital importance in one season might be atrophied or irrelevant in the next, while new areas emerge. Post roads and Indian affairs might lose relevance or prominence, while the environment, telecommunications, or international economics become transcendent. At the same time, the substantive life of a member of Congress is channeled through his or her committees; the number and nature of committees, the number and nature of assignments, along with the jurisdictions, matter directly and enormously to all lawmakers.

Committees were once defined as "little legislatures." They are the primary means for Congress to divide its labor, develop expertise, consider policy areas and alternatives, translate ideas into bills, and receive information and wisdom from outside the chamber. Congress constantly has to guard against too much fragmentation in the committee system—too many committees and subcommittees, too many assignments for members, that remove the necessary focus on important policy areas and diminish the expertise and deliberative capacity of lawmakers (the latter a topic I will consider in more detail below). At the same time, Congress has to be careful not to create committees that are unbalanced, in ideology, in region, or in terms of policy bent, causing them to be unrepresentative of the chamber as a whole, too protective of narrow interests, or too parochial.

In the post–cold war era, it seems clear that global economic issues will be more significant than they have been; the major jurisdictional task of congressional reformers is to reflect that reality in committees. Another related task is to find ways to revitalize the Foreign Affairs and Foreign Relations Committees, broadening their scope and attractiveness so that they are full-fledged, broad based players in the policy process. The best way to accomplish both of those goals is to create stronger and more vibrant international economic jurisdictions within them.

Moving trade jurisdiction from the Ways and Means and Finance panels to the Foreign Affairs and Foreign Relations Committees, while also shifting jurisdiction over exports and international financial institutions from the two Banking Committees, is a logical set of steps to take. Trade was originally settled in the two tax-writing committees because tariffs were the major source of federal revenue. Now, of course, they are a minuscule revenue producer, and trade is far more significant for its geopolitical and macroeconomic implications.

To be sure, these steps are not without costs or risks. Over many decades, both Ways and Means and Finance developed a culture supporting free trade principles, and devised methods and techniques to discourage a natural congressional strain of parochialism and protectionism and to give the president necessary leeway in negotiating and expediting trade agreements.[5] It would be unwise to lose that culture and outlook for the sake of a narrow desire to improve committee balance. For this reason, moving trade to the Banking Committee and beefing up *its* international economic jurisdiction would be unwise. In Foreign Affairs and Foreign Relations, however, the sensitivity to trade's role in the domestic and world economy, and to the desirability of a free trade environment, is already strong and likely to stay that way, especially in a stronger and more prestigious committee.

Strengthening Deliberation

That jurisdictional step would make sense for Congress to cope with the international realities of the next decade and beyond. A much broader change is highly desirable in the committee system, though, for a much broader purpose. If Congress is to be a player in the society's necessary debate over America's role in the post–cold war world, it must improve its capacity to deliberate. Congress needs to be a chamber where debate, argument, and analysis are dominant features at all levels, so that ideas can be tested and forged into policies, interests can be balanced, and lawmakers and the public can be educated about the alternatives available and the costs and benefits of each.

The whole rationale behind a representative legislature rests on its deliberative capacity. Rank-and-file citizens do not have the time or inclination to focus on policy alternatives and vote on their choices, but if they did, they would not be effective forces in a republican form of democracy without the ability to debate, and to take individual views that have not been well formed, well reasoned, or grounded in expertise and form them into a broader collective judgment.

Congress works best and is appreciated most when it deliberates most deeply and effectively. The best recent example, of course, is the Gulf War; when Congress spent several difficult days in January 1991 discussing and debating whether to give the president authority to use military force in the Gulf, its public standing rose sharply.

That the institution would have such a debate over the prospect of engaging in a major war is not too surprising. The problem is that Congress in recent years has seemed to engage in serious collective deliberation only when a decision that momentous is in the offing. But if the institution is to overcome deep public suspicion and antipathy, while also proving capable of dealing with the new and changing policy realities of the post–cold war era, it must make debate and deliberation a regular and commonplace reality.

That process must begin in committees. Committees provide Congress with its division of labor, giving the institution the ability to consider many policy areas at once, in some depth, while also providing channels for individual energies and creating needed expertise. But if the committee system is too spread out and too fragmented, the deliberative advantages of the system dissipate. Too many committees and subcommittees fragment policy areas, reducing the ability to focus, and using much congressional energy to assert or protect turf. Too many panels also mean too many assignments for individual lawmakers, which in turn fragment their attention and create constant scheduling conflicts and reduced levels of expertise.

Committees, subcommittees, and assignments are currency for Congress—valuable commodities that translate into power, prestige, and political influence. Like other currencies, they face a constant underlying inflationary pressure; leaders hand out slots and chairs to members to provide favors and to gain support for other matters. As a consequence, the number of seats on committees and subcommittees has grown sharply in the past decade, as has the average number of member assignments—and every lawmaker now finds his or her day driven by a schedule with nearly constant conflicts, as committees and subcommittees meet, mark up bills, or discuss options. Attendance deteriorates, attention spans atrophy, and deliberation has nearly disappeared.

Perhaps the single most important step both houses of Congress could take to prepare for the next century would be to cut back sharply on the number of committees and subcommittees, their sizes, and the number of assignments. This need has been recognized by inside and outside observers across the political spectrum for decades. The Senate acted in 1977 to deal with the problem and in fact succeeded in eliminating a number of committees while reducing the number of subcommittees by a third and writing tough assignment limits into the rules. The subcommittee reductions took hold, but the assignment limits did not; currently half the Senate violates them.

An effective enforcement mechanism in the Senate, along with a rules change and enforcement procedure in the House, reducing assignments to a maximum of two committees and four subcommittees in the House and two major and one minor committee in the Senate, along with four subcommittees, would be a key step forward—with an effective cap on the overall number of slots on committees and subcommittees.

If members of the House and Senate had more sharply focused responsibilities, with a reasonable number of assignments in committees that had themselves an appropriate focus for the next century, the priorities of the individuals and their institutions would likely be set better, and more time would be available and attention paid to important issues and policy. Less fragmented committee and subcommittee schedules would improve floor attendance and deliberation, even as they would mean more members showing up at hearings and meetings. It is hard to deliberate if there is no one there to deliberate with.

Altering time commitments and reducing committee fragmentation are necessary steps to improve deliberation; they may not be sufficient. Two other steps should be pursued. First, committees and subcommittees need to explore different ways of gathering information, bringing in different viewpoints, and debating alternatives. The traditional hearing process—witnesses at a table reading prepared testimony to members on a dais, followed by series of questions, in individual five-minute blocks, from the members—may not be the worst form of deliberation, but it would be hard to think of many less efficient ones.

Seminar formats, structured debates, use of moderators, and the Socratic method, all should be used more frequently; President Clinton's economic summit in Little Rock in December 1992 showed one way in which a large and disparate group, with a skillful moderator and a targeted focus, could educate participants and C-SPAN viewers alike.

At the same time, Congress should move to supplement its current floor procedures with real debates—blocks of time set aside, with a different set of rules, for Oxford Union–style debates with designated debaters and rebuttals, followed by broader discussions, on important issues of the times. These debates might be conducted in prime time, and their topics could range from specific policy areas—say, aid to Russia, or the efficacy of the North American Free Trade Agreement (NAFTA)—to broader questions like what role for a superpower in the post–cold war era, or what kind of defense strategy is appropriate for the next decade.

These debates, of course, would not be shown live on commercial networks, preempting *Murphy Brown* or *The Simpsons*. But they would attain a serious viewership on C-SPAN, be shown on occasion on CNN and public television, and would be an impetus for other important public affairs shows to change their agendas. A debate on Tuesday on Russia, for example, might inspire *MacNeil/Lehrer* and *Nightline* that night to show excerpts, and have a discussion segment with the designated debaters. The debates would educate members of Congress about the alternatives available to them, and about the range of opinions existent on the issues; they would also help educate different publics about the same things, and about the role of Congress in setting the public policies that would follow.

Dialogue with the Public

At a time when old anchors and precepts are gone, and people are groping to replace them, Congress's role and legitimacy in the American political system are under serious challenge. The need to change the public's perception of Congress is great. More important is the need to refurbish Congress's role and responsibilities. Streamlining the process and improving relations and communications with the executive are key. But particularly urgent is the need to restore a real deliberative capacity to the legislature. Voters and policy makers are not even sure of the questions for the next decade, much less the answers.

Consider simply the following partial set of international issues that confronted Congress, the nation, and the world at the hundred-day mark of the Clinton administration: the future of Russia, and America's role in shaping it; NAFTA, along with the pending action on a multilateral trade pact, the possibility of other free trade zones, and negotiations with Japan over issues like minivans; the excruciating set of dilemmas facing the country over the war in Bosnia; the Middle East negotiations between Israel, the Palestinians, and various Arab states; the threat posed by North Korea's belligerent export of weapons of mass destruction to countries like Iran; Iran's own aggressive arms build-up; Iraq's continuing threat to the Gulf.

Debates are going on in the country on many of these issues, and Congress is playing some role in them. But by conducting its deliberations mostly through a fragmented series of traditional committee hearings, with the public attention on NAFTA focusing almost exclusively on the two appearances before congressional committees of H. Ross Perot and on the ad lib, gloomy remarks of Clinton Budget Director Leon Panetta, the debate has been anything but thoughtful, focused, or enlightening.

The mass media, especially through television talk shows, has been a more important influence than Congress in conducting a debate on action in Bosnia, including a debate on the *Today* show between Senators Joe Biden and John McCain, and similar give-and-takes on *Nightline* and the *MacNeil/Lehrer Newshour*. The same was true of the Russian crisis. No force in society, except an occasional obscure newspaper columnist, has even taken up issues like the Uruguay Round or North Korea and Iran.

Some of these issues, of course, will never capture public attention until they erupt into full-blown crises affecting American lives. But whether immediate or nascent, the issues are critical ones for defining a new world order and a U.S. role, and Congress should be at the center of discussion and deliberation. A Congress sensitive to its responsibilities in these areas, and attuned to deliberative means, would be far more constructive.

Carefully shaping Oxford-style debates on Bosnia or Russian aid, putting forward Congress's most articulate and knowledgeable spokespeople and thinkers, and timing the debates to mesh with subsequent media analyses would serve both to sharpen and deepen the deliberation on these critical issues, and to underscore the important role of Congress in making the policy decisions. At the same time, a seminar organized by the House or Senate, including a roundtable discussion akin to Clinton's economic summit, attended by lawmakers, administration officials, scholars, and others, would get a substantial audience of opinion leaders on C-SPAN, and would serve as a base of knowledge and detail for other, subsequent analyses in editorials, op-ed pieces, magazine articles, and scholarly journals. At least as important, it would serve to educate members of Congress about the alternatives and trade-offs, and the consequences of their policy actions.

These kinds of steps would renew and energize the primary institution responsible for translating public needs and wants into real public judgment. At a time when old anchors and shibboleths are gone, and new themes and dogma will replace them, the need to have the first branch of American government prepared to shape the national debate is especially urgent.

Notes

[1] Mayhew (1992).

[2] Many of the recommendations that follow come from the discussions and reports of the *Renewing Congress Project*, jointly administered by the American Enterprise Institute and the Brookings Institution, and directed by Thomas E. Mann and Norman J. Ornstein. See Mann and Ornstein (1992).

[3] Reported in the *Washington Post*, April 12, 1993.

[4] See Mann (1992).

[5] For a broader discussion of governing institutions and trade, see Destler (1992).

6

Adapting the Executive Branch to the Post–Cold War World

ARNOLD KANTER

Introduction: The Changing Face of U.S. Foreign Policy

T he phrase "post–cold war world" has become an almost instant cliché. Everyone agrees that the world has been transformed in fundamental ways. There is nearly as broad a consensus

---

ARNOLD KANTER is a senior fellow at the RAND Corporation. From October 1991 until January 1993 he served as under secretary of state for political affairs, the State Department's "chief operating officer" with responsibility for the day-to-day conduct of American foreign policy and for crisis management. He served as special assistant to the president for national security affairs and senior director for defense policy and arms control at the National Security Council from 1989–91. Mr. Kanter was at the RAND Corporation from 1985–89 where he was a senior staff member working on issues related to nuclear forces, arms control, and European security; director of the National Security Strategies Program; and associate director of the International Security and Defense Program. Mr. Kanter served from 1977–85 in the U.S. Department of State, including positions as deputy assistant secretary of state for politico-military affairs and as deputy to the under secretary of state for political affairs. He has been on the staff of the Brookings Institution and has taught at Ohio State University and the University of Michigan.

that the very purposes of U.S. foreign policy, as well as the process by which it is made, need to be changed as well. At the same time, the post–cold war world in which we find ourselves is not the one we envisaged after the fall of the Berlin Wall, the collapse of Soviet power in Eastern Europe, and the August 1991 Bush-Gorbachev summit when the two superpower leaders announced the end of their competition and the beginning of partnership.

The post–cold war world instead has turned out to be a complicated, unpleasant, and paradoxical place. Politicians, policy makers, and average citizens alike are still very much in the early stages of grappling with the magnitude, nature, and implications of the changes that have—and have *not*—occurred. There is a strong sense that our foreign policy priorities should be reordered, and that the foreign policy machinery created and refined to fight the cold war is not well suited to serving U.S. foreign policy interests in the post–cold war world, but no consensus either about how our foreign policy interests have changed or about how the foreign policy process should be modified to serve them better.

This chapter begins with a description of some of the key features of the foreign policy machinery that was put in place and then modified throughout the cold war. It then reviews changes that have occurred in the post–cold war world and the implications of these changes for U.S. foreign policy. After discussing some of the steps that the Bush administration took to adjust its foreign policy process to changing circumstances, it describes the foreign policy structure that the Clinton administration has put in place. It concludes with a discussion of how the Clinton administration has addressed the organizational dilemmas and hard choices that our political leaders face as they adapt the executive branch to new demands.

Making Foreign Policy during the Cold War

The literature on the postwar U.S. foreign policy process is extensive. There is no intention to summarize it here. The purpose instead is to highlight briefly—and starkly—some of the primary features of the cold war decision-making structure in order to provide a context for understanding and assessing subsequent developments.

The foreign policy process that emerged in the early stages of the cold war can be described as having been based on several key premises:

- The preeminent objective of our foreign policy was to protect our national security. Threats to our vital interests were seen to derive overwhelmingly from the Soviet Union and its machinations around the globe. Other foreign policy goals and domestic concerns were subordinated to this purpose. Indeed, "foreign policy" quickly became synonymous with, if not a subset of, "national security policy."
- National security was defined predominantly in military terms. Diplomatic, economic, and political instruments of policy were largely treated as adjuncts to military policy and requirements.
- The National Security Council (NSC) was established by statute at the beginning of the cold war. Policy was (and largely still is) coordinated and integrated through the NSC and its subsidiary bodies. Membership on these bodies was drawn heavily from departments and agencies with responsibility for the military and related security aspects of foreign policy.[1] Inside agencies such as the State Department, political-economic issues took a back seat to political-military issues.
- The foreign policy process was relatively closed and substantially insulated from the hurly-burly of domestic politics. National security was considered to be more or less the exclusive province of the president, his senior advisers, and military "experts." Following the enunciation of the Truman doctrine, the congressional role in national security policy was circumscribed, in large measure as a result of self-imposed limits. With the notable exception of war and peace issues such as Korea, public opinion was neither a substantial constraint on nor a clear guide to action. The public's views were rarely solicited or offered.

The foregoing description is, to be sure, something of a caricature. The process was never as clear, single-minded, or pristine as it suggests. From the outset, national security was never viewed in purely military terms. Thus the National Security Act of 1947 authorized the creation of the National Security Council "to advise the President with respect to the integration of *domestic,* foreign, and military policies relating to the national security. . . ." Through the 1970s and 1980s the definition of "national security" was gradually expanded to include not only an explicit economic dimension, but also a growing array of "transnational issues" such as counter-narcotics and environment.[2] This increasingly expansive definition was reflected both in new directorates that were added to the National Security Council staff (e.g., international economics, international affairs) and in the growing diversity of departments and agencies that were invited to attend meetings of the National Security Council and its subordinate bodies.

Indeed, the growing importance of the role played by the national security adviser—as well as the endemic competition between him and the secretary of state—usually is attributed to the need to have someone who, sitting in the White House and standing above the competing parochial interests of the departments, could integrate the various strands of national security policy from a "presidential" perspective.[3]

We also know that national security policy has not been insulated either from public opinion or domestic politics. In their survey of administrations from Truman to Reagan, Bock and Clarke document that: "Every president, either at the outset of his administration or shortly thereafter, has found it necessary to include domestic political aides in national security policy deliberations."[4] Public opinion has been an increasingly important element in decisions about the deployment and employment of U.S. military force from Korea and Vietnam to Desert Storm and Bosnia. As the "missile gap" issue illustrated in 1960, and the Vietnam issue showed in 1964 and 1968, moreover, national security issues also can play an important role in presidential elections. Between elections, the politics of defense contracts and military bases, as well as the concerns of various groups of "hyphenate Americans" regularly made themselves felt. Finally, there are issues such as arms control and most favored nation (MFN) status for China that, while not high on the public's agenda, have been ones in which Congress has played a central role.

These qualifications and refinements notwithstanding, there

was an underlying coherence to the foreign policy process and structure throughout the cold war era that derived from a clear and consensual sense of priorities: domestic policy was subordinated to foreign policy, and the military dimension of national security was the preeminent foreign policy objective and preoccupation. Put differently, the *process* by which we pursued our foreign policy objectives adapted over time, but the *objectives* themselves were relatively stable.

The end of the cold war and the collapse of the external and internal Soviet empires mark these foreign policy objectives and priorities themselves as candidates for wholesale revision. They likewise raise the question of whether the machinery of foreign policy decision making can be further adapted, or whether it too needs to be overhauled. How our foreign policy priorities should be reordered and whether the foreign policy process should be restructured, however, depend importantly on an understanding of what international changes have—and have not—occurred.

Some Paradoxes of the
Post–Cold War World

The post–cold war world, in many respects, is both transformed and unexpected. The superpower competition has ended, but the world is neither peaceful nor stable. Many old threats have disappeared, but new problems have taken their place. The American people and their leaders are shifting their attention to domestic priorities, but U.S. foreign policy shows little sign of becoming isolationist. Delineating some of these paradoxes will aid in understanding both the objectives of, and the constraints on, reorganizing the foreign policy machinery of the executive branch.

Paradox 1: The Persistence
of a "Soviet Threat"

The expansive, hostile, militarily intimidating Soviet Union that had been *the* defining issue in U.S. foreign policy for more than a generation has abruptly disappeared, but the economically weak and politically unstable states that emerged from its ruins remain a major strategic preoccupation of the United States. In particular, the future of political and economic reforms in a very large, proud, increasingly nationalistic, economically bankrupt Russia with 27,000 nuclear weapons remains perhaps the major national security concern of the United States. In stark contrast to the cold war era, however, it is a national security issue for which our traditional foreign policy instruments, particularly our military capabilities, are virtually irrelevant.

Paradox 2: The Immutability of Institutions and Habits

The international system is undergoing fundamental change, and American policy priorities are being reordered and redefined, but the institutions that structure issues within nations and interactions among them seem to be all but immune to change. International organizations are blossoming, particularly those such as the United Nations (UN), European Community (EC), Conference on Security and Cooperation in Europe (CSCE), Asia-Pacific Economic Cooperation (APEC), Group of Seven (G-7), and Association of Southeast Asian Nations (ASEAN) that are primarily concerned with nonsecurity issues and nonmilitary aspects of security concerns. Supranational entities such as the EC Commission are also growing in importance. The national identities and loyalties of multinational corporations likewise are becoming increasingly diffused and indistinct. Meanwhile, cold war institutions such as the North Atlantic Treaty Organization (NATO) struggle to redefine their purposes, if not reinvent themselves.

Nevertheless, the nation state remains the principal organizational unit of international relations, and virtually every international organization operates as collections of these nation states. There remains an overwhelming presumption against "interference in the internal affairs of other states," no matter how corrupt, negligent, or cruel their leaders. National sovereignty not only remains enshrined as a guiding principle, but actually is being reinforced as the inviolability of national borders is invoked to counter the centrifugal forces at work in Eastern Europe and the former Soviet Union.

Institutions within governments that have foreign policy responsibilities are likewise relatively rigid. Reorganizing the departments of the executive branch is constrained in part by the need to preserve a structure that can interact efficiently with foreign governments. That typically means maintaining a set of agencies that closely mirrors the way in which other governments have organized themselves. Reorganization also is limited by the obligation to obtain the political concurrence of, if not new legislation from, the Congress. Congress is often reluctant to approve such reorganizations because to do so would require redrawing the lines of committee jurisdiction, if not a formal restructuring of the committee system (see chapter 5). Finally, there is the reality that agencies' self-conception of their mission and their mix of career personnel both change only very slowly.

No matter how much the world and U.S. foreign policy priorities are changing, any plans to restructure the foreign policy process must face these organizational facts of life. They imply that wholesale reorganization is likely to be simply infeasible, and that the key leverage points for trying to change the way in which the government does its foreign policy business are (a) the personnel selected to fill the most senior positions, and especially (b) the interagency processes that affect both the relative visibility of various issues and relative influence that various agencies and actors can exercise. These implications will be explored further below.

Paradox 3: The Declining Influence of the World's Only Superpower

With the collapse of the Soviet Union, the United States has become the world's only remaining superpower, but it no longer is the undisputed leader. Economically, the United States ceased to be a superpower some time ago in the sense that it no longer enjoys the economic preponderance it once did. While we continue to have the world's largest economy, it no longer is so much larger than everybody else's as to be readily convertible into overwhelming political influence.

Militarily, we remain the strongest nation in the world. We also have unique power projection capabilities that will be indispensable in meeting many future peacekeeping and "peacemaking" demands. However, the very meaning of being a military super-power in the post–cold war world is being questioned both in the United States and elsewhere as the military capabilities (and especially strategic nuclear arsenals) that formerly set superpowers apart from other nations decline in political relevance.

Politically, U.S. leadership remains the indispensable prerequisite to the creation of international coalitions to deal with the security problems that plague the post–cold war world, as well as with the nonsecurity issues that are crowding the agenda. No other country or international institution seems to have the capacity to galvanize the world community into action. That said, the United States is much less willing and able to act alone than during the cold war. For reasons discussed below, moreover, the United States has become more reluctant to exercise its international leadership, and other countries have become less willing to follow.

Paradox 4:
Allies Who Compete with Us

More and more, our post–World War II security partners also are our economic competitors. Traditionally, the trade differences among us were subordinated to security concerns we shared. In any event, American economic preponderance meant that the United States rarely was put in the position of having to trade off its economic interests against its security interests.

With the end of the cold war and the disappearance of U.S. economic preponderance, however, the interests we have in common with our allies are becoming less important—or at least less salient—while the interests we have in competition with them are becoming more salient. Our allies rely less on our security guarantees and find the shelter provided by our nuclear umbrella less valuable because they no longer perceive the serious and proximate military threats to their security they once did. At the same time, the combination of growing economic interdependence and increasingly competitive economies has led to spreading trade friction and, more broadly, growing mutual suspicions about motives.

As a result of these developments, the exercise of U.S. leadership in the world requires more skill and effort, but meets with less success, than we came to expect during the cold war. One consequence is an increase in frustration with, if not resentment toward, our friends and allies. Another is a narrower, harder-nosed conception of American self-interest. The net result is a growing reluctance on the part of the American people and their leaders to exercise international leadership and, in particular, to assume the burdens that go with it.

Paradox 5: A World That Is Both Less Stable and Less Dangerous

Although the cold war is over, the world remains filled with crisis and instability. Threats to U.S. interests not only persist but abound. Force still matters in the post–cold war world. Our quantitatively substantial and qualitatively distinctive military capabilities remain a key instrument of U.S. foreign policy and a vital ingredient of American leadership.

All this being said, however, the fact is that serious military threats to vital U.S. interests have all but disappeared. With their disappearance, the touchstone for making and defending decisions to deploy and employ U.S. military forces has been removed. We know instinctively that we still need a strong military, but we have a difficult time articulating the exact reasons why, much less determining how much and what kinds of these very expensive capabilities we still need. After having told ourselves for more than a generation that we would only use force to defend our vital interests, we now are groping for new guidelines to determine whether, when, and how force should be used to defend *less*-than-vital interests.

Likewise, the organizing principle on which the cold war foreign policy process has been based no longer seems compelling, or perhaps even valid. If our security no longer is the subject of serious military threat, then American "foreign policy" no longer is a subset of "national security" policy. On the contrary, the reverse is now true. Similarly, we now need to ask how well the "NSC system" of decision making, with the national security adviser at its pinnacle, functions as a "foreign policy," not simply a "national security policy," process. Indeed, the very terms "National Security Council" and "national security adviser" suddenly sound rather anachronistic. As Secretary of State Warren Christopher remarked early in the Clinton administration: "Soviet Communism is dead. But so is the reference point that guided our policies for 40 years."

Implications for American Foreign Policy

The disappearance of serious military threats to vital U.S. interests is the core difference and key change that is driving a transformation of U.S. foreign policy. This transformation is as real as it is profound. It is, at once, liberating and confusing. Some wonder if we not only have lost our enemy, but perhaps also our foreign policy bearings. Others see new and expanded opportunities to promote both U.S. self-interest and American ideals, but grope for guidelines to help determine when, where, and how we will do so. Most discern that public understanding of, and support for, foreign policy decisions will become both increasingly important and increasingly difficult to obtain.[5]

The Growth of Public Involvement in Foreign Policy

For the reasons described above, the American people have come to take the national security of their country, at least as defined in traditional terms, virtually for granted. Now they want to know how U.S. foreign policy is going to improve their *economic* security. They are skeptically questioning the demands and burdens that national security requirements have imposed on them for more than a generation. They may still accept the proposition that there is no substitute for U.S. leadership of the international community and remain proud of the values for which their country stands, but they are more insistent that they be told *why* the United States should take it upon itself to exercise that leadership and make the sacrifices that it entails. They want to know how the United States is going to exercise its international leadership in ways that will improve their well-being at home.

In responding to those often skeptical questions, U.S. political leaders find that the old, familiar reasons no longer are persuasive, that their international partners often appear ungrateful, and that the benefits of international leadership have become elusive and uncertain. As Secretary Christopher commented: "We need a new strategy for protecting and promoting American interests in the new era. We need a strategy that answers the questions that most Americans are now asking."

Features of the New American Foreign Policy

Despite some speculation to the contrary, the changes that characterize the post–cold war world and America's role in it are unlikely to yield an "isolationist" American foreign policy, if only because the United States inescapably is a global power whose interests and stakes are inextricably connected to decisions and developments around the world. Rather, the trends and forces described above are likely to yield a new *kind* of U.S. foreign policy. This emerging foreign policy surely has different priorities, but perhaps even different purposes. It is characterized by a retreat from many of the burdens of the cold war combined with a still active, but perhaps more explicitly self-interested, style of international engagement.[6]

This new U.S. foreign policy will consist of multiple elements, not all of which will be mutually supportive, or even compatible. The result of these multiple and conflicting forces could be U.S. foreign policy behavior that appears to be inconsistent, if not schizophrenic. There will be strong elements of continuity with our earlier foreign policy stemming from threats to U.S. interests arising from instabilities around the world. At the same time, a narrower, more concrete, and more immediate standard of U.S. self-interest is likely to be applied to specific foreign policy decisions, particularly those that require international involvement, risk, or sacrifice. Perhaps paradoxically, the shedding of various cold war constraints and compromises also is likely to lead to growing pressure to promote traditional American values such as support for democracy and respect for human rights.

Probably the greatest change in U.S. foreign policy is that it will become harnessed more closely and directly to U.S. domestic purposes, and will increasingly be judged by its domestic impacts and consequences. Not only is there likely to be a reversal of the respective priority assigned to domestic and foreign policy, but foreign policy increasingly will become an instrument by which to achieve domestic policy objectives. As a corollary, foreign policy will come to resemble the way in which domestic policy in the United States is made and judged, that is, in an overtly political manner. Put differently, politics no longer will stop at the water's edge, and public opinion about foreign policy issues will count for much more.

This change is nowhere clearer than in the U.S. approach to international economic and trade policy. As Secretary Christopher explained: "Our ability to prosper in this global economy depends on our ability to compete. That means harnessing our diplomacy to serve our economic goals abroad."[7] The most vivid example of this change is the U.S.–Japan relationship. From President Bush's ill-fated "jobs, jobs, jobs" trip to the Clinton-Miyazawa meetings in Washington and Tokyo, a key multifaceted, bilateral relationship has been virtually transformed into a U.S. domestic political and economic issue. As will be discussed below, the Clinton administration has recognized and reinforced this change by reorganizing the foreign policy machinery of the executive branch in ways that both highlight the priority assigned to economic policy and strengthen the linkage between domestic and international economic issues.

Changing the Machinery of U.S. Foreign Policy

As was noted above, both the concept of "national security" and the manner in which policy was made evolved throughout the postwar period. With the end of the cold war, these changes accelerated, often spurred by congressional action in the areas of human rights, nonproliferation, and trade. Some early, ad hoc adaptations to the post–cold war world could be discerned during the Bush administration. In an effort to address these issues in a more systematic fashion in anticipation of either the second Bush administration or the first term of his Democratic successor, two study efforts on reorganizing the foreign policy process were undertaken in 1992.[8] Influenced both by those studies and by its analysis of the Bush administration's practices, the Clinton administration has made several important changes in the foreign policy process.

Early Adaptations

By the time George Bush became president, this country's single-minded focus on resisting the Soviet Union and combating communism had given way to a much more multifaceted approach. An early Bush administration priority was to find resolutions to several Central American conflicts, both on the ground in the region and at home with the Congress. Meanwhile, a national drug policy that gave priority to curbing supply made counternarcotics a substantially more important *foreign policy* priority.

During the same period, increased numbers of personnel from "domestic" agencies such as the Justice Department, Agriculture Department, Treasury Department, Commerce Department, and Drug Enforcement Administration were assigned to U.S. embassies abroad. In many major posts, foreign service officers are now a distinct minority of the U.S. personnel assigned, in some cases as few as 10 to 20 percent. (Indeed, as some in the foreign service look out into the future, they see themselves becoming little more than landlords for overseas outposts that replicate virtually the entire structure of the government in Washington.)

The interagency process in Washington mirrored many of the same forces and trends. Representatives from a wide array of "domestic" agencies attended meetings of the National Security Council and its subsidiary bodies with increasing frequency as they took up a growing diversity of foreign policy issues that were unrelated to the Soviet Union, much less to the cold war. Subjects included whether to permit the lucrative sale of commercial aircraft to countries suspected of supporting terrorism, whether to license the sale of computers to countries suspected of having nuclear ambitions, and how to reconcile immigration, foreign policy, and humanitarian considerations in formulating a Haiti policy. Similar concerns led to the establishment of the National Space Council and its charge to improve interagency coordination so that U.S. commercial and economic interests were better integrated with our national security and intelligence objectives.

The area of economics and trade provides a good illustration both of the attempts at, and the shortcomings of, these early post–cold war adaptations. On the one hand, there were clear efforts to make international economics and trade a more important and an integral part of U.S. foreign policy. For example, in the directive establishing the NSC system and procedures for his administration, Bush mandated that the secretary of the treasury (as well as the director of the Office of Management and Budget) should attend all NSC meetings except in exceptional circumstances. The National Security Council staff included a Directorate of International Economic Policy that was responsible for integrating economic interests with other national security concerns. (It also is noteworthy that when the NSC's Soviet specialist—who had a political-military background—departed, a conscious decision was made to replace her with someone who had strong economic credentials.)

Similar efforts could be seen in the agencies themselves. The United States trade representative (USTR) increased in stature, importance, and interagency influence. She used these assets with single-minded determination to increase access by American producers to, and competitive advantages in, foreign markets. The deputy secretary of state made export promotion a personal priority and instructed all U.S. ambassadors to make it their personal priority as well. The intelligence community reviewed its collection and analysis priorities and debated the issue of collecting economic intelligence on allies.

On the other hand, for the most part these activities were grafted onto, rather than made an integral part of, the foreign policy process. By training, experience, and mandate, the staff and leadership of the National Security Council remained overwhelmingly focused on the political and security aspects of foreign policy. The interagency process for coordinating international economic policy—the Economic Policy Council (EPC)—was chaired by the secretary of the treasury. Operating outside the NSC structure and the White House, the EPC could not by itself coordinate economic policy with other aspects of foreign policy. For the same reasons, it was severely hampered in its efforts to shape the economic message the president would deliver in his meetings and phone calls with various foreign leaders. It also had a circumscribed charter that did not encompass key trade issues that were taken up variously in the NSC system as "technology transfer" issues, or in the National Space Council as "space policy" issues.[9]

The general consensus is that the EPC did not function effectively in the Bush administration as a mechanism for coordinating international economic policy, much less for integrating economic policy with other aspects of foreign policy. Instead, alternative structures each took up part of broad policy issues. The Trade Policy Review Group, chaired by USTR (and nominally reporting to the EPC) addressed specific trade policy issues. By late in the Bush administration, the White House based Policy Coordinating Group chaired by Clayton Yeutter assumed an increasing role for coordinating policy on various international economic issues. National Security Adviser Brent Scowcroft also assumed a larger (albeit largely informal) role as an "honest broker" to reconcile interagency differences on particular trade issues, especially those related to the Uruguay Round of the General Agreement on Tariffs and Trade (GATT) talks. The result was a largely ad hoc, fragmented process that fell well short of adapting the foreign policy process to some of the key developments of the post–cold war world.

Designs for the New Foreign Policy Machinery

In recognition of the fundamental changes that were occurring in the post–cold war world and in anticipation of the 1992 presidential election, two separate efforts were launched to analyze and make recommendations about how to improve the foreign policy process. One was an internal State Department study that resulted in *State 2000: A New Model for Managing Foreign Affairs.* The other was a study conducted by the Carnegie Endowment for International

Peace, which produced two volumes. The first, *Changing Our Ways: America and the New World,* was an assessment of the implications of the end of the cold war for the purposes and priorities of U.S. foreign policy. With that analysis as background, a second study group produced *Memorandum to the President-Elect: Harnessing Process to Purpose.*

What is perhaps most striking about these two exercises is the similarity of their diagnoses and objectives, including the factors they emphasized, the organizational models and guidelines they used as references, and the issues they tended to overlook or minimize. For this or other reasons, the organizational changes made by the Clinton administration are closely patterned after many of their recommendations. It therefore is instructive to summarize their analysis and proposals.

Both studies begin with the premise that the end of the cold war requires changes to the foreign policy process. The Carnegie report insisted: "As in 1933 and 1947, new circumstances and new policies require new machinery. . . . Reorganizing the government for the post–Cold War world is a necessity, not a luxury."[10] Both advocate a much more integrated approach to foreign policy that takes full account of economic and "transnational" issues, as well as better integration of foreign policy with domestic policy and politics. As the State Department report observed: "First, we must integrate our foreign policy. . . . Second, and even more importantly, we must integrate foreign and domestic policy. We must learn, in fact, to see them as two parts of one whole."[11] They likewise agree that the new process needs to be centered in and run out of the White House. Finally, both studies view the NSC system as a successful model either to be emulated (Carnegie) or expanded (State).[12] In effect, then, both groups have the same appreciation of what the ad hoc adaptations and EPC of the Bush administration were intended to accomplish, and the same diagnosis of why they fell short.

The two studies, however, recommend different approaches for accomplishing their common objective. These differences highlight an organizational dilemma that every proposal for redesigning the foreign policy machinery ultimately confronts. The State study recommends continuing to use the NSC as "the catalyst and point of coordination for this new, single foreign policy process."[13] It seeks to achieve a balance among, and integrated approach to, competing foreign policy objectives by establishing two deputy national security advisers, one for the traditional agenda of "political/military" issues, and the other for the new post–cold war agenda of "economic/global" issues, both reporting to the national security adviser.

It rejects the alternative of having separate processes for security and international economic issues each reporting to the president, because it would mean "the President will either face options at the extremes of sound policy or be forced to establish yet another forum to forge consensus."[14] On the other hand, it *would* create a separate process to handle domestic policy. The results of the two processes would then go up through the chief of staff to the president who would somehow make the trade-offs between domestic and foreign policy priorities, and inject the appropriate political calculations.

The Carnegie study takes a somewhat different and arguably more radical approach. It proposes that the National Security Council be maintained and that two additional, coequal bodies modeled after the NSC be created: the Economic Council and the Domestic Council. The NSC would continue to emphasize its traditional political/military responsibilities. The Economic Council would be responsible for coordinating and integrating domestic and international policy. The Domestic Council would have primary responsibility for coordinating noneconomic domestic issues. The heads of all three councils would have the same senior rank, and would report directly to the president. The president's chief of staff would be kept fully informed by them, and would be expected to play "the critically important coordinating role" as well as ensure that all the relevant domestic political considerations had been incorporated.[15]

If the State approach gives priority to achieving an integrated *foreign* policy by expanding the competence of the NSC, the Carnegie approach emphasizes the integration of the domestic and international aspects of *economic* policy by creating a separate structure parallel to the NSC. If the State design understates the problem of integrating and trading off domestic and foreign policy priorities, the Carnegie design minimizes the problem of integrating and trading off international economic and other foreign policy (as well as domestic policy) priorities. In both approaches, the coordination and integration problems that the analysis shortchanges are left to the president and his chief of staff miraculously to solve. In doing so, they give their implicitly different answers without explicitly engaging the essentially unanswerable question of how to strike the right balance among integration, specialization, and manageability.

The difference in the answers, however, not only reflects different views about the purposes and priorities of the new foreign policy, but also has important consequences. Under the State approach, our policy toward a given country (e.g., China) would be designed to pursue diverse foreign policy objectives such as increasing trade, improving human rights, curbing proliferation, and securing Chinese support in the UN Security Council on critical votes. We would make trade-offs among these various goals to achieve the net maximum benefit. To overstate the case, the consequences for overall domestic and international economic policy would be a by-product of these trade-offs. Under the Carnegie approach, by contrast, our policy on trade with China would be a by-product of our overall domestic and international economic policy.

Compared to the State approach, the Carnegie design would make it harder to trade off Chinese concessions on trade for Chinese cooperation in the UN Security Council, but easier to trade off Chinese trade concessions for government subsidies to domestic producers. In the former case, economic policy is the instrument by which to achieve other objectives. In the latter case, economic policy itself is the objective.

The point is not that one approach is better than the other. The point rather is to emphasize (a) it is humanly impossible to coordinate, much less integrate, all the aspects of government policy that are related to one another, and (b) which subset of objectives a particular organizational design gives priority to integrating has itself important policy consequences. If it is true, as was argued above, that U.S. foreign policy will become harnessed more closely and directly to domestic purposes and objectives, this suggests that the Carnegie approach will be better suited to that foreign policy. There is one other feature shared by the two studies that is noteworthy. While both reports stress the increasingly strong linkages between domestic affairs and foreign policy, and while both would expand the circle of officials and experts who participate in the foreign policy process, neither devotes much attention to the role of public support, much less to specific mechanisms for gauging and shaping public opinion.[16] In fairness, both studies refer to the need to integrate domestic policy and politics into foreign policy. Both, however, simply rely on the president, the chief of staff, and otherwise unstated processes to achieve this goal.

In doing so, they implicitly fall back on the political instincts and informal practices that have been more or less part of the foreign policy process throughout the postwar period.[17] If it is true that foreign policy process is coming to resemble the domestic policy process and, as a consequence, is becoming infused with domestic politics, then existing political mechanisms for public involvement may automatically encompass foreign policy issues. That said, routine public involvement in foreign policy is a still unfamiliar, if not novel, concept that would seem to warrant explicit attention in the design of new foreign policy machinery, including consideration of new mechanisms for explaining the public's direct and immediate stake in various foreign policy issues and outcomes. Against the backdrop of otherwise far-reaching recommendations in the State and Carnegie reports, omission of this subject is striking.

The Foreign Policy Process
in the Clinton Administration

In addition to the obvious personnel changes throughout the senior levels of the government, the Clinton administration has made small but potentially significant organizational modifications. Taken together, they suggest that the administration will concentrate on human rights, nonproliferation, and trade issues in the formulation of its foreign policy. In particular, an integrative approach to economic policy will be accorded special prominence. At the very least, such organizational changes will give added weight and prominence to these issues in U.S. bilateral relationships around the world.

Promoting American Values and Protecting American Security

The Clinton administration has made clear that the promotion of American values and ideals, as well as U.S. interests, will be a central theme of its foreign policy. A new under secretary of state for global affairs has been established and formally designated as one of Secretary Christopher's principal advisers. This new under secretary's explicit responsibilities include the promotion of democracy and human rights, as well as a broad range of other "transnational" issues such as counter-terrorism, counter-narcotics, and environment. One of the bureaus reporting to this under secretary has been redesignated the Bureau of Democracy, Human Rights, and Labor, and has been charged to provide initiatives and policies to promote democracy.

Parallel organizational changes also have been made in the Pentagon. The position of assistant secretary of defense for democracy and peacekeeping has been created. Reporting to this new assistant secretary will be the newly established deputy assistant secretary of defense for democracy and human rights. A new $50 million line item for "democracy" also has been added to the Defense Department budget.

The major arms control and security concerns of the Clinton administration come together in its emphasis on policies designed to inhibit and counter the spread of weapons of mass destruction. Reflecting these substantive policy priorities, organizational changes have been made to sharpen the administration's focus on nonproliferation. New nonproliferation responsibilities have been assigned to senior officials in the State Department, particularly the assistant secretary of state for politico-military affairs. An under secretary of state also is being formally redesignated to emphasize the priority the Clinton administration assigns to this issue.

Likewise in the Pentagon, the position of assistant secretary of defense for nuclear security and counter-proliferation has been created. Finally, a newly established nonproliferation directorate in the White House's National Security Council staff will coordinate and integrate government-wide nonproliferation policy.

Integrating Economic Policy

Nowhere is both the transformation of U.S. foreign policy and the growing linkage between foreign policy and domestic policy clearer than in the area of economics. President Clinton himself has explicitly underscored this relationship by emphasizing that improving the American economy and the economic well-being of the American people will be a major objective of his foreign policy, while observing that success in achieving the objective of an economically stronger America will make our country a more influential and successful leader of the international community. It also is noteworthy that many of President Clinton's most influential advisers now hold government positions related to economics and trade.

Nowhere have the changes in the Clinton administration's foreign policy machinery been more far-reaching than in the area of economic and trade policy. Perhaps most important has been the creation of the National Economic Council (NEC) in the White House. The NEC has responsibility for coordinating and integrating U.S. trade and economic policy, both domestically and internationally. The "NEC system" is parallel to, and is consciously modeled after, the National Security Council. It chairs interagency meetings on subjects ranging from "Japan" to "U.S. trade policy" from which the U.S. trade representative receives guidance. Its head has the same rank and status as the national security adviser. Both report directly to the president. In brief, the Clinton administration's foreign policy organization closely resembles the "Carnegie approach" described above.

Although it is too soon to know how effective and influential the new institution of the NEC will be, it could have far-reaching implications for U.S. foreign policy, as well as for trade and economic policy. In particular, these organizational innovations may make it easier for the Clinton administration not only to achieve a better integration of its domestic and international economic policy, but also to put foreign policy more directly and effectively at the service of U.S. economic interests. At the same time, they may make it more difficult for the Clinton administration to achieve an integrated foreign policy and to make trade-offs among competing interests and objectives in particular bilateral relationships. These outcomes could result for two related reasons. First, the NSC process no longer has overall responsibility for foreign policy coordination and integration. The NEC process will exercise that responsibility with respect to international trade and economic issues. Similarly, the national security adviser no longer is the president's primary point of integration and synthesis for the competing interests and perspectives of the various government agencies whose responsibilities have foreign policy implications. The head of the NEC now has that responsibility with respect to the economic aspects of foreign policy. On the other hand, the NSC still remains primarily responsible for preparing materials—including on economic issues—for the president's exchanges with foreign leaders.[18]

Second, and perhaps more important, the NEC is responsible for coordinating economic and trade policy *across* rather than within the domestic and foreign policy spheres. That is, the NEC's job is to ensure that there is a well-integrated U.S. economic policy, rather than—and perhaps even at the expense of—a well-integrated U.S. foreign policy. It therefore is a process that is better able to make trade-offs among competing domestic and international economic objectives than among competing foreign policy objectives, especially in particular bilateral cases in which economic interests have to be traded off against noneconomic foreign policy objectives.[19] To overstate the point, the NEC process tends to make foreign policy a means by which to achieve U.S. economic objectives, rather than using economic instruments to achieve U.S. foreign policy objectives.

The NEC process also is quite consistent with the new kind of, and approach to, U.S. foreign policy described above. In the Clinton administration, "national security" no longer is the predominant organizing principle for foreign policy. Foreign policy no longer is coordinated and integrated exclusively through the "NSC system," and the national security adviser no longer ranks first, or even first among equals, in responsibility for imposing a "presidential perspective" on foreign policy issues. Instead, the Clinton administration has put in place a process that reflects a broader, even different, conception of foreign policy priorities, that is structured to make different kinds of trade-offs, and that leaves primarily to the president himself the task of managing the strong centrifugal forces it generates.

Time will tell how well suited this new executive branch organization is to meet the new demands of the post–cold war world.

Notes

[1] The National Security Act of 1947 reflects this bias. It designates the president, the vice president, the secretary of state, and the secretary of defense as statutory *members* of the NSC, and the chair of the Joint Chiefs of Staff and the director of the Central Intelligence Agency as its statutory *advisers*.

[2] See, for example, *National Security Strategy of the United States* (1991).

[3] See, for example, Mulcahy (1986).

[4] Bock and Clarke (1986), p. 273.

[5] See, for example, Carnegie (1992a), p. 4, and Warren Christopher, "Remarks to the Chicago Council on Foreign Relations, the Mid-America Committee, and the Executives' Club of Chicago, March 22, 1993.

[6] See, for example, Carnegie (1992a), pp. 2–4, and Christopher (cited above): "All Americans have every right to demand a foreign policy that serves their interests in concrete ways."

[7] In the speech cited above, Christopher drew attention to the fact that "building American prosperity" forms the first pillar of the Clinton foreign policy.

[8] The Carnegie Foundation study produced two major publications: *Changing Our Ways: America and the New World* (Carnegie 1992a) and *Memorandum to the President-Elect: Harnessing Process to Purpose* (Carnegie 1992b). An internal State Department study resulted in *State 2000: A New Model for Managing Foreign Affairs* (U.S. Dept. of State 1992).

[9] The EPC also faced virtually insurmountable obstacles in persuading other agencies that it was performing an honest broker role rather than simply advancing parochial Treasury Department interests. Treasury's reluctance to use the EPC to address any issues that it thought were its own responsibility was an additional burden.

[10] Carnegie (1992b), p. 1.

[11] U.S. Dept. of State (1992), p. 3. See also p. 19; Carnegie (1992a), pp. 2–3; and Carnegie (1992b), pp. 1–2.

[12] U.S. Dept. of State (1992), p. 19; Carnegie (1992b), p. 5.

[13] U.S. Dept. of State (1992), p. 4.

[14] U.S. Dept. of State (1992), p. 19.

[15] Carnegie (1992b), pp. 5–6.

[16] This omission is more striking in the case of the Carnegie study, since it was based on Carnegie's own *Changing Our Ways* volume that emphasized the growing importance of public support for a sustainable foreign policy. For example:

"Today foreign policy can . . . raise or lower the cost of your home mortgage, create a new job or cause you to lose the one you've got" (p. 2). Also: "America cannot sustain an effective foreign policy unless the American people are confident that our efforts abroad serve our interests at home. This must be the bedrock of any new consensus" (p. 4).

[17] See Bock and Clarke (1986), pp. 258–279.

[18] The Clinton administration is trying to mitigate these problems by designating NSC staff as members of NEC chaired committees, and vice versa. It also sometimes resorts to the device of having meetings and studies cochaired by NSC and NEC.

[19] Assigning senior officials specific responsibilities in such functional areas as human rights and nonproliferation also will tend to increase the difficulty of making foreign policy trade-offs in specific cases. Maintaining the Agency for International Development and the Arms Control and Disarmament Agency as separate institutions could have the same effect.

7

Double Diversity: The Intersection of Big Changes at Home and Abroad

ERNEST J. WILSON III

Introduction

The United States now faces an unusual and difficult political challenge whose resolution and consequences will reach well into the next century and significantly affect our leadership position in the world. This challenge can be simply stated, though not simply resolved, as responding to and creatively managing the intersection of domestic diversity with international diversity and pluralism.

The world beyond our borders is changing radically. The once stable architecture of postwar world power has shifted from rigidly bipolar to multipolar. Political and economic power is less concen-

ERNEST J. WILSON III is a member of the staff of the National Security Council. Prior to joining the Clinton administration he was associate professor of government and politics at the University of Maryland. From 1988 to 1992 Dr. Wilson was the director of the Center for Research on Economic Development at the University of Michigan. He is the editor of *International Economic Reform: Theoretical and Comparative Perspectives,* and the author of *Politics and Culture in Nigeria,* as well as numerous articles.

trated. Simultaneously, within our borders, American society has also shifted radically, experiencing dramatic changes in the structure of the economy and the distribution of political and economic power across regions and classes. Overlaying these important shifts are equally substantial demographic and cultural changes, as the United States becomes more black, more brown, more yellow, and less white.

The *intersection* between these twin changes—growing domestic pluralism and diversity, bumping against growing global pluralism and diversity—is prompting often fractious debates among American intellectuals over the meaning and value of multiculturalism, standards of excellence, and how to provide greater gender and ethnic equity. Simultaneously, journals debate the place of U.S. power in a post–cold war world, and how best to achieve U.S. economic and strategic security. These parallel debates are now conducted separately. This chapter will try to join them, for it is the interaction of domestic and world pluralism that will exert powerful pressures on the design and implementation of U.S. foreign policy. How will those with responsibility for managing international transactions—government officials, corporate managers and strategists, interest group and political leaders—respond to this new challenge?

From World War II onward, U.S. foreign policy was based on the old organizing principle that U.S. national security rested on containment and anticommunism. The anchor to this policy was the actions of the USSR. The stakes of the struggle were the European heartland, the richest region outside the United States. This political and economic strategy was buttressed by the cultural origins and orientations of the overwhelmingly white, Anglo-Saxon, and Protestant U.S. foreign policy elite. A well educated and relatively outward looking cadre of internationalists nurtured the vision of a prosperous and democratic Euro-centered world.[1]

With Europe the other main source of world power, it was not surprising that the Euro-centered policy was the product of children of Europe. It is unlikely that such a culturally and strategically unified vision will be carried into the next century. The country—and its elites—are more heterogeneous. Indeed, the thesis of this chapter is that too much carry-over of the old vision will poorly serve our national interests. Instead, a new world at home and abroad requires a broader and more inclusive vision of what the United States and the world can become. Making such a vision reality requires opening up U.S. foreign policy making to new groups. The reinvented government called for by President Clinton needs new and better channels through which to listen to what all Americans are saying about their interests and concerns. Foreign policy making must be democratized at home, especially where new local and international forces intersect. Labor unions, chambers of commerce, the League of Women Voters, and city councils insist on playing larger roles in international transactions.

The intersection of domestic and global diversity may prove especially volatile in the years ahead because it touches not only objective conditions of national income and economic well-being, but also the more subjective, equally important side of political life as lived by individual men and women. This means issues of values, people's sense of identity and culture, profound matters of race and blood, indeed, of what it means to be an American. As such, "double diversity" presents nearly unprecedented challenges to foreign policy makers and all Americans.

In part these changes and our responses to them reflect the blurred dividing line between foreign and domestic policy. Driven by the expansion of so many transnational ties, private organizations on the local level are reaching out to their counterparts in other countries and are busily creating their own mini–foreign policies. Nongovernmental organizations (NGOs) in South Carolina deal directly with NGOs in South Africa or South America, bypassing the U.S. Department of State. American businesspeople insist that the investment climate in dozens of "foreign" countries will make or break their businesses. What then is "foreign policy"? What is domestic politics?

As significant as these trends are, we do not claim that they are completely unique and without historical precedent. After all, the decade of the 1980s was not the first time that immigration accelerated and helped to reshape American society at the same time as the international environment changed as well. From 1900 to 1910 the United States was flooded with immigrants, who added about 1 percent to the population each year. In the late 1800s and early 1900s also, old empires crumbled as new ones were created. We need only remember the unsettling internal consequences of those "distant" global changes to realize that growing double diversity will be a challenge to our foreign policy, especially at a time when global interdependence is greater.

Support for U.S. foreign policy after the cold war will be significantly shaped by the expansion of interests of African-Americans, Asian-Americans and Latinos, as well as women, in the design and implementation of foreign policy.

Since the changes in the international arena, and those here at home, have been widely described, analyzed, and evaluated, I will not repeat them in detail here though I will sketch their most important outlines. Instead, this chapter concentrates on the intersections of the international and the domestic changes, since they have received far less attention. These intersections are multidimensional, and operate through channels that are social and demographic as well as explicitly political and economic.

The International Changes

U.S. policy makers now confront a world grown more disorderly and unpredictable. There are far more global players, both state and nonstate, and they are tied to one another in more complex and crosscutting ways. Once weak states in Asia and Latin America now possess undreamed of economic and political clout. In this sense the globe has become more politically plural, and economically and technologically integrated. Financial and other markets operate literally around the clock. The international game has also become more culturally diverse, since many of these new actors lie outside the familiar North Atlantic Euro-American core. Once, the commonalities of a shared Judeo-Christian, largely Anglo-Saxon culture and its attendant ease of communication helped smooth our manifold relations with Europe. Arguably, the same automatic ease will be missing in our relations with Japan, Korea, and China, countries with cultures very different from our own. The opportunities for misunderstanding grow apace. It is the simultaneous expansion of new patterns of economic power, backed up by greater political and cultural pluralism, that is at the heart of the "double diversity" challenge.

Since the international changes of the past several years have been widely described in journals like *Foreign Affairs* and *Foreign Policy,* I will not go into great detail here. In summary form they include:

1. The break-up of the Soviet Union into a loose collection of newly independent states, with Russia at the core.
2. The shift from a bipolar to a multipolar (or nonpolar) structure of global political power.
3. The growing economic influence of countries with non-Western cultures, especially in East Asia, as economic dynamism there contrasts with sluggishness in Europe and America.
4. The eruption of latent nationalism and ethnic conflicts in virtually every part of the globe, but especially in the ex-Soviet Union and Central and Eastern Europe.
5. The ongoing globalization of technology and markets. The net effect of these changes is a new world system more politically plural and culturally diverse than its predecessor.

A number of particularly challenging global issues have forced themselves onto our foreign policy agenda. They include immigration, drug smuggling and use, population, the environment, and health concerns (such as AIDS): issues in which many minority groups have a special interest. Overriding all these is the imperative of dramatically improving aggregate U.S. economic performance.

Are these foreign or domestic policy issues? It is increasingly difficult to distinguish between them, since all spill over between the two arenas. The links from the outside to the inside can be as direct as the challenges to U.S. citizens posed by Columbian drug smugglers or Japanese automakers. Or, they can be as indirect as the collapse of the Soviet Union and the reduced need to maintain military spending at historical levels, freeing resources to be allocated to other domestic uses. Whether indirect or direct, these international transactions are likely to have differential impacts on different groups of the population.

The Domestic Changes

Given the focus of this chapter, I devote more attention to domestic conditions than international ones. After describing recent
domestic demographic and socioeconomic changes, I will turn to
their intersections with the global system.

We must interpret the recent explosive changes in U.S. demographic patterns against the background of our recent past, when
immigration was relatively low. One expert reminds us that

emerging from World War II into the McCarthy era, the share of the
population that was foreign born was declining. As those who entered the
United States in earlier years aged, and immigration restrictions excluded
entire regions of the world, the proportion of foreign born dropped from
almost nine percent to five percent in the 1950s. In the 1960s, before the
immigration policy reforms, the share fell again to historical lows; less
than 5 percent of the total population was foreign born.[2]

The greatest wave of immigration since the early 1900s found
7.3 million people coming to the United States between 1981 and
1990. As distinct from earlier immigration waves that were predominantly European, fully 85 percent of recent immigrants came
from Latin America, Asia, and the Caribbean (35 percent, 38
percent, and 12 percent, respectively). Over 2.5 million Latin
Americans and almost 900,000 immigrants from the Caribbean
came to the United States during this period. Almost 3 million
Asians immigrated as the Asian population in the United States
nearly doubled. The Latino population also increased 53 percent
over the ten-year period. These changes in the number and origins
of immigrants pose tremendous challenges to the United States.
For example, some employers are now struggling to adapt to the
now-common situation where their employees and customers do
not speak English. In Los Angeles, for example, 30 to 40 percent of
the population speaks a language other than English at home.

Perhaps the single most striking development of the current
domestic wave of growing diversity is the increasing differentiation
within the population of non-whites. This new differentiation
greatly complicates the domestic sources of U.S. foreign policy.
The great American divide between black and white is being

blurred and complicated by a mosaic of cultures and colors. Americans are no longer just "black" or "white," minority or majority, with the latter usually richer and the former almost always poorer. For example, within the Asian population, Koreans, Chinese, and Japanese-Americans are enjoying considerable economic success, and along many welfare indicators are ahead of white Americans on average. Within the Latino community education and income rates also differ substantially.

There are also important differences in residential and work patterns. Since 1900 the United States has reversed its percentages of urban and rural residents. At the turn of the century only 39.9 percent of Americans lived in cities; by 1990 fully 75 percent did. These changes also complicate the conduct of foreign policy, as urban populations more than rural ones are typically more directly involved in foreign affairs.

The most recent of these demographic and societal changes come in a difficult economic environment. In brief, the American economic pie is growing only slowly, and the distribution of the shares has become much more skewed. For the working population as a whole, real average weekly earnings have actually declined in recent years.[3] For African-Americans, these figures are compounded by a tremendous racial maldistribution of income, as the black-white median gap has remained steady over the past several decades—African-Americans' median income is only around half that of whites. The intersection of slow growth, less economic equality, and increased ethnic differentiation gives the current period its peculiar character.

These economic changes will greatly shape the subjective meanings that different groups give to raw demographic changes. Groups that feel themselves losing economically will respond differently to demographic upheavals than groups that win. There is no longer a neat black-white divide, as different non-white groups are winning and losing at different rates. The differing sentiments that result will, in turn, translate into debates over foreign as well as domestic policy.

Areas of Intersection

The global-domestic intersections that interest us are just barely visible, and their future shape almost unimaginable. They are each composed of complex economic, political, and cultural elements. Trying to predict their future would not be especially fruitful. Therefore, we will assume that there are not one but several plausible scenarios that can flow from these complex intersections. For each of three dimensions—economic, political, and cultural—we suggest a utopian and dystopian view of what the future may hold. This chapter makes the alternative futures as stark as possible by drawing out alternative "good news," "bad news" scenarios of the intersection of "double diversity." The *utopian* scenarios assume constructive and positive-sum gains, with favorable impacts on U.S. foreign policy. The *dystopian* scenarios assume zero-sum conflicts and negative impacts on foreign policy. These scenarios are not predictions, but an exercise in imagining alternative paths of where our current ethnic conditions could lead us. By so doing, we can alert policy makers to the kinds of emerging diversity issues that will confront them.

Both views, "good news" as well as "bad news," can be found in our society. On the bad news side, for example, a 1993 report on the relationship between immigrants and established residents concluded that "the current transformation of the American political economy [through immigration] has rekindled fears of social disorder, disorganization, conflict among newcomer and established groups, and fragmentation of the entire social fabric."[4] Will there be many more Los Angeleses in our future, or will the rise of intergroup competition, mistrust, and hostility give way to more effective integration and cooperation, and ultimately to an innovative and improved foreign policy?

Economic Issues

What major economic issues are raised by double diversity? A central one is the way that changes in the demographic composition of the United States affect domestic processes like savings, investment, and productivity, in an international environment that has grown sharply more competitive and threatening. For example, will the demographic changes just described affect savings rates, capital investment, and labor force quality? A separate issue is how recent demographic changes will affect economic management at the level of the firm, and microeconomic efficiency. Especially important is how the changes will affect our capacity to shift more resources to investment and away from current consumption.

Diversity will affect international transactions as well. Diversity may help or hinder our trade relations with other parts of the world. Will the U.S. international competitive position be enhanced by the presence in Miami and Los Angeles of millions of people of Central and South American origins? Or overseas Chinese with China and East Asia? African-Americans with oil-rich Nigeria and Angola?

Conversely, to what extent will overseas "cousins" seek deliberately to link up with their local cousins for business purposes. Some now argue that overseas Chinese or Indians constitute a distinct, qualitatively new subsystem of the world economy, with its own rules and structures. A related question: at the margins will these populations find the United States a more attractive and hospitable place for investment and flight capital, because of the presence of a culture or subculture with which they feel more comfortable? The flip side of this issue is that overseas economic changes will increasingly affect local ethnic relations, influencing such issues as China's control of Hong Kong.

Utopian-Dystopian Visions of Economic Intersections

Let us take simply one or two of these economic issues, and briefly explore their more positive utopian, and more negative dystopian, possibilities.

A *utopian* vision of U.S. demographic changes and their impact on future economic relations is that growing diversity will help U.S. competitiveness as entrepreneurially minded immigrant Americans enhance the quality of our services and manufactures at home, and develop strong and advantageous commercial ties with their homelands in Latin America, Asia, or Africa. Also, immigration provides a pool of poor and ambitious workers willing to accept lower wage rates than native-born Americans, thereby holding down labor costs. American consumers will benefit from lower prices, and employers from a lower wage bill, the savings from which they can plough back into expanding their businesses. Language skills and enhanced sensitivity to other cultures could also help make U.S. firms more competitive in overseas markets.

A *dystopian* view of our future concentrates on the inefficiencies that might arise from a workforce that, increasingly, speaks less English, knows less math, and reads and writes less well. Management for the foreseeable future will be mainly white and male; employees are increasingly female and brown, black, or yellow. Management-employee relations will be more strained when the latter are culturally distinct from the former. Efficiency and competitiveness will suffer. This is exacerbated when, as Robert Reich writes, white collar–blue collar gaps are growing, in terms of income and technological sophistication.[5]

The difficulties of a diverse workforce are compounded, arguably, in an international marketplace where the competition in Japan, Korea, or China is unencumbered by the historical legacy of a multiethnic population. Cultural homogeneity makes stable economic growth easier. Orders are given, trust is developed, skills are imparted more quickly and with greater acceptance. In this dystopian view, productivity declines, and competitiveness weakens. More and more income is shifted to consumption. The economy spirals downward.

Political Intersections:
Utopian and Dystopian Views

Economic dystopia could be reinforced by political dystopia. Certainly the post-1960 political mobilization of African-Americans and other ethnic groups wrought enormous changes in the U.S. political system, from the election of black mayors and members of Congress to Richard Nixon's crafting of a conservative, mainly white political coalition. This coalition, hostile to further African-American advances, was further nurtured by Reagan and

Bush with Willie Horton–type appeals, playing into a national politics of racial resentment. In such a climate, the next several years could bring ultra-chauvinist appeals to racial and ethnic solidarity and memories of ethnic homelands, the risk of rising terrorism, and continuing policy gridlock that could further balkanize and disable U.S. foreign policy making.

In the dystopian vision the political antipathies between suburban and urban voters in cities like Detroit and Los Angeles will heighten as the suburban areas become more culturally white and economically strong, and the inner cities further deteriorate into black, brown, and yellow ghettos without jobs and without hope. Television and movies show the urban ethnics what they cannot hope to have, as they show suburbanites what they do not want. The result is the politics of resentment between city and suburbs, between the poor and the rich, between white communities and communities of color.

Dystopians argue that urban ethnics may turn for solace and support to their ethnic homelands in Latin America, Africa, or Asia. The dispossessed will look back toward their regions of origin instead of forward to their American future. They risk falsely glorifying their past achievements and using past glories to justify further self-segregation. In an extreme dystopian future, immigrant chauvinism and sympathies for the "homeland" may merge with resentment toward white America, producing violence and terrorism against U.S. foreign policy in the Middle East or elsewhere.

Ethnic foreign policy goals (say, ending apartheid) can serve as a rallying cry for community mobilization. But the deliberate mobilization of ethnicity for political ends is not unambiguously or equally good for all members of the group. Not only will different *groups* have different interests, but different strata within one group will have different interests—African-American members of Congress and African-American garbage collectors, Latino businesspeople and Latino fruit pickers. Businesspeople and fruit pickers will be affected quite differently, for example, by the North American Free Trade Agreement (NAFTA). Middle class ethnic mobilizers may press their own narrow interests under the guise of a universal ethnic good. Working class ethnics may get diverted from bread and butter issues by international campaigns.

Another dystopian view is that in substantive areas of domestic and foreign policy, the further mobilization of ethnic groups in foreign policy could lead to even more policy gridlock, as groups with narrow but well articulated interests grab and capture very small pieces of turf in the policy process. We are already familiar with the intensity with which Irish-Americans promote Ireland (and sometimes the IRA), Cuban-Americans oppose Castro's regime, and Jewish-Americans lobby for Israel. Will we find that African-Americans gain a de facto veto over U.S. policy toward Africa and the Caribbean, while Latinos get to veto policy toward Latin America? If so, then U.S. foreign policy will lose any hope for the coherence it needs to engage properly with Third World societies.

The political risk is whether the inevitable jockeying and bumping together of different groups in a democracy will help produce a more perfect union for our time, or whether culture will be so politicized and highly contentious that ultimately it disrupts the health of the body politic. Certainly the opponents of "multiculturalism" see this dystopian future ahead.[6] Other dystopians predict that race riots and mutual intolerance will produce a United States of America more like the violent and gritty film *Mad Max* than the "city on the hill" imagined by the Puritans.

A more utopian political picture sees the melting pot metaphor as driving the eventual assimilation of Cambodians and Nigerians just as it did the successful earlier integration of Irish, Italians, and Jews, groups also shunned and despised by earlier generations of white Anglo-Saxon Protestants (WASPs). The creative energies of new immigrants will reinvigorate the political process and American democracy, bringing it new creativity and new ways of mobilizing all Americans. Latino and Asian leaders will follow African-Americans into the traditional political process. Also, despite what the dystopians predict, the mobilization of groups of color into the foreign policy process may not contribute to gridlock since hyphenated Americans from poor countries, whose own U.S. communities are poor, will be less inclined to hammer away at foreign policy than to focus on immediate domestic economic and welfare imperatives. Divisive conflicts over the details of regional policy are less likely than generalized pressures to do something in the region, including appointing ethnic representatives to regional positions. Therefore these groups' direct impact on foreign policy may be modest. Still, as groups become more middle class, they eventually become more directly concerned with foreign policy issues and diversify their concerns beyond the strictly bread and butter issues of jobs and services. We can anticipate, therefore, growing interest in foreign policy among these groups.

Utopians would argue that increased U.S. engagement in new regions is positive. For example, U.S. policy toward Israel has certainly been strengthened by Jewish leadership on Middle East issues. This has given the United States a strong presence in the region that it might not have otherwise had.

However, the position that any particular ethnic group takes on a substantive foreign policy issue is far from obvious. The NAFTA treaty is a case in point, especially among Latino-Americans for whom there exists no formal consensus over the treaty's impact on the American Spanish-speaking communities. Chicanos and Cuban-Americans hold different positions, and the anticipated impacts will differ by industry and for those close to or far from the U.S.–Mexican border. Many Latinos agree that they would likely be the first to suffer job loss, as half of Latino-Americans live in states that border Mexico and many work in the low-wage positions that risk moving south. But this fear does not prevent many Latinos from conditionally supporting some form of free trade agreement. Views range from advocating renegotiation of the treaty to inserting safeguards in the implementing legislation. The expected costs in job loss and environmental quality are tempered for some by the belief that as the image of Mexico improves in the United States, so will the image of Latino-Americans. In their eyes, Mexico for the first time has been treated as an equal partner with the United States.

Across the border, the Mexican government has begun to reach out to Latino-Americans in novel ways, pushing greater economic and cultural integration between Mexicans and Americans of Mexican origin. For example, in July 1992 the Mexican government established a cooperative agreement with U.S. Latino organizations to establish a $20 million loan program for joint ventures between Mexico and Latino-Americans. The Mexican govern-

ment has also opened an office in its embassy to work solely with
Latino-Americans to foster interaction and exchange. There are
parallel efforts by African governments to reach out to African-
Americans through economic ties as well as through cultural links.
For example, there have been annual African-American summits
in 1992 and 1993 where African heads of state and political leaders meet leading African-American politicians and businesspeople.

Cultural Intersections:
Utopian and Dystopian Visions

This is probably the most obvious and yet the most difficult area
on which to comment. Cultural intersections are obvious in mate-
rial manifestations like spicy restaurant menus and exotic clothing
styles. Equally important are the less immediately obvious aspects
of culture. Ethnic groups and races are not simply collections of
people who happen to be the same color. They have cultural
particularities as well that give deepest meaning to our lives and
actions.

Utopians would argue that America's unique mosaic of immigrant cultures creates its own national supraculture that fosters
greater crosscultural understanding. Our many cultures nurture
interpersonal skills that enable Americans to navigate with aplomb
the difficult waters of ethnic neighborhoods and racial boundaries
in the United States, and by extension, internationally. Many
commentators point to the optimism and openness of Americans
overseas, and to American firms' greater ability to incorporate
local people as workers and managers.

Furthermore, the growing mix of cultures might help to complicate the historically difficult and defining fault line of black and
white, muting this basic, binary conflict and channeling some of
those energies into considerations of "multiculturalism."

Cultural clashes are the flip side of cultural sharing and learning. America's capacity to coopt and incorporate may break down
under the pressure of new immigrants. We have described some of
these possibilities under the political dystopian vision, and need
not repeat them here.

Direct and Indirect Foreign Policy Impacts

This chapter is ultimately concerned with United States foreign policy. We know that "double diversity" will bring changes, but we do not know whether they will be modest or monumental. Nor can we know the precise foreign policy areas they will most affect. In other words, we know neither the magnitude nor the direction of the impacts that will surely come.

There are at least two ways to think about these impacts. The more conventional way traces the direct influence of interested and mobilized ethnic elites on foreign policy. This can range from the influence of Polish-Americans on U.S. policy toward Poland, to the influence of Jewish-Americans on U.S. policy toward the Middle East. This classic "foreign policy" paradigm poses the issue in terms of direct "politics in/foreign policy out." In these terms the new "double diversity" impacts are likely to be modest on the design of overall U.S. foreign policy, but will have greater effect on U.S. regional policies.

Under the last two Republican administrations, African-American interest groups were almost entirely frozen out of any serious foreign policy channels (with the exception perhaps of the development oriented AfriCare). African foreign policy experts were apparently made to feel less than welcome in the foreign service, witness the Republicans' serious reductions in senior African-American officers and the law suits and administrative actions brought by African-Americans against the Department of State. By the end of the Bush administration African-Americans were appointed to only seven out of 170-odd ambassadorial posts, and only one of the top fifty positions in the State Department. Organized African-American leverage over substantive foreign policy matters was comparably low. Latino figures and effective influence were even lower. There was no indication that African-American input was seriously considered under the Republicans.

Ethnic Americans with Third World roots will expand their lobbying for more favorable policies across the board toward their home regions whether Africa, Latin America, or Asia. This could certainly involve more liberal immigration policies. Groups will also press for more foreign assistance to "their" areas, more state visits by presidents from these areas, and probably greater support from the Export-Import Bank and other agencies for more private investments. There may be less pressure for military intervention in these areas. Some of the new attention will remain in the relatively neutral arena of culture—museums and visiting dance troupes. These are the specific substantive areas that will be most affected by the diversification or "ethnicization" of foreign policy. In general, these individuals and groups will seek more high-level attention to developing areas as a whole, irrespective of their country of origin.

However, foreign policy has historically been the domain of elite or upper middle class politics. The Latino and African-American middle classes are still relatively small, and their attention more attuned to domestic socioeconomic issues. Foreign policy is unlikely to be a major preoccupation. But with Latino and African-American and Asian middle classes growing, we will see greater international interest and more attempts to exercise direct influence. They are likely to seek most radical policy changes as much as more attention (conventionally defined) to these parts of the world. Perhaps there may be greater emphasis on direct "people-to-people" exchanges among NGOs. Certainly the history of Congressional Black Caucus (CBC) interest in Africa is instructive, since the CBC was largely responsible for the regular increases in U.S. Agency for International Development funding for the continent, and provided backing to create the African Development Foundation. Also, African-American support for sanctions against South Africa had an important influence on Congress's decisions to impose them on that country. With an increase in 1993 to thirty-nine African-American members of Congress, their views on Africa carry more weight since the administration will need those votes on other issues. (The number of Latino members also rose in 1993, to a total of nineteen.)

In a general sense, more direct lobbying and public agitation by these groups is likely to introduce into U.S. foreign policy greater sensitivities to their home areas and the people who live there. Americans (policy officials as well as the average citizen) might gain a more nuanced appreciation for non-European countries and peoples.

However, there is potentially a far more important, if indirect, link between the behavior of black, yellow, and brown citizens and U.S. foreign policy. These links are more structural in nature. It is certainly no secret that the most wretched, rejected, and rebellious elements of American society are disproportionately black and brown in number. The poorest of the poor are disproportionately concentrated in our inner cities, and they are people of color. Observers from progressives like Professor William Wilson to conservatives like Charles Murray agree on this point. As the Kerner Commission reported twenty-five years ago, the United States is still a society divided between black and white.

Black-white economic and spatial segregation is reflected in black-white attitude differences. Survey research polls show substantial gaps between black and white opinions along important political dimensions. While there is certainly ample evidence of black-white cultural homogenization and ethnic crossover, there is also evidence that many younger African-Americans remain enclosed in an angry, antiestablishment urban culture that scorns standard "white" notions of economic and political success. This is especially true for young African-American males. The ladders of upward mobility, those well-paid, low-skilled positions that once let earlier ethnics climb out of Italian or Irish ghettos, have themselves been pulled up and tossed away. Unlike some of its European counterparts—and here is the critical point for public policy—the U.S. economy has been unable to provide new ladders of upward mobility to its lowermost citizens, especially through apprenticeship programs. African-Americans are especially hurt here, but the Latino communities are affected as well. Recent books by Studs Terkel, E.J. Dionne, and Thomas and Mary Edsall demonstrate the ways that race and ethnicity risk paralyzing our polity and economy, as some whites are reluctant to support policies they feel would benefit African-Americans disproportionately and give them something for nothing.

U.S. foreign policy in the 1990s and beyond will be decisively affected, however indirectly, if there is further consolidation of an American underclass disproportionately black and brown. A growing underclass will be a terrible weight on the economic recovery of America. Sharp divisions of race and wealth will stunt the possibilities for a full and creative foreign policy. In the short term and the long we need to allocate scarce and expensive capital, and scarce and expensive leadership attention to domestic priorities to ensure that America does not select this dystopian path to the future. Reallocations from consumption to investment, and from less directly productive investments to other more productive ones, will be difficult politically and financially. Yet it is becoming painfully obvious to more and more Americans that the growing inequalities and disaffection has become unacceptably expensive for them, in societal, moral, and economic terms. Deteriorating racial relations, and a stagnant economy partially stalled by racially motivated policy paralysis, will spill into our international relations as well, both diplomatic and economic. As international economist Robert Hormats and others ask, can a great nation with great ambitions abroad meet those ambitions, and its obligations, if it contains within itself a terrible drain on its moral standing and its economic strength?

Conclusion

In this chapter I have analyzed and described the new differentiation within and between ethnic groups and races in the United States, and how this domestic differentiation intersects political pluralism and cultural diversity internationally. I also speculated on how the intersection of domestic and global change ("double diversity") might evolve along economic, political, and social dimensions, and how over the coming years these might be expressed through utopian or dystopian paths.

Diversity—both domestic and foreign—is not something we can ignore. It is not a choice, but a condition of life at home and abroad, and we ignore it at our peril.

In this period of profound domestic and international structural changes, the role of leadership becomes especially important. These are rare historical moments when more possibilities open up than are usually available under more "normal" times. With our choices greater in number, progressive leadership plays an important role in shaping future paths, especially in setting new agendas for action.

For America to retain its international leadership position, our political and civic leaders must grasp the full implications of the two scenarios. They can lead by telling the American people that these two potential futures are before us. They can lead by pointing out the terrible costs of the dystopian future. They can lead by insisting that Americans need to pursue the positive scenario, while doing everything possible to avoid the dystopian "bad news" scenario. They can lead by drawing on traditional American democratic values of inclusion and openness. Diversity must be defined by the leadership as opportunities to be seized, not as terrible burdens to be shed, or intractable problems to be avoided.

To make progress in this area, the leadership needs to catch up conceptually to our increasingly diverse social realities. The Clinton administration has pursued gender, racial, and ethnic diversity in its appointments, including those in the foreign policy area. Longer to develop are changes in the content of policy, aimed at reflecting these different forces of diversity in a post–cold war foreign policy framework more cognizant of the changed structures of domestic and international politics.

For new leadership to emerge, the traditional foreign policy establishment must open up and become more representative of the new diversity of gender, ethnicity, and race. Foreign policy appointments should reflect the growing interest in global issues found beyond the Boston–New York–Washington corridor, in the Far West, the Midwest, and the South. The State Department as much as the Labor Department should have a leadership team that in President Clinton's words "looks like America." The ultimate purpose is not a bean-counting exercise of meeting affirmative action numbers. Instead, embracing diversity means drawing on the talents of all Americans, especially those who may bring different perspectives of global change than the traditional foreign policy elite. Those with responsibility for making foreign policy should consult more frequently with nongovernmental organizations and groups that are primarily domestic but have international potential. Similarly, new ways must be found to listen to new international voices. Presidents and prime ministers have views, but in Zaire and Burma and elsewhere, so do democratic nongovernmental organizations. Their views are likely to be the views of the future.

It is not only the federal government that must respond to these major domestic and international changes. Other large American institutions (universities, foundations, corporations, and so on) also need to develop new strategies to benefit from this "double diversity" as well.

At this critical point in our history, where utopian and dystopian paths lie ahead, the country badly needs to concentrate on commonalities and the points that unite us, even as we explore the cultural and other differences between groups or individuals that distinguish us from one another. Indeed, it is precisely the search itself that is so uniquely American. Groups of color need to devote energy to strengthening and enriching the common bonds that link all Americans, just as Anglo-Americans need a more sympathetic understanding of the perspective of the outsiders and the underdogs. The theme of Americans reinventing themselves is, after all, a dominant one in the literature and intellectual history of America, from the colonists reinventing themselves as a people separate from the British, to individuals like Ben Franklin reinventing himself several times, to the recent enormous popularity of the film *Malcolm X*, whose hero, like so many quintessentially American characters before him, worked hard at continual self-transformation. Here at the intersection of dual diversity, in a post–cold war world, never was the need greater for such transformation.

Notes

[1] See Destler, Gelb, and Lake (1984) and Michael Clough, "Global Changes and Institutional Transformation: Restructuring the Foreign Policymaking Process," The Stanley Foundation, October 22–24, 1992.

[2] Robert Bach, *Changing Relations: Newcomers and Established Residents in U.S. Communities,* A report to the Ford Foundation by The National Board of the Changing Relations Project, 1993, p. 3.

[3] Average U.S. wages in private industry fell (in constant 1977 dollars) from $184 per week in 1975 to $169 per week in 1987. See Wright (1990), p. 298. The total income of the wealthiest 20 percent of Americans increased from 41.5 percent to 43.7 percent of total U.S. income between 1977 and 1987. In contrast, the income of the poorest 20 percent decreased from 5.2 percent to 4.6 percent. See Burtless (1990), p. 1.

[4] See Robert Bach, cited above, p. 29.

[5] Reich (1991).

[6] Schlesinger (1992).

8

Breaking the Adversarial Tradition: Cooperation and Competition in the Twenty-First Century

B.R. INMAN AND
DANIEL F. BURTON, JR.

We operate in 47 countries around the world. Nowhere do we have as adversarial a relationship with the government as we do here in the United States.—senior U.S. auto executive

Over the past century, the United States has developed an impressive array of institutions and traditions that have paved the way for its emergence as a superpower. Unfortunately, it has also developed an adversarial government-industry relationship that threatens its future performance in the international

Admiral B.R. INMAN served in the United States Navy from 1952 until his retirement in 1981. He was director of naval intelligence from 1974–76, director of the National Security Agency from 1977–81, and deputy director of the Central Intelligence Agency from 1981–82. From 1986–90 he was chairman of the board and chief executive officer of Westmark Systems, Inc., Austin, Texas. Admiral Inman is a trustee of The American Assembly.
DANIEL F. BURTON, JR. is president of the Council on Competitiveness. Prior to joining the council, he was the executive director of the Economic Policy Council, UNA-USA, and a fellow in the U.S.–Japan Leadership Program. Mr. Burton has edited three books on the global economy and written numerous articles on international economics.

economy. Some of this is rooted in the deep-seated mistrust of government that is part of the American political tradition, but it would be a mistake to accept it as a permanent feature of our heritage. This chapter briefly reviews the causes of the adversarial U.S. government-industry relationship that emerged during the twentieth century. It also looks at the new kinds of partnerships that we will need in order to compete in the twenty-first century. Most important, it explores how to mobilize public opinion to support this cooperation.

We argue that the rise of international competition and the collapse of the Soviet Union have radically altered the climate in which U.S. government and industry operate. If the United States is to maintain its economic leadership into the next century, it must develop a new, more productive alliance between these two groups.

The Origins of the
U.S. Adversarial Tradition

The U.S. adversarial tradition can be traced to three factors: (1) America's geographic isolation and relative international economic strength, (2) the legacy of the Depression, and (3) the military-industrial complex that was created during the cold war.

Geography has played a major role in the evolution of the U.S. government-industry relationship. Because of the sheer size of the U.S. economy and its relative isolation, U.S. government and industry have tended to view their roles primarily in domestic terms. In the absence of a foreign economic threat or the need to penetrate overseas markets, there was little reason for the public and private sectors to cooperate closely on international economic issues.

In the late 1800s, Germany and Britain were the world's unquestioned economic leaders. As the industrial revolution took root in the United States, however, America quickly surpassed them both. By 1913 the United States was the world's largest market for manufactured products. Ten years later, when the huge price that Europe had paid for World War I became apparent, the United States accounted for 45 percent of the world's industrial output, including half of its steel, electricity, and crude oil, and 80 percent of its automobiles. The size and diversity of the U.S. market and the fact that it was relatively self-sufficient caused both business leaders and government officials to think in domestic terms rather than to view the economy from an international perspective.

The Depression left a lasting imprint on government's relationship with industry. In the mind of much of the American public, Wall Street and big business were to blame for the excesses that led to the Depression. The government responded by redefining its role in the economy. Roosevelt's New Deal was predicated on a new bargain between government and industry. In the future, the federal government would aid the business economy through deficit spending in order to stimulate aggregate demand during recessions, but it would also carefully scrutinize and regulate business activity in order to protect consumer welfare and the rights of workers.

World War II lifted the U.S. economy out of depression and restoked the engines of industry. By the time the war ended, America's economic dominance was even more pronounced. In 1950 the United States accounted for one-third of world gross national product and completely dominated international technology and manufacturing markets. In the face of such dominance, government's concern was regulating U.S. industry and making sure that it served America's new national security needs, not stimulating U.S. industrial competitiveness in world markets.

From the vantage point of the early postwar period, the U.S. economy looked impregnable. American industry had escaped the devastation visited on Europe and Japan; Keynesian economics had seemingly ironed out any problems with the demand function; and the government had established a social welfare net to address the needs of workers and consumers. Consequently, neither government nor the private sector gave much thought to the impact of their adversarial relationship on America's industrial base.

The defense procurement system and the rise of the military-industrial complex also had a major impact on U.S. government-industry relations. What began as a constructive collaboration between government and industry to meet America's military needs during World War II, over time mushroomed into a massive bureaucracy of procurement, specification, and oversight. The implications of this system were cogently outlined in the 1993 report of the Carnegie Commission on Science, Technology, and Government: *A Radical Reform of the Defense Acquisition System.*

Central to the government's relationship with the U.S. defense industry is the regulatory, cost based government procurement system. At present about 40 percent of the Department of Defense (DOD) acquisition budget goes to management and control of the acquisition process, compared to only 5–15 percent in commercial industry. This total, which amounts to about $50 billion annually, is testimony to the mountain of laws and regulations that Congress and the Defense Department have created to eliminate waste, fraud, and abuse. These laws detail how every defense system is to be developed and procured. They have led DOD to create a horde of acquisition officers who oversee the process, and have led industry to hire a shadow army of accountants and auditors to work with the government bureaucrats.

The dominant characteristics of the defense procurement system are cost-plus contracts, high overhead costs, quality control based on inspection rather than design, highly specialized product requirements, limited production runs, long cycle-times, and restricted markets. They stand in stark contrast to commercial industry's preoccupation with flexibility, total quality control, volume manufacturing expertise, lean production, rapid cycle-time, and access to many different markets.

The Defense Department's system of procurement and oversight has led to growing separation of defense and commercial industry in recent years and fueled heightened tension between these two sectors. This is not to say that U.S. industry has not benefited from government defense programs. Jet engines, semiconductors, computers, and numerically controlled machine tools—to name just a few—were all given a significant boost by DOD development and procurement programs. But in the mind of many industry executives and much of the American public, the $800 toilet seat has replaced the computer as the symbol of DOD's contribution to the civilian economy.

The distrust that exists between government and industry is compounded by the public's distrust of each of them individually.

The Founding Fathers were deeply suspicious of a powerful central government and set up a system of checks and balances to prevent any one branch from seizing too much power. These concerns are still deeply felt by the American public today. During the 1980s they found expression in President Reagan's pledge to "get government off your back and out of your pocket." More recently, they were reflected in the broad popular support for Ross Perot in the 1992 presidential election.

America's distrust of a powerful central government is mirrored by its distrust of powerful business interests. Despite the celebration of free enterprise, most Americans are wary of unregulated business activity. They are concerned that without careful monitoring of the marketplace, business will be only too tempted to exploit consumers and manipulate markets for private gain. A 1991 ABC/*Washington Post* poll, for example, revealed that 42 percent of the public blames major business corporations for the country's current economic problems. Moreover, according to a 1991 Council on Competitiveness poll, two out of three Americans believe that a major reason for America's inability to compete is that top executives pay themselves excessive salaries, even when their companies are not performing well.

Few Americans would dispute the depth of the adversarial tradition in U.S. politics. Although such a tradition may have been acceptable when the American economy was strong and relatively isolated and when national security concerns dominated U.S. public policy, it is unacceptable in a post–cold war world of fierce international competition.

The New Economic Agenda: Cooperation for Competition

During the 1950s and 1960s, solid economic growth, rising personal incomes, strong industrial performance, low inflation, and low unemployment were the hallmarks of the American economy. The seemingly automatic nature of America's robust economic performance caused many policy makers to concentrate more on distributing economic benefits than on assuring long-term economic growth.

After the first oil shock in 1972, however, the U.S. economic engine began to falter. High inflation rates were the first sign of trouble. Unemployment rates also increased dramatically. Although it was not widely appreciated until the 1980s, these trends were accompanied by an even more insidious problem—poor productivity growth. From 1972 to 1981 the annual rate of U.S. manufacturing productivity growth averaged only 1.6 percent, only about half the growth rate achieved in the 1950s and 1960s.

During the 1980s, more signs of economic distress accumulated. The U.S. economy racked up $1 trillion of trade deficits and almost $3 trillion of budget deficits; key industrial sectors, such as steel, autos, consumer electronics, and semiconductors, were hammered by foreign competition; and unemployment rates averaged 7 percent for the decade. For most Americans, however, there is an even more disturbing fact—real wages have not increased for almost twenty years.

The net result has been increasing frustration, anxiety, and uncertainty on the part of the American public. According to a 1991 Hart/*Wall Street Journal* poll, by more than a two to one majority, Americans do not believe that life for their children will be better than it is for them. According to a 1991 ABC/*Washington Post* poll, nearly two-thirds are worried that they will not have enough savings for retirement. These sentiments have combined to shift attention from wealth distribution to wealth creation. They reflect the growing conviction that unless the American economy can improve its ability to produce economic growth and create good jobs, everyone will suffer.

Just as poor economic performance has led government to reevaluate its relationship with the private sector, so has fierce foreign competition led industry to seek a new alliance with government. This change in attitude stems from the belief of much of U.S. industry that it cannot compete with the close alliances that exist between government and industry in other countries. In 1986 the President's Commission on Industrial Competitiveness issued a report that highlighted the growing challenge of foreign competition and called for bold government action to strengthen America's performance in the international economy. The report was embraced by Congress, but ignored by the administration. As problems mounted during the latter half of the 1980s, however, more and more people in both the public and private sector began to share this perspective.

In a national poll that the private sector Council on Competitiveness conducted in the fall of 1991, two-thirds called for a more activist government role in the economy. Democrats favored this proposition by a four to one margin. Even more striking was the fact that Republicans favored this position by three to one. This poll data is interesting since the Republican party, with its emphasis on limited government intervention in the economy, has traditionally been viewed as the party of the business community. Yet Republicans were calling for more, not less, intervention in the economy.

In part, this poll reflects the public's frustration with the administration's handling of economic policy during the recession, but it also reflects the growing public sense that a new public-private compact is necessary to compete in the international economy. The extent of this shift was highlighted in a 1993 Ernst and Young poll of senior U.S. manufacturing executives, which revealed that 77 percent believes that a national industrial policy that focuses on strengthening U.S. economic performance is needed.

These changing attitudes on the part of the private sector played an important role in the 1992 presidential election. Many conservative business leaders began to call for a more activist government, a position usually associated with the Democratic party. In response, the Democratic party, which has traditionally focused on issues related to social welfare and income distribution, began to recognize the need for wealth creation and found itself more closely allied with the U.S. business community. This shift does not mean that the business community has lost its faith in the dynamism of open markets or that it welcomes heavy-handed government intervention. Nor does it mean that the Democratic party has rejected its traditional social agenda. But it does show that the new emphasis on economic growth offers the potential for powerful new political coalitions.

The 1992 presidential election highlighted the extent to which the American public is focused on the new economic agenda. According to a 1992 Gallup/*USA Today* poll, the economy ranked as the number one issue in the campaign. Ninety-three percent of the public cited it as very important, while only 43 percent cited national defense as very important. Presidential candidates Paul Tsongas, Bill Clinton, and Ross Perot all responded to this concern by focusing their campaigns around economic issues.

Other polls have revealed that foreign competition is driving much of the public's concern about the economy. According to a 1991 Associated Press poll, three-quarters of the American public believes that U.S. business has lost ground in competing with foreign imports. According to a 1992 poll by Americans Talk Issues Foundation/Market Strategies, 82 percent believes that making the country more competitive with Japan and Europe is an important goal. And according to a 1991 *Money Magazine*/Willard and Shuman poll, 83 percent of Americans think that competition from Japan is a serious threat or one of the biggest threats to the economic well-being of the country.

Most Americans, however, are convinced that the root cause of our economic problems can be found at home. By margins of almost five to one, the public believes that the United States should not think so much in international terms, but in terms of its own national problems. Indeed, one reason why so many Americans believe that we are having so much trouble with the economy is because of our preoccupation with foreign policy. According to a Gallup poll, 65 percent of the public believes that the best way to improve U.S. performance in the new global economy is to pay less attention to world affairs than we have in the past and to focus on things here in the United States.

These trends demonstrate just how pervasive the concern about U.S. economic performance is and just how impatient the public is with the status quo. They have set the stage for a fundamental shift in the relationship between government and industry, one built around the need for greater cooperation to strengthen U.S. economic performance.

Four New Goals

Although both industry and government are anxious to forge a more constructive partnership to stimulate U.S. economic performance, each has misgivings about the motivations of the other.

Industry is concerned that government intervention in the economy will be dominated by pork barrel politics rather than sound economic policies. Government, in turn, is concerned that corporations will play a shell game, transferring any gains from government incentives overseas, and thereby minimizing the benefits to the country while maximizing the benefits to their companies. In order to fashion a new alliance, it will be important to move beyond these concerns. Four goals should guide this effort: (1) an international economic perspective, (2) a new priority on savings and investment, (3) a determination to make the U.S. workforce the most highly skilled in the world, and (4) an integration of the civilian and defense industrial base.

First, it is imperative for government and industry to view their relationship in an international context. With the exception of the two world wars, the U.S. government's attitude toward industry has been dominated by a domestic agenda for most of the twentieth century. To a large extent, this preoccupation remains true today. The antitrust suit that the government brought against IBM in the 1970s did not take into account international competition, nor did the decision to break up AT&T or deregulate the airline industry in the 1980s. Not that these actions were wrong per se, but they were taken without consideration of the implications for America's international competitiveness. We can no longer afford that luxury.

Second, we must stimulate systematic savings and investment in the United States. High savings and investment rates underpin the productivity growth that is central not only to U.S. industrial competitiveness, but also to a rising standard of living. The need to stimulate savings and investment was reflected in the administration's FY 1994 budget with its emphasis on deficit reduction. The administration plan approved by the Senate in March 1993 would raise $295 billion in additional revenue while reducing spending, entitlement, and debt payments by $332 billion. This package is not a panacea (even with the proposed spending cuts, the cost of government will continue to rise from $1.5 trillion in 1994 to $1.7 trillion in 1998), but, as bond markets have signaled, it is a step in the right direction.

Third, government and industry must work together to assure

that the U.S. workforce is the best educated and best trained in the world. We have a long way to go. American high school students rank poorly in international tests of math and science. One-fourth drop out of high school. Over two-thirds do not attend college. There is no systematic program to aid in the transition from school to work. There is only haphazard support and training for workers who have lost their jobs. Non–college bound young people in the United States rank among the least prepared to work of those in any advanced industrial nation, and older U.S. workers often do not have the skills necessary to compete.

Fourth, we must integrate the defense and civilian industrial base. In many ways, the government's defense procurement system is the most blatant example of the adversarial relationship that exists between government and industry today. It has systematically distorted the defense sector's perception of innovation and efficiency and compounded the hostility between government and the private sector. In order to integrate the defense and civilian industrial base, we must replace defense acquisition practices with common commercial buying practices. The key is to convert the regulation based system to a market based system. Such a reformation would eliminate the cost-plus contracts and allowable overhead that have undermined efficiency and created a massive bureaucracy that does not add value to the production process.

Working toward these four goals would have a major impact on U.S. government-business relations. They would help each party recognize that the other is a partner to be cultivated rather than an adversary to be thwarted. Progress, however, will not come easily. It will require a new spirit of cooperation on the part of both government and industry, as well as a mobilization of public opinion.

Opportunities and Obstacles

There are several signs that both the American public and leaders in U.S. business and industry are beginning to recognize the need for a new partnership. First, there is a widespread recognition that the current adversarial relationship is unsustainable. For most Americans, this is the real lesson of Japan. When they look across the Pacific, they see a country structured around partnership, shared gain, and shared sacrifice whose economy has outperformed the United States during the past two decades. According to a 1991 Council on Competitiveness poll, 77 percent of the American public believes that the United States is behind Japan in terms of economic strength and the ability to compete in world markets. Although they may not know exactly how Japan works, they sense that it benefits from a spirit of cooperation that is lacking in the United States.

On top of this recognition, there is a growing sense of urgency. During the 1970s, Americans watched as U.S. heavy industry and consumer electronics were hurt by foreign competition. During the 1980s, many high-tech firms met the same fate, and in the early 1990s, some of America's largest companies, such as GM, IBM, and Sears, have eliminated hundreds of thousands of jobs. This growing list of problems has prompted many citizens to insist on a new partnership between government and industry that will strengthen the U.S. industrial base.

Moreover, there are signs that both government and industry are willing to experiment with new cooperative programs. Perhaps the most widely recognized is the Semiconductor Manufacturing Technology Corporation (Sematech), which is a joint effort between several U.S. semiconductor manufacturers and the federal government. Sematech has proven to be instrumental in the turnaround of the U.S. semiconductor industry. Similarly, the host of cooperative R&D agreements (CRADAs) that has been signed between U.S. industry and the federal laboratories is testimony to the willingness to enter into cooperative ventures. Two new programs at the Commerce Department—the Advanced Technology Program and the Manufacturing Extension Program—also attest to this new spirit of cooperation.

Although there is still a lively debate about how to structure and manage such programs, public opinion appears to have undergone a fundamental shift. For many Americans, there is the growing conviction that we have no choice. If we are going to compete in international markets against foreign firms that have close ties with their governments, we need to find a way to establish similar ties at home.

Forging such a partnership will not be easy. To succeed, we must overcome three obstacles: a long history of distrust, a lack of appropriate institutions, and the need to balance the concerns of a multitude of diverse interest groups. The first issue is perhaps the most important. Unless government and industry can establish credibility with each other and with the general public, any attempt to establish a new alliance will fail. Each group must demonstrate that it is willing to look beyond its own parochial interests to the broader national good. For government, this will mean a renewed focus on issues related to strengthening economic growth and creating wealth. First and foremost, it must get the federal budget under control and stop living beyond its means. Business also faces a challenge. In addition to watching the bottom line, companies must demonstrate their willingness to make systematic investments in people, equipment, and research and development in ways that strengthen the U.S. industrial base.

Another complicating factor is that the government is not organized to work closely with private industry. Conflict of interest laws under the Federal Advisory Committee Act prevent an intimate government-industry dialogue about issues related to economic competitiveness. Moreover, agencies are not organized to address issues related to U.S. industrial performance. Instead, they are set up to focus on broad national missions, such as defense, space exploration, health, and energy. Although we have long applauded the incidental, spillover economic benefits that these activities yield, in the future it will be necessary to refocus them so that they directly address issues related to competitiveness.

Finally, the sheer number of players means that policy debates are subject to a degree of complexity and public scrutiny that makes consensus building difficult. Unlike the national security arena, where a few major government agencies set the agenda, the economic policy debate involves virtually everyone. In the federal government, Congress, the Federal Reserve Board, Treasury, Commerce, Labor, the Office of Management and Budget, the Trade Representative's Office, the Council of Economic Advisers, and even the State Department have a hand in formulating policy. The debates within the federal government, however, are only the tip of the iceberg.

State and local governments also play a major role. In many ways, state governments are well ahead of their counterparts at the federal level. The states have long recognized that their economic growth depends on a policy climate that favors investment and economic growth. States like North Carolina, Ohio, and Texas have been at the forefront of this trend. Recently, even states like California, which once assumed it was immune from the pressures of economic competition, have discovered the need to establish policies that favor investment, education, and business performance.

In addition, a broad cross-section of the private sector is involved. Although much of the attention goes to a few widely respected corporations, thousands of other companies, industry associations, labor unions, consumer groups, think tanks, universities, and professional societies are deeply involved in discussions about the formulation and execution of U.S. economic policy. Needless to say, these groups do not speak with a common voice on economic issues.

Finally, the press plays a pivotal role. In many ways, it is the watchdog of the public interest. In addition to exposing improprieties, however, the press can also be instrumental in pointing the way to progress. In addition to highlighting the shortcomings of government and industry, the press can also help articulate the new agenda that springs from the public's growing concern with the economy, and encourage the new partnerships that are necessary to address this agenda.

If we are to put U.S. government-industry relations on a more cooperative footing, we must seize on the sense of opportunity and urgency that the new economic agenda offers to overcome these obstacles. Only when many different groups feel that they share a common purpose will they be willing to put aside their differences and work together in a spirit of cooperation.

How to Rally Public Support

With the collapse of communism in the Soviet Union, the goal that drove much of U.S. policy for half a century was achieved. The sense of national relief and accomplishment, however, was muted by growing concern about America's ability to compete in international markets. In order to inspire and focus America's energies so that it can succeed in the new world economy, leadership will have to come from the top.

Senior government officials and private sector executives must demonstrate that they understand the primacy of the new economic agenda and are willing to forge new cooperative alliances to achieve them. One of the Clinton administration's most forceful statements about the need for a new partnership came from Warren Christopher in his January 13, 1993, confirmation hearings before the Senate Committee on Foreign Relations. He stated:

First, we must advance America's economic security with the same energy and resourcefulness we devoted to waging the cold war. . . . The Clinton administration intends to harness our diplomacy to the needs and opportunities of American industries and workers. We will not be bashful about linking our high diplomacy with our economic goals.

This explicit proposal to link statecraft with U.S. international economic goals is a clear signal that the federal government intends to restructure its adversarial relationship with the U.S. private sector.

The public is clearly willing to embrace a new economic agenda. The extent of its willingness to do so was reflected in the fact that the economy was the number one issue in the 1992 election. In order to generate broad support for a new public-private alliance, however, both government and industry must demonstrate anew their legitimacy in the eyes of the American public. They must show that they are willing to look beyond parochial interests to the broader national interest.

Two issues will have a pivotal impact on the ability of government and industry to mobilize public opinion behind this new agenda: investment and jobs. During the cold war, policy makers were fond of speaking in terms of "guns versus butter" decisions. In the future, they will be forced to focus more on "investment versus consumption" decisions. Although there is growing support for greater investment, the trade-off is especially sensitive because at some level it is a zero-sum game. A dollar that goes to investment is not available for consumption and vice versa. Therefore, in trying to stimulate more investment, government must pay careful attention to issues of equity and work closely with industry to assure that savings and investment incentives stimulate economic growth within the United States.

If anything, jobs are an even more important issue. While the public at large may not fully understand the complexities of macroeconomic policy debates or international trade theory, they can easily comprehend the employment picture in their communities. They will not tolerate nor long support a government that fails to deliver good jobs, nor will they support a private sector that they believe is exporting American jobs overseas. If U.S. policy enhances U.S. productivity and the competitiveness of American firms but fails to generate new jobs, there will be a backlash on the part of the American public that will further erode confidence in the legitimacy of government and industry as agents of the national interest.

In fundamental ways, then, investment and jobs are the touchstones of the competitiveness debate and the real test of new public-private partnerships. If government and industry are to gain public support for a more cooperative relationship, they must demonstrate that they are willing to increase investment and employment in the United States and thereby raise the U.S. standard of living. Any solution that ignores this need will not withstand the scrutiny of public opinion.

Fortunately, the contours of a new compact between government and industry are beginning to take shape. For government, it starts with the recognition that business is a solution to pressing socioeconomic issues, not just a source of problems. Government understandably remains wary of providing incentives to industry since there is no guarantee that these incentives will result in concrete public benefits, not just private gains. At the same time, however, there is a growing realization within government that unless it helps create a strong U.S. business climate, America's social and economic problems will only get worse.

For industry, the new compact begins with the realization that actions that strengthen the U.S. industrial base are also good business. Industry remains skeptical of heavy-handed government intervention in the market, as it should. But within the private sector,

there is also increasing recognition of the fact that unless it helps
address the broader socioeconomic problems confronting the
United States, its future will be severely compromised.
One area in which the shape of the new compromise can be
seen most clearly is in the federal R&D budget. Here, the private
sector is resolved to restructure federal R&D programs so that, in
addition to supporting basic research and mission oriented R&D,
they aggressively advance practical applications with commercial
potential. In response to the private sector's concern that the federal R&D budget underfunds many technologies that are critical
to America's economic performance, the Bush administration
launched a series of national technology initiatives. The Clinton
administration followed by releasing a technology policy that targets economic performance and establishes a new balance between defense and civilian R&D. To the extent that this program
creates economic growth and jobs, it will be supported by the
American public.

The public-private partnerships that are being formed to promote technology and competitiveness point the way to the new
kinds of alliances that can work to the benefit of both parties. The
challenge we face is to extend this collaboration to other areas in
order to build a new sense of shared purpose. Education, training,
and infrastructure development also hold potential for greater cooperation, and successes here could set the stage for progress elsewhere. Poll after poll demonstrates that the American public is
prepared to try new approaches to address the international economic agenda facing the United States. Neither government policy makers nor private sector executives can afford to allow an
adversarial tradition that has its roots in our past to interfere with
the need to seize the future.

9

Building a New Economic Relationship with Japan

WILLIAM A. REINSCH

Introduction

"**W**hy Japan?" is the appropriate question to begin this chapter. It is the only bilateral relationship given this much attention in the book, an unintended slight to the Europeans, if not the Mexicans, Canadians, and other Latins and Asians. It is also somehow less cosmic an issue than the future of the environment or global security. U.S.–Japan aficionados deal with the grubby daily realities of trade—steel, oranges, automobiles, baseball bats, semiconductors, and supercomputers, to name

WILLIAM A. REINSCH is legislative assistant to Senator Jay Rockefeller (D-WVA). He is responsible for the senator's work in foreign trade, international economic policy, foreign affairs, and defense. From 1977 to 1991 Mr. Reinsch served on the staff of the late Senator John Heinz, focusing on foreign trade and competitiveness policy issues. Prior to 1977, Mr. Reinsch was legislative assistant to Representatives Richard Ottinger and Gilbert Gude and acting staff director of the House Environmental Study Conference. Since 1990, Mr. Reinsch has been adjunct associate professor at the University of Maryland University College, teaching a graduate course in international trade and trade policy.

a few famous tension points—but this is somehow not quite the same as nuclear arms reduction, global warming, famine, or population growth.

The answer to "Why Japan?" lies both in what this book is—and is not—about and in the peculiar symbiosis that has developed in the relationship over the past forty years. This book is intended as more than a laundry list of current problems and possible solutions; rather, it is a discussion of American public opinion and how to develop the necessary consensus to produce coherent policy actions that further our national goals. From that point of view the U.S.–Japan relationship can serve as a paradigm for other relationships, in part because it is so difficult. If we can develop policy cohesion and consensus on Japan, we can do it for anybody.

There are also some specific reasons why this relationship as opposed to any other was chosen. Japan is not only both our major economic rival and our partner, it exemplifies a model of economic policy and consensus based decision making that may well be more suited to today's trading system than our own model. Certainly it is more popular, as numerous countries in Asia—Korea, Taiwan, Singapore, Thailand, and others—borrow from it and see their own growth explode.

Thus the United States finds itself challenged not simply by people who may be doing what we do *better* than we do it, but by the idea that there might well be another, better way to do things than the way we have been doing them. This comes as a profound shock to American generations used to global dominance and permanent prosperity and growth. Under those circumstances, it has not been hard to assume we must be doing something right. While the question of whether the Japanese really are in any sense "better" is hotly debated, the implications of that debate differ depending on whether one believes they have succeeded because their system is superior, or because they have simply worked harder than we have and have had some help along the way in the form of U.S. assistance and technology. As shall be seen, uncertainty over the accuracy of the premise, as well as sharp differences among those who accept the premise, as to why it is true, are at the core of American ambivalence about Japan and are key obstacles that policy makers must overcome.

Resolving this debate takes on added urgency due to the consensus that there are some things seriously wrong with the American economy. The 1992 election was fought over those things—a declining standard of living, growing social and economic polarization as middle class stability erodes, and intractable budget and trade deficits, which people feel are wrong whether or not they can explain why in terms of economic theory. Summed up in the statement that by a ratio of more than two to one Americans believe their children will likely be the first American generation to have a lower standard of living than their parents, this "malaise" (Jimmy Carter was ahead of his time) helped elect Bill Clinton, and it remains the fundamental challenge of his presidency.

It is common in such situations to blame the foreigners. It is, after all, easier than blaming ourselves, and Japan is the most obvious foreigner to blame, in view of its economic success and the oft-disruptive impact it has had on jobs in America.

It is also frustrating for Americans to realize that in our case, the foreigners' success is in part attributable to our help. The basic premise of America's postwar policy was first to rebuild Europe and Japan and then integrate them into a strong Western alliance to contain the spread of communism. That policy, by and large, succeeded. The world is hardly free of trouble spots, but we now have a cadre of strong, developed industrial democracies in Europe and Asia—precisely what our policy makers in the 1950s wanted and precisely an example of the old proverb, "Be careful what you wish for; you might get it."

It would be nice if these prosperous trading partners who, by virtue of catching up with America economically, have effectively ended the era of U.S. hegemonic leadership (as is explained in detail in Robert Gilpin's *The Political Economy of International Relations*) now would be prepared to step in and assume greater responsibility for maintaining the international system. That particular millennium does not appear to be at hand, however, a fact that contributes to the American dilemma. We perceive, and to some extent accept, the change in our global status, but our inherent optimism is tempered by our awareness that the evolving status quo is not an improvement. Problems persist throughout the world, and others are not stepping forward either to solve them or to help us deal with them.

Right in the middle of this sea of inner doubts and frustration lies Japan, hardly without its own doubts and frustrations, but nevertheless the most effective economic challenge America has faced since it became an international power. Japan's presence touches all our lives, positively through its products in virtually everyone's home, negatively in the homes of those who have lost their jobs precisely because of those imports. For older Americans there is an inevitable undercurrent of mistrust going back fifty years. Japan did, after all, attack us, and we lost thousands of lives in a long, difficult, but ultimately successful war. More than a few Americans suspect that we won the war but have lost the peace, and there is no doubt that many Japanese have reached the same conclusion from the opposite perspective.

While many of these frustrations are not specific to Japan—that older generation remembers the Germans as well as the Japanese—there are a sufficient number to warrant a closer look at the bilateral relationship. We compete vigorously with Europe, which also accounts for substantially more investment in the United States than Japan does, but somehow that is different. We do better against them, although that was not as true ten years ago, but more important, Europe does not challenge our world view or our way of organizing ourselves economically. We compete with them the same way we compete with ourselves, sometimes winning, sometimes losing.

Japan is perceived as different. The relationship does not respond in the same ways to changes in macroeconomic variables. We have successes there, but they seem always to be at the margin, achieved at the cost of huge expenditures of business and government time and energy. The *system* challenges us as much as the individuals, and therein lies the difference. Because that challenge comes in the midst of our own economic problems and our growing self-doubt, it is all the more compelling and dangerous.

This chapter will examine these mixed feelings, attempt to identify how they are dispersed, and then discuss the means by which consensus might be achieved. This is not a discussion of policy options per se, but rather an effort to suggest how we can build consensus on a set of options—in other words, a frame of reference for policy makers. That, of course, necessitates some analysis of the

"Japan problem" and what to do about it, which, hopefully, will be neither painful nor redundant.

Public Perceptions of Japan

Public opinion about Japan has been extensively studied over the years. While the data reflect some changes over time, they also show remarkable consistency on basic conclusions.

The most fundamental conclusion from the data year after year is ambivalence. Americans are acutely aware of Japan as a problem—a country that imperils jobs here through its imports yet in many areas itself remains closed to our products and services. But we admire the Japanese people for their many good qualities, including hard work, family values, honesty, and devotion to quality and service. We are also more than ready to blame many of America's competitive problems on ourselves and our neighbors. In other words, Japan may be unfair, but it is also a better competitor and thus cannot be wholly blamed for our problems. According to Daniel Yankelovich:

In response to a question in which people were given five alternative causes to America's problems in trying to compete economically in the world, Japan ranks fourth, at 14 percent. The first three most frequently cited reasons, selected by 80 percent of those surveyed, were "Short-sighted attitudes of American corporate management," "The failure of the government to provide a plan for competing with Japan and other countries," and "Low productivity of American workers."[1]

Yet when Americans are asked why American products have trouble penetrating the Japanese market, 40 percent blame it on Japanese restrictions on market access by U.S. companies, while the rest attribute it to other reasons, including lower American quality and lack of U.S. effort.

One problem with the data is separating out Japan-specific concerns from larger worries about declining American hegemony. The latter decline is indisputable, if only because other nations have caught up with us economically, but Japan's role in and responsibility for it are more in dispute.

According to Yankelovich:

77 percent of the American public believes the United States is falling behind Japan in economic strength. Three-quarters believe our economy is stagnant or declining. . . . 8 percent . . . rate America's ability to compete as "excellent," which is higher than the paltry 2 percent who rate as excellent the quality of America's job training and the job opportunities for young people starting out.[2]

At the same time that they maintain that pessimistic view, "more than two-thirds of the public agrees with the statement that 'Americans are too inclined to blame Japan for problems of our own making.' "[3]

In a survey of reasons why the United States has international competitiveness problems, only 19 percent chose "countries like Japan are out to be number one economically, and they ignore the principles of free trade in order to get ahead." Yet at the same time, "Six out of ten (63 percent) agreed with the statement "we are allowing other countries like Japan to own and control too much of our manufacturing and real estate," and 75 percent said they would support a presidential candidate who favored "imposing new restrictions on the sale of Japanese products to protect American jobs, even if it meant higher prices for consumers."[4]

These attitudes may be linked to Americans' feelings about how they are doing competitively. Bad economic times skew public opinion. Just as a rising tide lifts all boats, in the world of public opinion an ebb tide causes a lot of them to run aground. But beyond the immediate worries of jobs and inflation lie long-term perceptions of competitive trends. When Americans feel better about themselves, they also feel better about Japan. In that regard, it will be interesting to see if recent positive developments in the U.S. auto and semiconductor industries become reflected in lessened American concern about Japan.

Attitudes about Japanese investment are also mixed, where each major Japanese acquisition (Rockefeller Center, for example) leads to semihysterical outbursts, while far greater investment from Great Britain or Germany produces a large public yawn. (Japanese owned companies and assets are 17 percent of foreign investment in the United States, compared to Great Britain's 30 percent.) This concern has not been applied only to Japanese. There was a wave of anti-Arab sentiment in the late 1970s when their equity investments began to increase as part of their efforts to recycle petrodollars. According to Daniel Bob:

... almost two-thirds of Americans say that their views of Japanese direct investment are somewhat or very different from those they hold toward other foreign investors. The distinction is not due to any large bias against Japanese people or culture, but rather to a sense of economic challenge posed by Japan, coupled with a belief that Japanese investors have more influence in the United States than investors from other countries. Only one-fourth indicate that they view Japanese investment as different because they sense that the Japanese are less likely to fit into American culture than other foreigners.[5]

At the same time, Japanese firms surveyed "believe that community views toward them are as favorable as those toward other foreign investors and even toward American companies."[6]

Paradoxically, the same consideration has constrained policy makers from taking too hard a line against Japan. While public opinion surveys provide the cover of anonymity, politicians are public figures who must bear the consequences of opening their mouths. American politicians do not want to be accused of prejudice, and the Japanese have learned to be quick to make accusations of "Japan bashing," although their own politicians' record of bigoted public statements is far worse than our own.

One area where public opinion is clearer is in its perception of what everyone else is thinking. According to Yankelovich, 65 percent of Americans believe that anti-Japanese feelings are increasing in the United States, 58 percent think Japanese are prejudiced against Americans, and 67 percent believe that most Japanese look down on Americans and that the bilateral relationship is getting worse.[7]

Interestingly, a separate poll only three months earlier found that only 33 percent of the respondents believed that anti-Japanese attitudes were increasing (*Washington Post*, February 14, 1992). In fact, if there is any trend in public opinion at all, it is in an overall negative direction. A question on whether or not Japan is a dependable ally of the United States, which has been asked regularly since 1960, showed only 44 percent saying "yes" in 1991, the lowest number since 1974. Conversely, 39 percent answered "no," the highest number since 1960 except for 40 percent in 1990. Similarly, in a series of Gallup polls, the number of respondents indicating a very favorable or mostly favorable attitude toward Japan declined from 69 percent in March 1989 to 47 percent in February 1992. Roper and Harris polls showed similar results.

Americans admire the Japanese and appear more than ready to blame themselves for their problems but at the same time, they are not reluctant to see the Japanese partly at fault, to blame them for looking down on Americans, and to support economic restrictions on them, regardless of fault. It is also likely that American attitudes are influenced by economic conditions. Recession has magnified the negative views of Japan.

Policy Maker Perceptions of Japan

Taken as a whole, the opinion of the policy elite is equally ambivalent, but with the experts we have the luxury of extensive public debate and written work elaborating on their views. From that it is possible to identify schools of thought into which most of them fall, and into which members of the public also fall, whether they know it or not.

Fundamentally, there are two large groups on the question of Japan, popularly known as the apologists and the bashers, or soft- and hard-liners, respectively. While the labels are overdrawn— which itself is part of the problem—as with many stereotypes, there are elements of truth in them. At the same time there are many variations within each of the two groups, creating a broad spectrum of views about Japan as people attempt to deal with the bilateral relationship in their own way, based on their historical and personal experience.

The soft-liners, perhaps best personified by Mike Mansfield, Bill Bradley, Gary Saxonhouse, and Hugh Patrick, take a moderate approach to Japan growing out of one or more of the following hypotheses.

(1) *There is no problem.* Transitory blips in the relationship are inevitable and are a function of macroeconomic factors. If the United States increases savings and investment, brings the dollar to the appropriate level, and reduces its budget deficit, our bilat-

eral problems will go away. Besides, the relationship brings benefits to the United States in the form of investment and high-quality consumer goods. This approach was very popular as the dollar's value was peaking against the yen in the mid-1980s but is less in vogue in the 1990s, as trade problems and worries about technology transfer with Japan persist despite shifts in macroeconomic variables in favor of the United States.

(2) *Japan does engage in unfair trade practices, but they account for only a small fraction of the bilateral trade deficit, and should not be, therefore, of primary concern.* This variation of the macroeconomic school was best exemplified by Fred Bergsten and William Cline of the Institute for International Economics in their October 1985 monograph, "The United States–Japan Economic Problem," which concluded that eliminating all Japanese trade barriers, intangible as well as overt, would increase U.S. exports only $5–8 billion, at most some 20 percent of the bilateral deficit. The obvious implication is that a vigorous U.S. attack on Japanese trading practices is misplaced, because it will address only a small part of the problem. The better solution, one that deals with the other 80 percent of the problem, is attention to macroeconomic variables.

(3) *There may be problems, but they are as much or more our fault as they are Japan's.* Japan can be a difficult market to penetrate, but many American companies have succeeded (Procter and Gamble, Schick, Polaroid, IBM, Pepsi Cola), and those that have not have not tried hard enough. In fact, there is substantial anecdotal evidence on both sides. Numerous American companies, primarily in retail sectors, have had significant success in Japan. Others, particularly manufacturers of components or other intermediate goods, have had much more difficulty, despite employing a wide variety of tactics, largely because they are more vulnerable to the *keiretsu* relationships that characterize Japanese manufacturing. (A *keiretsu* can best be defined as a large group of industries tied together by interlocking ownership through common directors, cross-holdings of shares of stock, and other links. *Keiretsu* members buy, sell, and borrow from within the group whenever possible, generally on terms more favorable than the market would provide.)

(4) *There may be trade inequities in the relationship, but they are less important than our broader foreign policy and national security interests.* This

is a continuation of the basic U.S. policy of the 1950s and 1960s—integrating Japan into the Western alliance and promoting Western-style democracy and economic growth, in part through maintenance of open markets for Japanese products. Proponents of this line of reasoning, which have been heavily represented in the State and Defense Departments and the Council on Foreign Relations, believe economic issues are subordinate to security issues and are not persuaded that the world has changed sufficiently to warrant a major shift in policy.

(5) *There may be inequities, but the fact remains the Japanese have been financing our budget deficit through their investments here, and the economic consequences of disturbing that relationship would be worse than the costs of the inequities.* This argument is rarely articulated publicly and does not appear to be a factor in public opinion surveys; yet there remains a good deal of suspicion in Washington that it was, if not the rationale for our Japan policy during the Reagan administration, at least a significant check by the Treasury Department on those who urged a more confrontational line.

The hard-liners can also be divided into categories.

(1) *Japan's goal is global power, and it engages in deliberate, planned efforts to out-compete the United States economically, and politically neutralize its American opponents to achieve that goal.* Government works in concert with large businesses to plot competitive tactics and to manipulate economic resources to support the plot's goals. Some adherents of this school of thought, such as Kevin Kearns of the U.S. Business and Industrial Council, focus on the economic implications of it. Others, like Pat Choate, focus on the political effects.

(2) *Government and industry may not directly plot together, but Ministry of Trade and Industry (MITI) "visions," government-industry consultations to make these visions realities, and Japanese corporate activities on their own have had the same effect.* The difference between this argument and the first is primarily one of intent. In the first, the Japanese government is predatory; in the second, merely efficient. A variation of this argument, reflected among other places in Michael Crichton's novel, *Rising Sun,* is the idea that Japan is not so much predatory as efficiency out of control. The government is aware of the difficulties Japanese competitive activities cause overseas and of the hostilities that are engendered, but is unable or unwilling to do anything about them.

Japanese corporate tactics—infant industry protection at home and seeking market share rather than profit abroad—are effectively predatory tactics designed to maximize Japanese company gains and decimate the competition. *Keiretsu* relationships play an important role in limiting foreign access to the Japanese market. In contrast to the others, this school of thought is not concerned with government plots or policies, and instead emphasizes actual Japanese business practices and views them as at odds with comparable Western practices. Akio Morita of Sony has begun to make similar, though more restrained, arguments, notably in his January 1992 article in *Bunjei Shunju,* but before that in a speech at the Honolulu International Forum on January 3, 1992:

> The end of the war gave birth to a new Japan, and the policies of government, the practices of business, and the assistance of the United States were all aimed at nurturing this new infant member of the global community. But those days are over, and the old ways of doing things can no longer apply. . . . people . . . believe that the way Japanese corporations compete in the marketplace does not fit in with the approach taken by other countries.
>
> I will not go so far as to say, as some have, that Japan pursues "adversarial trade," but Japanese preoccupation with market share is very strong. Japan's corporations have, in many cases, sacrificed potential and legitimate profits in an effort to secure a strong place in the market, taking razor-thin profit margins which no Western company would be able to tolerate.

(3) *Trying to dissect motivation and assign blame is a pointless exercise. We should just agree that Japan is, as its government officials have frequently asserted, different, and the West is therefore justified in treating it differently.* Over the years there have been a series of embarrassing comments by Japanese officials using Japan's "differentness" to justify lack of market access. These comments include the "facts" that Japan has different snow (to justify not buying European and American skis), different soil conditions (to keep American construction companies out), and different intestines and digestive systems (to justify import restrictions on beef). At one time Japanese authorities opposed importing American magnetic resonance imaging technology on the grounds that it would not work on Japanese bodies. The "Japan is different" school of thought, typified by Clyde Prestowitz of the Economic Strategy Institute, tries effectively to turn

the tables on Japan's insistence that it is different by accepting the
statement and using it to justify a different, and usually tougher,
trade policy toward Japan.

(4) *It does not matter whether Japan is fair or unfair, different or the same.
U.S. policy should be designed to support U.S. interests, which lie in successful
economic competition with Japan rather than nurturing a defense relationship.*
This argument is a direct repudiation of the soft-line national security argument, but it begins with the same premise: the fundamental issue is not the character of the Japanese but the interests of
America. If we can identify those interests and reach consensus on
them, then the next step, developing policies to achieve them, is
much less difficult. In some respects this may be the least overtly
confrontational approach, inasmuch as it emphasizes what America needs to do for itself. Most of those things involve elements of
domestic policy—taxation, education, antitrust, worker training,
and so on—that do not necessarily get in the way of good relations
with Japan.

"Hard-liner" views are particularly prevalent among business
and labor groups hurt by Japanese competition and "revisionist"
scholars like Chalmers Johnson, but advocates of these views can
also be found among congressional trade specialists, frustrated
trade negotiators, and members of the high-tech defense community concerned about the erosion of U.S. technological leadership.
"Soft-liner" views are likewise spread rather widely. They are held
particularly, of course, by those with strong economic or other
stakes in the current U.S.–Japan relationship, but they are also
prevalent among free market economists. They are less likely to
find expression on Capitol Hill, where general frustration over
"the Japan problem" has been growing for many years. Within the
executive branch, soft-line views are typically centered at the State
Department and in general economic agencies like Treasury and
the Office of Management and Budget, with Commerce (and
sometimes the U.S. trade representative) taking the tougher line.

The diversity of these views sheds some light on why public
opinion is ambivalent about Japan. If there is no common understanding of the problem, it should come as no surprise that there is
no agreement on how to deal with it.

Nevertheless, there are some common themes that run through

these diverse attitudes. First, there are relatively few observers and policy makers who still argue that the Japanese are completely innocent of unfair practices or market access limitations. The arguments of most soft-liners are either that the number or significance of those cases are exaggerated or that, even if they are accurate, they simply do not make much difference in the context of overall bilateral relations. The hard-liners, while clearly more irritated at Japanese economic practices, differ primarily from the soft-liners in their evaluation of where U.S. interests actually lie and in the importance they place on micro- rather than macroeconomics in making that calculation.

Japan is intrinsically a more important problem to the hard-liners because they look at the sectoral economic effects of Japanese competitive tactics and believe they are more important to our economic and political position than cold war foreign policy goals. Further, if such economic effects are important, then it is a short step to argue for a more confrontational policy than that advocated by those who acknowledge the practices but dispute their importance.

As noted, while the intricacies of these various schools of thought are articulated by policy elites, U.S. public opinion reflects many of the same disagreements. Harsh judgments of Japanese unfair competition are tempered by recognition of American flaws as well—poorer work ethic, low productivity, lower quality, focus on short-term rewards rather than long-term savings and investment at both personal and corporate levels. This willingness to be fair and objective leads to ambivalence about desired outcomes. The people perceive a problem—indeed, they perceive many problems—but they don't know what they want to do about them.

At the same time, we are faced with a political landscape where there are strong pressures against public articulation of some of the darker suspicions about the Japanese and policy elite pressures against the advocacy of "tough" anti-Japanese measures. The Japanese have been adroit in developing tactics—a willingness to call any criticism "bashing," a reluctance to take any official, tough, anti-American trade actions, willingness to follow our political leadership, sustained efforts to keep channels of communication open and to improve the bilateral dialogue—that discourage criticism in the United States and convey the impression of a loyal and docile ally that accepts U.S. global leadership. The United States finds it difficult to respond to such an approach that reaffirms our own image of what our country's global role ought to be.

The result, at least for the past fifteen years, has been an effort to "manage" the relationship rather than to address the problems in it on any permanent basis. Unfortunately, that is no longer likely to be a viable approach.

The Management Alternative

Although the bilateral relationship is the subject of a good deal of comment and analysis, it cannot be characterized as in a state of crisis. We have muddled along for years, and there is a credible argument that we can continue to do so indefinitely. The Japanese are clearly more obsessive about the relationship than the Americans, perhaps reflecting their perception that they have more to lose than we do in the event of a serious rupture. Their scramble to develop connections to the incoming Clinton administration following their miscalculation through the spring of 1992 that George Bush would be reelected bordered on the comical. At the same time, they have shown no particular inclination to take initiatives that would produce breakthroughs on the sore points in the relationship. That should come as no surprise: the status quo has been quite successful for them. Any resolution that would satisfy the Americans who complain would require significant Japanese concessions. If the Americans are disinclined to force the issue, it is unrealistic to expect the Japanese to do so.

As Israeli politicians have said for years about the Middle East, some problems cannot be solved; they can only be managed. That, of course, is a one-sided argument—their Arab adversaries would very much like to "solve" the problems in ways Israelis would oppose. The *intifada* can be regarded as an Arab effort to increase the cost of management to the point where it exceeds the cost of settlement. "Management," in contrast, usually ends up trying to keep conflict at an acceptable level rather than trying to eliminate it.

The U.S.–Japan relationship is more distant and less personal.

While people may feel strongly about it, and there is no shortage of American workers willing to attribute the loss of their jobs to it, there are few who regard it as an immediate threat to be defused. That creates both flexibility and danger for American policy makers. The flexibility is that they can postpone any lasting resolution and, so long as they stay within acceptable parameters of public opinion, manage the relationship in perpetuity. As the soft-liners understand, but the hard-liners prefer not to, one set of those parameters is largely defined in the public's mind on the basis of macroeconomic criteria. If the economy is healthy and growing, problems with Japan recede into background noise. Recession produces a surge of protectionist feelings and efforts to assign blame.

The other set of parameters involves keeping the number of specific disputes below some undefined unacceptable level, both in terms of number and importance. Congress has historically been a bellwether for this measurement, pressing on the president new obligations and authorities when it believes the existing ones are not being adequately exercised.

A classic example of this phenomenon was the "Super-301" debate that culminated in enactment of a provision in the 1988 trade bill that was implemented in 1989 and 1990. (The provision expired automatically after two years.) In the years leading up to its enactment, Congress identified a growing number of bilateral trade disputes, primarily with Japan—semiconductors, pagers, cellular telephones, rice, beef/citrus, baseball bats, leather, and so on, and perceived an administration reluctance to pursue solutions aggressively. That led to congressional efforts to put "teeth" into section 301, the provision of the law that provided a petition mechanism to request the government to address violations of trade agreements and other unfair or discriminatory acts by other countries.

That effort succeeded in the 100th Congress with bipartisan support. The most persistent advocate of tougher action against Japan was Senator John Danforth, a Republican from Missouri. The provision ultimately enacted, so-called Super-301, required the president to identify countries or sectors where unfair practices were injuring Americans. While generically phrased, it was intended to force a more aggressive posture with Japan. As Senator Danforth stated on the Senate floor on April 23, 1990, referring to the forthcoming second set of decisions on Super-301:

The test is coming literally within the next week. Is Japan going to be designated again as a Super-301 priority country? I said last year that when the Congress created Super-301, we did not believe that Super-301 encompassed only Japan. But we could not imagine that it encompassed anything less than Japan.

Two days later in a Finance Committee hearing, Danforth told U.S. Trade Representative Carla Hills, "I just cannot conceive of not naming Japan as a Super-301 priority."

The administration's initial response—not identifying Japan as a country, but rather three Japanese sectors (wood products, supercomputers, and satellites) as Super-301 targets, temporarily defused congressional pressure, only to have it flare up again in 1990, when no additional Japanese sectors were identified.

Overall, the Bush administration's use of this provision was a classic effort to manage both the bilateral relationship and the Congress by taking the minimum actions necessary to avoid further congressional action, yet not disrupt relations with Japan. There was no interest in using Super-301 either creatively or aggressively.

The danger of a management approach is that since it assumes stasis in the relationship, it can become a long-term as well as short-term strategy that may not be adequate to the task of addressing the periodic "abrasions" that occur in any bilateral relationship, but that are particularly frequent in this one. It allows us to avoid the debate over the larger issues that divide the two countries.

Obviously, any bilateral relationship changes over time. While the specific crises of a relationship will change and can be managed one by one, focusing only on them, as a short-term management strategy does, risks ignoring larger economic and political developments that change the balance of power between the parties.

In the case of the United States and Japan, forty years of hard work, technology acquisition, and development have taken Japan from a defeated, war-devastated nation to a technology and manufacturing leader that has sharply altered that balance. Some of that was both inevitable and desirable, the product of our own policies. But it is hard to believe that leaders in 1950 or even 1970 envisioned the manufacturing, technology development, and export success Japan has had. It is easy to obtain public support for a management strategy because it requires no vision and little leadership, but it does not by its very nature address these larger developments.

At the same time, management strategies often ultimately fail because they do not achieve even their own limited objectives. That is, they do not manage very well. If one examines U.S.–Japan trade fights going back as far as textiles in the 1960s, one sees a long series of settlements and agreements that were sufficient to turn attention elsewhere temporarily, but which did not in the public's judgment solve many of the problems.

That should be no surprise, since it is the very definition of problem management. What it leaves in its wake is a series of grumbling American industries. The 1986 Semiconductor Agreement stopped the dumping but did not achieve its market share target. The subsequent 1992 agreement only met the same target after enormous pressure and publicity and amidst widespread suspicions that the achievement would prove a temporary aberration. Agreements President Bush reached on auto parts, paper, and glass during his January 1992 trip to Japan produced zero to modest results in their first year. Despite an agreement on Japanese public sector supercomputer procurement, obtaining new contracts continues to be a major struggle. The one agreement that appears to have been an unqualified success is on tobacco, where the international share of the Japanese market has increased from 2.8 percent when the agreement was signed to 18.4 percent in 1992.

The consistency of outcomes in these situations is particularly interesting in light of the diversity of processes employed. Some cases grew out of section 301 complaints, others out of the Super-301 process. Some were the result of presidential level intervention; others were working level agreements. Some, such as the automobile Voluntary Export Restraint, were ostensibly unilateral and voluntary. Others were part of the MOSS (Market Oriented, Sector-Specific, also popularly known as More of the Same Stuff) talks or the Structural Impediments Initiative (SII). The latter was intended as a different approach focusing on large structural differences rather than specific disputes, although at least one of the topics, the Japanese distribution system, led to the legal changes that permitted Toys 'R Us to open in Japan.

While experts might argue nuances of difference in the outcomes of the various tactics employed, and many view the fact that the Semiconductor Agreement only had any effect after sanctions were imposed as the most important lesson of the past fifteen years, to the public at large the lasting impression is of the intractability of an endless parade of largely similar problems. Huge expenditures of time, energy, and resources by both business and government seem to produce only marginal results. While few are interested in every case, most are interested in at least one, and at least dimly aware of others. Frustration grows as much at the perception of our failure as over the facts of any specific case. This suggests that a management approach over the long term will be a dry well simply because of our continuing inability to manage in ways the American people regard as successful.

Finally, a management approach is also deficient because it discourages debate over the more serious long-term problems that define our relationship. By definition, a management approach addresses the short term. Rather than permanently solving problems, it focuses on finding ways to lay them aside. In any complex relationship, that can nonetheless take enormous amounts of time and energy, with nothing left over for the even more demanding task of solving the problems. That was clearly the experience of many of our negotiators during the 1980s.

Potholes on the Road
to Policy Consensus

What we need is a strategy that will find a way to get these constant sectoral irritants off the table and develop a better mutual understanding of our two countries' global roles. Doing that, however, will depend on our ability to forge consensus both among the policy elites described above and between those elites and the general public over how we will define the "Japan problem" and on how we will deal with it.

Three recent developments work together to make the achievement of that goal more complicated.

First, the end of the cold war significantly changes the nature and importance of our security relationship with Japan. The United States' focus will be on preventing single-power dominance in Asia rather than on maintaining unity against a monolithic Communist threat. That does not reduce Japan's importance, but it makes its changed nature clearer. There are only two likely regional hegemonic powers in Asia: China and Japan. In the case of the former, we will need close relations with Japan as a bulwark against the Chinese and as a partner in facilitating China's economic and political transformation to internationally acceptable systems. In the case of Japan itself, its "threat" in Asia is one of economic rather than military dominance. Our ability to prevent that outcome will depend on our ability to compete economically, not on our military relationship.

Both cases weaken the argument of those who see security relationships as paramount. As is often the case for those who focus on defense to the exclusion of everything else, it will take some time for reality to penetrate perception, but the new set of facts in the wake of the Soviet Union's disintegration forces a reevaluation whether anyone wants it or not, and undercuts the arguments of those schools of thought who favor subordinating economic policy. That provides an opportunity to build a new consensus.

The second factor is the growth of elements that stereotype or polarize the debate—the media and extreme elements in both countries. To the daily press and television there are only two sides: free traders and protectionists, apologists and Japan bashers. It is axiomatic that there is no news without conflict, and the media has been adept at identifying it, whether it is there or not. For example, numerous articles speculating about President Clinton's selection for U.S. trade representative focused on "Washington's trade policy factions":

... the various sides in the "free trade-fair trade" debate have taken turns pushing their favorite candidates and elbowing rivals, distributing poison-pen memos and otherwise inflaming the hypersensitive, highly personalized trade issue. . . . The passions over this appointment echo the national tensions over trade and tariffs, which are older than the republic itself. Since the late 1970s, when the Japanese economic miracle began to cost Americans their jobs and U.S. manufacturers their market share, the debate has been recast simply in terms of America versus Japan. Criticize Japan and your opponents brand you a protectionist—or a "Japan basher," if they want to be really nasty. Urge caution in confronting Japan and you're a naive "free trader," blind to the realities of global competition. Work for a Japanese client and you are a foreign "agent of influence," in the terminology of author Pat Choate. . . ."[8]

Japanese politicians have contributed to the problem by regularly referring to any U.S. criticism as "bashing" regardless of its legitimacy or the way it is presented. Americans have also not hesitated to get into the fight. The same *Washington Post* article quotes Herbert Stein, former chair of the Council of Economic Advisers, calling those who favor a tougher policy toward Japan "economic skinheads."

Polarizing forces, however, often appear without the media's initiative:

America has renewed its bluster in the last year. . . . Criticism of Japan by U.S. politicians has taken on a rather hysterical tone these days. . . . [U.S.] politicians indicated that since both Americans and the Soviets are white, at a final confrontation, they might gang up against a non-white Japan. Japan should never give into such irrational threats. Japan also holds very strong cards in high technology capabilities which is indispensable to military equipment in both the U.S. and USSR. . . . America wants to steal Japanese know-how. . . . That is why America is applying so much pressure attempting to force Japan to come to American terms.[9]

The United States has paid an extremely high price for its relationship with Japan. The U.S. has permitted Japan to close its consumer and capital markets to American companies, while allowing Japanese companies access to American markets. . . . We can therefore see quite clearly that there are underlying reasons—economic, political, and military— that must put the United States and Japan on a collision course. . . . the growing respectability of the view that Japan is a danger to America is symptomatic of a fundamental change in relations between the two greatest economic powers in the world. . . . the U.S. must, in part or in whole, exclude Japan from the American market.[10]

Michael Crichton's novel, *Rising Sun*, although fiction, also contributes to the polarization by painting a picture of a sinister Japan taking over America.

Statements like these make the development of policy consensus more difficult because they help polarize the debate, but they also serve as an incentive to mobilize the moderate forces in both countries who reject destructive approaches. In fact, the controversy that followed publication of *The Japan that Can Say "No"* produced immediate backpedaling by Shintaro Ishihara's coauthor, Akio Morita, as well as efforts to discourage its translation into English. By showing the extremes of public sentiment and the dangers that go with them, these polarizing tracts can encourage responsible parties to assert themselves in the debate.

Ironically, those most intimidated by these tactics are the politicians, who are often afraid to speak their minds for fear of being labeled and placed in one camp or the other. That fear paralyzes the debate on Japan, except among academics, who apparently either have no fears or don't care what anyone else thinks, and makes it difficult to open a frank and honest dialogue with Japanese.

The public, however, as reflected in opinion surveys, has not been taken in and seems not only capable of some objectivity with respect to problems in the relationship but also of worrying about the perceived deterioration of relations. The fact that the public is ahead of the politicians in this regard creates an opening for leadership that will press for a rational dialogue without labels. There will not be a shortage of followers if leaders can be found. For reasons discussed below, they will more likely be found in the United States than in Japan.

The third factor is the phenomenon of the weak government, which has characterized virtually all developed-nation governments in the late 1980s and early 1990s. In the case of Japan, a combination of continuing campaign finance scandals that at various times have implicated most of the senior Liberal Democratic party (LDP) figures and a weak economy has produced: (1) a series of prime ministers with abbreviated tenure (Takeshita, Uno), weak ties to major LDP factions (Kaifu), or amazingly low public support levels (Miyazawa); and (2) a divided Diet where a combination of opposition parties has controlled the upper house, an opportunity they have used to embarrass the LDP regularly. In addition, the Japanese style of consensus leadership forces a process of negotiation among LDP factions on important decisions that makes bold initiatives virtually impossible. The result has been a weak and divided government with little popular support in which the various factions attempt to take turns at the prime ministership. The system continues in power largely because of the absence of alternatives.

The situation in the United States has been better, but not by much. The same party has not controlled both the presidency and the Congress since Jimmy Carter left office in 1981, and his administration was notable for its difficulties with Congress despite his party advantage. George Bush faced a Congress controlled entirely by the other party throughout his term, as did Ronald Reagan in the last two years of his presidency. The resulting gridlock, aided by Bush's lack of a positive agenda of his own and his penchant for using the veto, and coupled with a sagging economy and no apparent plan to deal with it, led to his defeat in the 1992 election.

The arrival of the Clinton administration provided some hope of change in this regard, as the same party would once again control both branches of government, and Clinton had a reputation as the kind of executive who will work closely with the Congress. Moreover, his election could be interpreted in part as a sign of public frustration with government gridlock and a mandate to exercise stronger leadership. If the Congress receives the message, then the opportunity exists for new initiatives to address long festering problems, including the U.S.–Japan relationship.

These developments, while not all positive, nevertheless taken together suggest an opening door, a developing critical mass of people who reject cold war rhetoric and polarizing arguments and are ready for more than management in the relationship, with at least one of the two governments prepared to lead in that direction.

Producing Policy Consensus—
Where Are We Going?

A leader's willingness to walk through the door, however, also requires some understanding of what one hopes to find on the other side and some sense of how to persuade the public to follow. Achieving such a consensus in the United States necessitates showing the public how Japan policy relates to domestic economic policy and our long-term government goals of growth and job creation and preservation, as well as dealing with the anxieties created by declining U.S. hegemony.

Relating Japan policy to economic concerns responds directly to the American public's fears about the Japanese and the consequences of continuing our present bilateral policies. While public opinion is fairly objective about the causes of Japan's successful economic impact here, it clearly perceives the Japanese as constituting an economic challenge (pessimists would say threat) for the American worker and corporation. While the element of challenge is a fact that cannot be denied, building policy consensus requires convincing the public that: (1) the challenge also provides opportunity in the form of Japanese investment and job creation in the United States that is good for both our economies; and (2) the challenge occurs within the limits of generally accepted economic "rules of engagement."

In other words, we must both cooperate and compete—the former in areas where our interests coincide; the latter within the ground rules the public accepts.

Dealing with Americans' post–cold war anxieties is a more complicated task that goes far beyond the question of Japan and the scope of this chapter. While those anxieties are often expressed, as has been shown, in economic terms, our postwar experience inextricably links our prosperity with our position of global leadership. One sustains the other, and the evident decline in our international position is seen as having clear, and adverse, economic consequences for us.

At one level this presents an opportunity for policy makers to lead the public in accepting the short-term sacrifices that are necessary to restore the country's health. At another level, since the days of U.S. hegemony in the 1950s and 1960s are clearly gone, the public must be led to understand that there are many stages on the continuum between primacy and irrelevance, and that most of them leave plenty of room for U.S. economic and political leadership.

Those stages can best be achieved through close cooperation among economically developed countries working together to promote world economic growth and political stability. A cooperative relationship between Japan and the United States is an integral part of that effort, and policy makers must articulate it to the public.

Thus the foundation for a new policy and a winning strategy is one that enables Americans to understand: (1) the immediate opportunities a better relationship provides; (2) the importance of such a relationship to our global position in the long term; and (3) the fact that vigorous competition can occur within such a relationship.

Producing Policy Consensus—
How Do We Get There?

Achieving the above objectives begins with identifying positive elements of public opinion we can build upon to achieve a more constructive relationship, as well as those attitudes and perceptions that we must confront and address rather than manage. Each of the schools of thought identified earlier contributes to that process.

Politics

Foremost among the perceptions we must confront is the view both our peoples have of Japan's place in the world system that discourages it from playing a more responsible international role. Americans tend to see Japan variously as a defeated former adversary better off kept that way, as a significant economic challenge that can be met partly by neutralizing it politically, or as an important but potentially uncertain ally that needs care and feeding. All three create an approach-avoidance conflict for Americans. We demand Japan play a larger international role, particularly in terms of economic assistance; yet when it does, we complain, often correctly, that it is too little too late, or we secretly worry that it might be too much. We seem simultaneously to want a more active Japan but not an assertive one, a Japan that assumes a greater economic burden internationally, but that still allows us to maintain political control. It is no wonder the Japanese see mixed signals.

For the Japanese, international activism is a problem because it focuses world attention on them, often negatively, and calls on them to exercise if not leadership, then at least bold decision making. The nature of Japanese government makes that a difficult task that is easiest to avoid if one is simply not in a position where one is expected to act. The provision of the Japanese constitution relating to the use of force and the military appears to have grown deep emotional roots in the country as well, creating public pressures on the government not to assert itself. The decision to participate in the UN peacekeeping operation in Cambodia and the ongoing campaign for a permanent UN Security Council seat are signs this attitude is changing, but it will undoubtedly be a slow process, particularly since mixed signals from the United States more often than not discourage any major change.

One element of this problem is the issue of *gaiatsu*—foreign pressure. Japanese frequently, off the record, welcome and even recommend *gaiatsu* as a means of pressing the Japanese government to do the "right" thing as far as the bilateral relationship is concerned, and Americans often play this game because they believe it may be the only one that works. Unfortunately, such tactics only serve to further absolve the Japanese of responsibility for their own actions. *Gaiatsu* allows them to perpetuate the public image of a weak Japan giving in to American pressure, thus permitting the government to avoid having to demonstrate leadership.

Moving beyond our mixed signals and ambivalence begins with putting the relationship on a businesslike basis and demonstrating consistency in our approach to Japan. We must move beyond the patronizing tone of a senior partner–junior partner relationship to one of equals who share some common interests but also diverge on some issues of importance. We must send the same signals regularly. They should emphasize the legitimacy of a greater Japa-

nese global role and the characteristics of that role that provide a
foundation for cooperation in other areas.

Achieving agreement on elements of the latter is the best way to
contribute to the former. Several areas that appear acceptable,
because they are constructive and benign, are greater involvement
in UN led programs, including peacekeeping, assistance to Russia,
and environmental protection. All present the opportunity for
commitment of financial resources, which Japan has available, as
well as opportunities for government and individual leadership.
All have been the subject of interest and debate within Japan, and
none necessarily raises fears elsewhere of a renewed effort at regional hegemony or even more aggressive economic competition,
although the latter could turn into a race to corner the world
market on environmental technology.

Economics

Second, looking at perceptions of the economic relationship, we
should meet the two challenges identified above by building on
those public attitudes that reinforce common interests and the
need for cooperation, and by reaching agreement on the rules of
competitive engagement.

One important common interest is the job-creating and sustain-
ing role Japan can play in our economy through investment in
productive facilities in the United States. The Commerce Department, for example, estimates that Japanese affiliated companies
employ over 500,000 Americans. In recent years, of course, this
has sometimes been for political rather than economic reasons.
The Japanese automobile and television industries, for example,
responded to protectionist pressures in the United States in part by
shifting some of their production and/or assembly to this country.
That not only created some public support in those areas where
the investment was occurring, it also helped reduce imports of the
finished products by substituting American-made versions.[11]

While these investments are usually popular in the areas where
they occur, they are often met with suspicion elsewhere because
they are perceived as more beneficial to Japan than the United
States. Transplant factories that merely assemble Japanese com-

ponents into finished products that are American in law but not in spirit do little to increase American appreciation of what Japan can contribute to our economy, and they are not convincing evidence that Japan's chief objective is cooperation rather than disguised dominance.

More successful models have been those that are genuine joint ventures that involve the transfer of technology, management practices, and worker training in both directions. There are some of those in the steel industry and in the electronics sector, to cite two examples, but they appear to be characteristic of individual company policies rather than government policy. Increasing their number requires the Americans to be more knowledgeable about and open to what they can gain from Japan besides capital, and it requires the Japanese to understand Americans' desire for business relationships that are equitable and truly collaborative.

Clarifying the rules of engagement means dealing with public perceptions that Japanese economic success here might be the result of unfair actions, and it means bringing some civility to the debate. This is a problem in both countries. Americans display clear sensitivity to perceived Japanese unfair trade practices. Japanese, in turn, tend to reject American criticism as "bashing" that reflects a lack of understanding of Japan and the way its economy and society operate.

Governments can take the lead in sanding the rough edges off these attitudes, but the truths at their core also need to be addressed. That is best done by focusing on actions rather than motives, which is where many of the "experts" go wrong. Debating whether Japanese actions are "predatory," because of government design or corporate policy or a conspiracy of both is not the way to come to consensus. Instead policy makers should concentrate on facts—on actions in the marketplace—rather than trying to divine intent. In this respect, advocates of the "Japan is different" school make a major contribution because of their moral neutrality, their businesslike approach, and their emphasis on the positive development of policy in the American interest.

While much of the "expert" debate in this area relates to improving access to the Japanese market, which, presumably will both rectify inequities and bring our trade relationship into better balance, the more common source of frustration among the American public is Japanese imports into the United States and the job losses they cause. The U.S. government needs to do a better job of insisting that Japanese comply with our unfair trade laws rather than complain about them or circumvent them, the latter being a growing problem. In turn, Americans should be helped to understand that not all Japanese penetration of our market is unfair, and that when it is fair, the proper policy response is not import exclusion but improved competitiveness here at home. Having clear rules, both in domestic law and in the General Agreement on Tariffs and Trade (GATT), would help. Japanese efforts to undermine that process in the Uruguay Round, unfortunately, do not help achieve that clarity.

With respect to market access issues, a businesslike relationship will treat them as commercial problems to be solved rather than sins to be expiated. In that sense, the debate over a rules based approach versus a results based approach misses the point, since the latter often is little more than a means of measuring the success of the former. We have a long history of agreements with Japan that have not achieved their intended or expected results. Agreements that quantify the expected results enable Americans to determine their degree of success, and it puts the Japanese under a healthier pressure than *gaiatsu*—that of keeping their own commitments. If the Americans negotiate wisely, as in the semiconductor case, the Japanese commitments cannot be kept without meaningful changes in their system and its rules. This is in keeping with the American public's lack of interest in theological debates. Keeping the discussion focused on the bottom line helps remove the tone of moralism that so easily creeps into these debates, and helps keep the relationship on an equal, businesslike basis.

Sometimes, of course, that approach fails and emotion takes over. When anti-Japanese actions occur, as when a group of House members held a press conference to destroy a number of Toshiba consumer products—a literal example of "bashing" if there ever was one—it should be promptly condemned by U.S. opinion leaders. While most opinion leaders do not engage in such activities, they are not always quick to declare them unacceptable and to steer others away from them. Similarly in Japan, the political leadership has often been conspicuously silent when one of its number makes an offensive statement about America or a particular group of Americans.

It also should go without saying that pursuit of intelligent economic policies that promote growth in both countries will make a major contribution to building consensus. While different schools of thought place different weight on macroeconomic policy, all give it a place of importance that cannot be ignored. As noted above, the poll data appear to reflect a deterioration in American sympathy for or support of Japan that coincides with our slide into recession. As—or if—we come out of recession, we can expect public opinion to shift again, this time in a more favorable direction. To the extent the government fails to meet that economic challenge, favorable public perceptions of the bilateral relationship will continue to erode and scapegoating of Japan will grow.

Likewise, Japan's record 1992 trade surplus of over $110 billion, $49 billion of it from the United States, is certain to further antagonize both Europeans and Americans, even though it appears that Japan's decline in imports was due to its recession and its gain in export value largely reflects exchange rate movements. However, if the Japanese government and business community seek to end their recession by expanding exports rather than stimulating domestic demand, as they have done in the past, it will validate foreign perceptions of Japanese economic aggressiveness and retard the consensus-building process.

Technology

Third, Americans must deal with their perception that Japanese technology threatens our competitiveness and thereby our international stature. While this debate also relates to the unfair trade issue, it is clear that the American public is equally ready to blame itself—or more likely, each other—for the country's competitive shortcomings. The public understands, though perhaps American politicians do not, that the fact that Japan has chosen to organize its economy differently from the United States is not by itself an unfair act.

On the contrary, Japan's willingness to have its government

guide industrial and technological developments through a variety of means is seen as a strategy that Americans might usefully emulate in appropriate circumstances. A consensus-building approach would take a page from the school of thought that emphasizes pursuing policies that are in America's interest. It would deal with our shortcomings through domestic economic and industrial policy rather than more confrontational trade policy actions.

The Reagan and Bush administrations rejected for ideological reasons the idea that Japan's approach to technology development and preservation of its manufacturing base might be better than ours. That possibility conflicted with their deeply held fondness for noninterference in the market. Ironically, by closing off that range of "industrial policy" options, the Reagan-Bush attitude encouraged Americans to view what the Japanese were doing as an unfair trade problem. The advent of the Clinton administration provides an opportunity to look at technology competition more as a challenge to American domestic policy than to the U.S.–Japan relationship. If President Clinton successfully changes this focus, then he will have brought American policy up to date with public opinion, which will help defuse one of the most difficult issues in our bilateral relations.

Education

Fourth, educators and students of both countries need to do more to help both publics understand that economic differences are often the product of different social systems and modes of personal behavior that cannot be easily changed. The school of thought described above that uses the "differentness" of the two societies as justification for different treatment has a point. Whether or not different policies are justified, the societies are different, and mutual recognition—and tolerance—of that fact will inevitably contribute to better relations and more effective policy development in each country.

One interesting and hopeful sign this idea may be taking root is the *kyosei* debate in Japan. In this context, *kyosei* translates as "living together" or "symbiosis," but it has become a code word for proposals to harmonize Japanese practices with those of the West—a way to produce peaceful coexistence, to give new life to an old cold war term.

Should Japanese companies put less emphasis on market share, and more on profit? Should Japanese work fewer hours and take more holidays? Should Japan offer an accommodation to its main rivals—the U.S. and Europe—by which all sides would modify their business practices? These are some of the issues being discussed under the kyosei label.[12]

Convergence

The *kyosei* debate also raises the long-term issue of convergence, which deserves some attention. Some analysts, while acknowledging a wide variety of differences between Japan and the United States in social systems, economic policy, and values, believe that those differences are eroding and will ultimately largely disappear. They argue that the globalization of transportation and communication increasingly makes isolation impossible, erodes efforts to maintain cultural or political uniqueness, and ultimately leads to a kind of world cultural stew, where societies may retain differences in some outward characteristics but increasingly share fundamental core values and ways of conducting political and economic business. The end of the Soviet empire and the drive of the successor states toward democracy and free market economies, albeit not all at the same pace, have given added weight to this idea.

In addition, some argue that demographic changes in particular will lead to economic convergence between the United States and Japan. America's aging population, as the baby boom era moves into middle age and ultimately retirement, will place renewed emphasis on savings, investment, and long-term growth. The generation that will next come to power in Japan, in contrast, grew up in the 1960s and 1970s and is arguably more consumption oriented than its predecessor generation, which endured the privations of the war and its aftermath.

Both these arguments may turn out to be correct over a period of twenty to thirty years, but that does not make them particularly useful observations for policy makers trying to deal with the bilateral relationship in the remainder of this century. Keynes said, "In the long run we are all dead," a reminder that convergence theories are of limited relevance to current problems.

They do, however, inspire us to think more creatively about long-term solutions, including larger structural changes in the relationship. The most prominent one to creep into the debate, inspired by EC 92 and the North American Free Trade Agreement (NAFTA), is that of either a U.S.–Japan or Pacific Basin free trade area. Although responsible arguments can be made for further economic integration in the region, much of the impetus for the idea comes from Japanese fears of being left out in the economic "regionalization" of the world, with obvious consequences for their ability to export. Initial proposals for a bilateral free trade area, when examined in detail, also seemed to focus on the removal of unfair trade laws, which would disadvantage the United States vis à vis Japan, which only fueled U.S. fears that such an agreement would exacerbate rather than remedy existing imbalances.

Subsequent proposals, particularly those that focus on the entire region, have corrected some of these problems, but there is not yet a consensus in either country on regional trade blocs as a desirable policy generally. This would be a necessary precursor to discussion of a new Pacific region structure, which would almost certainly be much more controversial even than NAFTA, itself a divisive issue.

Despite the change in our hegemonic position, Americans, particularly opinion leaders, have not relinquished their support for a multilateral open trading system. Regional blocs can be justified as an instrument of that policy—as examples that can pull otherwise reluctant governments along the path of freer trade—but they can also be market-closing and protectionist, depending on how they are constructed. At this point, however, these proposals are more likely to evolve out of policy consensus than to serve as instruments to achieve it.

Conclusion

One of the problems in building consensus on a delicate and controversial matter is that messy reality gets in the way. While poll data on Japan reflect a surprising degree of consistency over time, there is nevertheless always some movement in it, accompanied by uncertainty as to whether this time it reflects a new trend rather than a small shift within acceptable parameters. An increase in the bilateral trade deficit as occurred in 1992, a particularly controversial investment acquisition, a new market access crisis, or the next version of Japanese snow or digestive systems not only produces changes in public sentiment that may or may not be lasting, but distracts policy makers from the task of building a long-term relationship.

The system and the media compel us to react, comment on, and chew on each of these incidents, more often than not making things worse rather than better. The fact that the Japanese have shown themselves to be both obsessed with and exceptionally sensitive to U.S. public opinion encourages the process of excessive reaction. It is easy to become preoccupied with the short-term game of sending the Japanese a message when they have a long history of reading them very carefully. At the very least, we should be able to do a better job of making such messages consistent, so that we can minimize the "abrasions" that are poisoning the atmosphere and concentrate on building consensus on policy in relative peace.

Even under those circumstances, however, the process will not be an easy one. The many schools of thought on the subject are sharply divided, and their adherents are committed to their views. Perhaps more important, the public itself remains ambivalent, simultaneously praising and blaming Japan, willing to support strong actions against it but recognizing that those actions may not be solutions to the problems. The advent of a new administration in Washington, which offers the promise of better relations with Congress and a more proactive approach to the domestic economy, provides both the opportunity for a fresh start at showing the leadership necessary to build consensus and the possibility that the skills may actually be there to do precisely that.

The Japanese picture, as usual, is murkier. The government's capacity to lead remains as much in doubt as ever. Increased discussion of serious political reform, driven by the departure of Tsutomu Hata and Ichiro Ozawa from what had been the largest LDP faction, is a sign of hope, as is the growing *kyosei* debate, which involves both Japanese government and business figures. It may well be that in the end it is the Japanese business community, which has led the way on so many changes in Japan since the war, that takes the lead in building a consensus for change in Japan. That would be no small irony, but a welcome one nonetheless.

Notes

[1] Yankelovich (1992).
[2] Yankelovich (1992).
[3] Yankelovich (1992).
[4] Yankelovich (1992).
[5] Bob and SRI International (1990), p. 23.
[6] Bob and SRI International (1990), p. 23.
[7] Yankelovich (1992).
[8] *Washington Post,* December 19, 1992, p. C 7.
[9] Shintaro Ishihara and Akio Morita, "The Japan that Can Say No," Kobunsha Kappa-Holmes (unofficial translation), p. 52.
[10] Friedman and LeBard (1991).
[11] Job creation data, of course, are tricky. A new plant may create jobs at its location but displace them somewhere else, either directly through consolidation of the company's resources or indirectly through successful competition with other firms that subsequently lay off people. There also is the issue of job value—high-wage technologically advanced jobs vs. low-wage assembly jobs. These issues, however, also apply to American firms, particularly multinationals that transfer much of their production overseas.
[12] Rowley (1992), p. 52.

10

Security in the New Order: Presidents, Polls, and the Use of Force

CATHERINE McARDLE KELLEHER

Introduction

T he crisis over Bosnia raises anew a debate that reaches back to the first days of the American republic: under what conditions will and should the United States be willing to use military force? It is a debate that most presidents have tried to avoid or to

CATHERINE McARDLE KELLEHER is a senior fellow in foreign policy studies at the Brookings Institution. She was formerly professor at the School of Public Affairs and founding director of the Center for International and Security Studies at the University of Maryland. Professor Kelleher was a member of the National Security Council staff in the Carter administration and has taught at the National War College, Columbia University, and the Universities of Denver, Michigan, and Illinois. She presently serves on the Council of IISS, as president of Women in International Security, and as vice chair of the National Academy of Sciences Committee on International Security and Arms Control. She wishes to thank Holly Spiller of the CISS for research assistance on this chapter and Steve Farkas and Michael Canavan of the Public Agenda Foundation for a wealth of polling data, various additional sources, and their willingness to share opinion survey results.

dominate quickly; President Clinton is no exception. Yet for Bosnia or a new contingency, it is a debate that must now be joined as a superpower United States, clearly superior in military capability and far from its isolationist past, searches for new relations with former friends and foes, with competitors and clients, with the strong and the weak.

For much of the cold war era, the arguments and the answers to these questions seemed reasonably straightforward; the United States must be prepared to use force whenever and wherever an implacable ideological foe challenged its fundamental interests and those it shared with its free world partners. In retrospect, Berlin, Korea, and Cuba appear predictable, if not necessarily inevitable, and in the tradition of World War II, "the good war." The worldwide threat of communism in all its forms meant the United States could no longer afford the luxury of slow, considered mobilization, of withdrawal to its hemisphere, or of shunning entangling military alliances.

But the decade of Vietnam and its aftermath, the debate over U.S. military intervention and the legitimacy of both service and protest, divided the nation and ultimately marked a generation. Throughout the 1970s, most issues—military, political, and ethical—were left undiscussed or unresolved. The 1980s yielded few answers as arguments raged over whether to use American force in Nicaragua and Libya, and over the impact of military victories and defeats in Lebanon, Grenada, and Panama.

The debate over Bosnia goes to the heart of American assumptions about the utility of force and the factors that now must shape U.S. foreign and defense policy. What, in this post–cold war era, are the appropriate yardsticks and instruments for U.S. national interest? How narrowly can or should we choose to interpret this concept? How are we now to balance our long-revered tradition as democracy's "city on the hill" and our proud claim as the first practical, nonideological polity in our approach to international issues? What of our legacy as the arsenal of democracy and the champion of human rights? What of our heritage as pragmatic problem solvers, faithful to case-by-case analysis and the trade-off of costs and benefits? Regarding Bosnia itself, how do we now choose between what some portray as our moral responsibility to intervene to prevent further atrocities and protect the innocent, and what others argue should be our principled avoidance of an involvement in an uncertain quagmire?

This chapter attempts to illuminate the critical aspects of this debate and to place it in a wider context—the structures and trends in domestic support for the use and maintenance of military capabilities in the post-cold war international order. It focuses first on the official actors who have structured postwar public debate and decision making—overwhelmingly the president but also increasingly the Congress and the military and foreign policy-making bureaucracies. It then turns to what past and present polls can reveal about the long-term nature and evolution of American opinion on these issues.

Who Structures Debate and Decision?

The President

In defense as in foreign policy, American tradition accords the president the greatest role in the structuring of debate and decisions. Some of this reflects the president's unique and encompassing constitutional powers—as head of state, as chief executive, and more importantly, as commander-in-chief sworn to defend the United States against all enemies, domestic and foreign. Much more results from the repeated presidential use of the "bully pulpit" on questions of peace and war, of moral obligation and pragmatic calculation.

But by far the dominant factors in questions of defense are the recent traditions of the "imperial presidency." The president is the center, the setter of agendas, the driving force of debate and action. He sits astride intelligence, diplomacy, and capability—all, as the Irangate debacle demonstrated, sometimes more loyal to his ideas and preferences than to constitutional mandates or congressional prescriptions. More importantly, in an age of global communication, his is the most prominent and credible national voice—galvanizing interest, explaining events, interpreting motives, asking support. Increasingly, this role extends not only to

American deliberations but also affects and sometimes conditions the decisions reached by other leaders and other publics.

Nowhere is this more true than in decisions about military intervention. In every instance since the end of World War II, it has been the president who has been interventionist, calling on a sometimes reluctant Congress and the electorate to support his plan for the use or threat of use of military force. More often than not, he has been obliged to explain clearly and carefully how this action relates to the national interest, how it accords with national values and moral principles, how the conflict role will be initiated and hopefully terminated. There have also been presidents who, like democracies in general, were slow to act or react—Eisenhower and Carter perhaps most notably. But within these limits, most presidents have seized leadership and prevailed. Few have failed to get a "rally 'round the flag"—that is, overwhelming support on grounds of patriotic duty and national unity, at least in the initial phases of conflict or intervention.

But most presidents have also discovered the risks and costs involved. Whether just or not, it is the president's war, his responsibility. Failure, long engagement, or even limited success has often led to electoral punishment, as a row of Democrat presidents from Truman to Carter has discovered. It was true even for a George Bush who was unable to translate his enormous popular success in the Gulf War into positive support for reelection.

Moreover, in the post–cold war era, the president faces inherent limits on his exclusive ability to structure and explain the national defense agenda. There is no longer one great overriding threat to which all can be related, one simple explanation for enduring friendships and implacable enemies. Rather, the list of potential threats is more diverse and less certain in importance. Conflicts are perhaps becoming more frequent but occur at far lower levels of armament and violence. Most are local or regional in character, with far less direct implications for the United States than in the era of probable escalation of any dispute with superpower involvement, including to the level of all-out nuclear war.

Instantaneous global communication means the president's unique intelligence assets now race CNN's pictures and interpretation that evoke popular emotional reaction and turn popular attention almost with lightning speed. Whether it was the suffering of the Kurds in northern Iraq, the starvation in Somalia, or the horrors of Bosnia, the response of American viewers is to demand that the president act—or at least explain why he cannot. These may also be the same voices that call for the recovery of a peace dividend, for a halving of the present defense budget, or for the withdrawal of most U.S. forces from overseas. But it is the president who must find and strike the acceptable balance. It has always been the presidential task to sort out competing pressures for action, but the "CNN factor" now makes this a constant occupation.

Over Bosnia, President Clinton discovered another disadvantage of the communications spotlight—the distortions and penalties of media focus when interagency consultation and diplomacy are not yet ripe. Learning from the Gulf experience, Clinton attempted to consult with allies over multilateral options, and therefore delayed a direct explanation and appeal to the American people. But however critical this was for coalition building, it left a yawning vacuum soon filled by opponents, pundits, and leaks of allied opposition. Announcements of Clinton domestic programs were overshadowed by the Bosnian drama and insistent press questions on the timing of presidential action. Moreover, once the press reported that the momentum for action had begun to build, any presidential hesitation or second thought was portrayed as weakness, if not a defeat. Before commitment or afterward, few presidents indeed have had the diplomatic skills or the consummate talents of a Franklin Roosevelt or even a Dwight Eisenhower for avoiding decision and deflecting political pressures.

The Congress

The Constitution, of course, formally accords to the Congress most of the critical powers to use military force and to develop and maintain military capabilities. The task of assuring the common defense and raising an army turned initially both on Congress's power to spend or deny spending and on its embodiment of deep-seated traditional American fears about exclusive executive control over military forces. Both reasons still remain true, although at far lower levels of intensity in the face of multiyear defense funding for major projects, military-industrial pressures for jobs, and increasing popular acceptance of presidential primacy and a U.S. global role.

Perhaps the most decisive power, congressional authority to declare and commit the nation to war, has declined in importance in the twentieth century, in direct proportion to the increasing presidential authority. In the postwar period, it has become a largely symbolic or formal function, given the existence under direct presidential command of large standing forces, stable overseas deployments, and high alert rates for immediate response, nuclear but also conventional. The post–Vietnam War Powers Act of 1973 attempted to right the balance, mandating congressional approval within ninety days for any military crisis deployments, and requiring timely presidential reporting on the objectives for which any forces are sent overseas in harm's way. In the 1980s the congressional Democrats sought even tighter, more specific prohibitions over not just the use of U.S. military assets, but also over military assistance and liaison with autocratic governments, especially in Central America.

But most presidents have energetically resisted these constraints, and few have met even the minimum reporting provisions. The Iran/Contra investigations reveal the awesome capabilities of the executive branch to evade or to honor only the letter of specific congressional restrictions. Congress questioned but did not challenge the fateful Marine deployments to Lebanon, and decisive resistance to President Reagan's wish to use military assets against the Sandinistas in Nicaragua came as much from the uniformed military as it did from the congressional leadership.

Perhaps the only significant direct result of the War Powers Resolution was the extended debate early in 1991 to gain congressional approval, however late, for the military build-up in the Gulf. Even that debate was portrayed by President Bush as a "courtesy to Congress," not something he was required to do. Opinion was clearly divided; there was full and careful consideration of moral imperatives and practical operations, of constitutional duties and political realities, of the utility of sanctions versus military force. In the end, despite many expressed doubts, a majority voted to support the president's use of military force, if needed. Not only was partisanship to end at the water's edge, but in crisis and uncertainty, priority was to be given to demonstrating national solidarity and resolve.

In the cold war crises, indeed, most members of Congress were more than willing to step aside and allow the president to assume the responsibility and the risks for military action. Few could or would claim the knowledge to challenge the president's interpretation of events; even fewer challenged the need for instant presidential reaction in the face of nuclear threat or the prospect of all-out conventional war in Europe. Given the early Vietnam experience (as the shunning of Wayne Morse after his opposition to the empowering Gulf of Tonkin Resolution), most feared the immediate political effects or even longer-term electoral consequences of "denying the president." The most cynical calculated that there would be time for questions and investigations once the conflict was over or as it wore on to declining popular support and changing international conditions.

Congressional reaction to Somalia and to Bosnia demonstrates considerable continuity from the cold war experience but also shows some similarities with Capitol Hill patterns before 1945. It is not just the familiar post-Vietnam argument that the United States should not be the world police officer; rather it is the widespread doubt as to whether there needs be a police officer at all. Throughout much of the fall and winter of 1992–93, there was only a handful of assertive voices for action. Most members of Congress expressed concern for the personal suffering, and support for humanitarian action and little else. Mirroring the trends in public opinion discussed below, there is now far greater skepticism about the feasibility of military solutions, far more resistance to any detraction from the domestic agenda. The House and Senate leaderships have proclaimed their willingness, as always, to support the president in unilateral or, preferably, multilateral action in defense of the national interest. But, as with the public, there are now even more insistent congressional demands for full presidential explanation and justification, a fairly detailed statement of goals and limits on risks and costs, a comprehensive plan for timing and for burden sharing.

The Professionals:
The Military and the Foreign Service

The debate over Bosnia reveals renewed efforts by what I call the professionals to structure and steer the debate over the use of force. Criticism and eventually resignations by cabinet members are not new. But not since Vietnam has there been such willingness among some members of the military and of the foreign service to assert publicly their concerns about policy making and their preferred conditions for policy implementation. The ultimate impact of the views of the Joint Chiefs of Staff (JCS) and General Colin Powell, or of the appeals of a group of mid-level desk officers, cannot be measured. Moreover, in the end, both groups must accede to presidential decisions or resign. But these have become clear points of reference for both the Congress and, to some measurable effect, informed public opinion.

The role of the JCS reflects in largest measure the continuing military sensitivities over Vietnam. But it also stems specifically from the controversies and the changes in the 1980s. In the early 1980s, in the case of Nicaragua, the JCS and particularly Army Chief of Staff Edward Meyer enunciated their own formula for the legitimate use of force: a stated objective, a predetermined measure of success, and convincing evidence of public support. Secretary of Defense Caspar Weinberger backed this effort and adopted these criteria as his own in other cases as well. In Nicaragua, even the ultimately popular Ronald Reagan did not overturn the opposition of the military and their allies in the Congress and among the attentive foreign policy publics.

But the new military voice also reflects the organizational changes in the JCS itself, and especially the new prominence the Goldwater-Nichols reforms give the chair as the president's principal military adviser. Both in Bosnia and Somalia, for example, the views of General Powell (somewhat at variance with many in the White House) were clearly and widely circulated, even before any formal congressional hearings or press briefings. The chair's choice ultimately may be "to salute or resign," but he now has far more leverage and visibility in the process up to decision. The president also faces a JCS with more incentives toward positive unity, and more vocal statements by theater commanders who are more regularly and openly brought into the debate of goals and means. Military skepticism and military reluctance to use force are traditional; specific public questions about the risks accepted and the operational limits are new. The broad public may still question and finally reject the military view, but it is clearly aware of and influenced by it.

The reaction among the foreign service to Bosnia may be more transitory, the result perhaps of the coincidence of a change in administration, and a commitment to more open access and debate. But the Department of State professionals, like the more senior military, may well also be reflecting the new opportunity for debate and dissent now that the imposed urgencies of the cold war are past. There seem to be greater room and time for choice, less insistence on consistency in the interests of overall deterrence, less value of particular geopolitical stakes, and more emphasis on overall stability. Declining budgets and fewer capabilities mean more need for choice and for consideration of consequences. For at least the foreseeable future, the mood of the public and its tolerance for military risk and costs appear hard to predict or even to gauge.

The Media

Mention of heightened media impact on issues of force and defense is now so commonplace that only a few comments about its structuring effects are necessary. It is clear that more and more Americans rely on television images as their international frame; the widening availability of CNN and other "instant reality" channels suggests this trend will continue. Television has become increasingly confident of its ability to devise "soundbites" even for the most complex conflicts and the most remote areas. The result may well be both oversimplification and a higher average level of information among attentive publics. There is clearly also a far greater emotional impact on the public as a whole.

The last three years have repeatedly demonstrated the structuring impact of television images on public debates and attitudes. Aid to the Kurds (Operation Provide Comfort) after the Gulf War was almost certainly conditioned by television mobilization of opinion first in Europe and then in the United States. Televised hunger in Somalia, not the comparable untelevised situation in the Sudan, became the object of public concern. The violence of Bosnia has been the evening fare for policy makers and public alike, whatever their initial policy preferences. Journalists indeed have become targets or treated as combatants, given their purported inability to report "the real story."

Although slower, the national print media have also been playing a more active role. Here again the end of the cold war means greater freedom for criticism, more questioning of established policy, and more direct appeals for action or for choice. Bosnia, for example, would have been far less of a national crisis without the day-in–day-out calls for moral judgment and political actions by a relatively hawkish *New York Times*. With few exceptions, editorials and commentaries called for intervention, for a direct response to the new opportunities now available through multilateral agreement and the United Nations, for action now or repentance later.

Public Opinion: Trends and Tendencies

The Post–Cold War Context

Understanding present trends concerning the use of force in Bosnia requires a step backward to more theoretical debates about the nature and disposition of American public opinion toward foreign policy more generally. The dominant postwar interpretation was that Americans were largely uninformed and uninterested in international issues and affected more by mood and domestic conditions than by adherence to coherent world views.[1] Like most democratic populations, they were seen as slow to anger and generally noninterventionist, especially in the affairs of other democracies. But once mobilized by their political leadership, Americans were prone to rash or "moralistic" action, or the "spasm" use of military force. They wanted immediate action, the effective and immediate application of all-out military power "to get the job done," and the fastest possible return at the lowest costs of life to the "normal" status of domestic tranquility. Successful problem solving was the operational task; the preservation of democratic values in an uncertain world, the national preoccupation.

Analysis done during the 1980s and 1990s challenged this interpretation as outdated and far more reflective of the assumptions of the immediate postwar and even the prewar climate of opinion.[2] Whether once true or not, this traditional view is undermined by the nature of the post–cold war international environment and the changing nature of domestic political patterns. Almost every general foreign policy survey shows the public is increasingly well informed about global issues, devotes attention to evolving international events, and has clear opinions on most major foreign and defense policy questions. Americans do take more account of moral issues in evaluating foreign policy choices than some other nationalities; they are more mobilizable for what William Schneider calls "valence" issues, or questions involving values, than for what seem matters of "position" or narrow policy advantage.[3] But they are overwhelmingly pragmatic in finally deciding on support for overseas initiatives, including the use of military force. Costs and risks count; case-by-case decisions outnumber the invocation of universal principles; short-term actions with a high probability of success are preferred to longer-term involvements with uncertain prospects for achievement. They are, in Bruce Jentleson's apt phrase, "the pretty prudent public."[4]

This reflects less the passing of the Communist threat than a gradual evolution of post-Vietnam thinking about America's role. Jentleson argues, for example, that popular support for U.S. military ventures before the fall of the Berlin Wall reflects neither the block solidarity of the cold war period nor the distraction and fragmentation of the "Vietnam trauma." Rather, Americans became more disposed to the use of military force for humanitarian ends or to counter blatantly aggressive behavior, while remaining resistant to military efforts at enforced nation building or intervention in civil wars.[5]

But the changes are clear even in public rhetoric or at the surface level of opinion. Unquestionably there is a special susceptibility in poll results to the manipulation of key words and symbols, but there is also increasing attention to practical utility—as is evident in recent surveys on attitudes about Bosnia. Americans are much more willing to offer their support for U.S. military involvement when it is mentioned in the context of an "allied" or "multilateral" or "UN" mission. This signals a fundamentally different type of U.S. involvement, from unilateral action to collective effort, and it is not surprising that favorable responses increase by as much as 10 percent. Americans respond more subtly to words that play on sentiment such as "moral" or "humanitarian," and those that play on emotion by conjuring up graphic images of "ethnic cleansing" or "raping and murdering." Mention of words like "innocent" or "victim" may slightly increase support for American intervention, and phrases such as "send ground forces" or "risk casualties" have the opposite effect. The patterns indeed are quite stable—and far less variable than those reported in the past.

Overview: Current Opinion on the Use of Force

In the abstract, Americans continue to view direct U.S. military involvement only as a last resort, reserved for the most desperate and extreme circumstances. The key descriptors are reluctance and caution. There is still a reservoir of support for the traditional U.S. commitment to the North Atlantic Treaty Organization (NATO) and to the use of military force to defend our allies in Western Europe. But there is an overwhelming reluctance, if not a fundamental aversion, to the use of force elsewhere. This dichotomy persists into the 1990s with two "hypothetical" exceptions. Americans report an increasing willingness to defend South Korea from an invasion by the North Koreans and Israel from an Arab attack.[6]

The Gulf War boosted public confidence in the military, and fueled a greater tendency toward championing the cause of weaker nations confronted by aggression, and toward defending the human rights of the oppressed. But the apparent constraint of Saddam Hussein and the end of the Soviet Union have given new room for concerns about the severity of the budget deficit and heightened pressure to divert badly needed resources from defense to domestic programs. A majority of the American public objects to providing military aid overseas, and support for military assistance even to traditional allies has suffered since the cold war ended. Despite the Gulf crisis, support has fallen for military and economic aid to Israel and Egypt, the two pillars of the Gulf strategy.[7]

Humanitarian assistance clearly outranks all other international initiatives in popular support—as it does in most European countries as well. The *Times Mirror* Center poll of October 11, 1990, for example, found that, while reluctant to send military aid, Americans are very willing to provide vital assistance to countries where basic vital necessities may not be available. Eighty percent of those surveyed responded that they would favor the United States offering "food and medical assistance" to those in need. By contrast, only 70 percent favored sending "economic and military aid to countries that are *important allies* of the U.S.," and only 75 percent favored aid to encourage the purchase of U.S. products.

There is a good deal of evidence that while Americans reject an activist role for the U.S. military, they consistently support nonmilitary international involvement. A survey taken by the Chicago Council on Foreign Relations reveals an interesting trend in public support for an internationally engaged America. There was a steady decline in support for an active international role for the United States, from an all-time high in 1956 (71 percent) to an all-time low in 1982 (54 percent). From 1982 to 1986, however, there was a resurgence in support (to 64 percent) for an active United States. Ironically, in spite of the heightened attention given to domestic/economic issues, the 1990 survey indicates that the percentage of Americans favoring an active international role for the United States fell only slightly between 1986 and 1990 (see Table 1).

Americans also now see U.S. military prominence as only one aspect of our international interest and commitment. The 1991 *Times Mirror* Center poll, for example, found that 92 percent of those surveyed agreed it is best for the future of the United States to be active in world affairs. When asked directly about the statement, "The best way to ensure peace is through military strength," only 52 percent agreed, while 45 percent disagreed. For the most part, though, Americans still believe that a strong military

TABLE 1. Percentage of the American Public "In Favor of Active Role"

1948	70%	1978	59%
1952	68%	1982	54%
1956	71%	1986	64%
1973	66%	1990	62%
1974	66%		

Source: Chicago Council on Foreign Relations, 1990.

is critical to the long-term security of the United States. In a CBS News/*New York Times* poll of October 5–7, 1991, 67 percent of Americans agreed that it is "still important for (the) U.S. to be on guard with a strong military," while only 30 percent felt that it is "possible to reduce military strength."

Americans divide almost evenly on whether the United States is more influential today than it was in 1980; in the 1990 Chicago Council on Foreign Relations poll, 37 percent said the role of the United States is now more important, 35 percent said the role of the United States is now less important, and 24 percent said it is equally important. It is interesting to note that, traditionally, the views of the public with regard to the U.S. role in global affairs have fluctuated along with perceptions of the U.S. military vis-à-vis the Soviet Union. American opinion now is more closely correlated with public perceptions of the economic standing of the United States vis-à-vis Western Europe and Japan.[8] This plus the disparity between those who agree that an activist role for the United States is wise and those who agree that military power is the best way to fulfill our global mission illustrate that Americans are increasingly aware of the importance of economic and other nonmilitary power in safeguarding our national security.

Attitudes of the American public toward the use of force are strongly affected by whether the military action is unilateral, multilateral, or part of a United Nations mandated effort. Throughout most of the cold war, the American public supported the leadership role of the United States to balance the Soviet Union. Americans are now more likely to support U.S. military involvement as part of a coalition than when the United States is acting independently, and the public is even more supportive when the United States is acting as part of a UN sanctioned effort. A Gallup poll taken December 3–4, 1992, found that 87 percent of Americans agreed that the "United States should commit its troops only as part of a United Nations operation," while 73 percent felt that the United States should commit "only with other allies." The percentage of the population willing to support U.S. military action "on its own in some cases" dropped to 62 percent.

A poll taken by Market Strategies and Greenberg-Lake between June 23 and July 1, 1991, found that 80 percent of Americans agreed with the statement: "When faced with future problems involving aggression, the United Nations should take the lead." In stark contrast to opinion at the height of the cold war, only 17 percent responded that the "United States should lead." Asked what they would prefer if the UN refused to act, many (54 percent) felt the United States should then take the lead, but a clear 40 percent believed the United States should still wait for others to act or "stay out of it."

Clearly, most Americans now are more wary of unilateral military action. They seem reluctant but willing to join a multilateral effort to put an end to a genuinely ominous and threatening situation, and they are more willing to participate in an effort to fulfill a mission endorsed by the United Nations.

The Use of Force in Specific Countries

During the cold war, the continuing East-West struggle gave many countries some strategic significance that they otherwise would have lacked. Americans now consider a few select nations to be of special or vital interest, but most to be relatively insignificant in terms of U.S. security. Long-standing prejudices and preferences towards other countries and people, such as historical experience or cultural likeness, continue to affect public opinion regarding the use of force. Nonetheless, public attitudes toward many countries have changed dramatically since the end of the cold war.

A Louis Harris and Associates poll taken in July of 1980 asked Americans which countries they felt "could be a threat to the

security and well-being of the U.S." Eighty-four percent responded positively that the Soviet Union could pose a threat to the
United States, while 56 percent cited Iran as a potential threat,
and 41 percent named Communist China. No other countries
were mentioned by more than 17 percent of those surveyed as
posing a potential threat to the United States. While the Soviet
Union was seen as a serious threat to the United States and as its
greatest rival during the cold war, Americans now view Russia as
being of critical importance to the United States. Whereas 84
percent of respondents in 1980 said the Soviet Union posed a
threat to the United States, by 1990, 83 percent mentioned the
Soviet Union as a nation of vital interest to the United States. In
the *Times Mirror* polls of 1990 and 1992 as well, the perception of a
Russian threat fell significantly from 32 percent in 1990 to 13
percent in 1992. Most striking was the increase in two years of the
number of respondents who named Japan as representing the
greatest threat to the United States—from 8 percent to 31 percent.
The focus of public concern on an economic competitor rather
than a traditional military rival suggests that the public has embraced the broader definition of U.S. security interests made a
reality by the end of the cold war.

The Chicago Council polls in 1986 and again in 1990 reflected
other changes in how Americans view specific political-military
relationships. Respondents who saw Saudi Arabia as vital to the
United States increased from 77 percent in 1986 to 83 percent in
1990. Those who said Japan was of vital interest to the United
States increased from 77 percent in 1986 to 79 percent in 1990.
Iran was mentioned by 51 percent in 1986 and 56 percent in 1990,
while Poland was named as vital to the United States by 35 percent in 1986 and 43 percent in 1990. All other countries considered in the survey were thought to be less vital to the United States
by 1990 than they had been in 1986. Most notably, the percentage
of Americans viewing the countries of Western Europe (including
Great Britain, Germany, and France) as vital to the United States
fell significantly between 1986 and 1990.

Clearly though, Americans retain a unique sense of commitment to our traditional allies in Western Europe. Although the
immediate Communist threat has receded, the special transatlan-

tic relationship has endured and the economic and political ties have grown ever stronger over the years. The Chicago Council poll indicates that this majority willingness to use force extends to only four other American regional relationships: with Mexico, the Middle East, Korea, and Eastern Europe, and then only under direct threat (see Table 2).

The Use of Force in Bosnia

It is interesting to contrast these general findings with the more specific opinion patterns in one particular time period with respect to the Bosnian crisis. Throughout the week of May 6, 1993, the day that the Bosnian Serbs rejected the Vance-Owen peace plan, a series of public opinion polls was conducted on the subject of U.S. military intervention in Bosnia. The results of three—a CBS News poll of May 4–5, a CNN/*USA Today* poll of May 6, and an ABC News poll of May 7—showed that Americans were paying closer attention to the crisis in the Balkans than they were earlier in the year, and that they were more supportive of President Clinton's efforts to bring a stop to the war. But although they were

TABLE 2.

"Favor Use of U.S. Troops Overseas"	Percentage
If Soviet troops invaded Western Europe	58%
If Iraq invaded Saudi Arabia	52%
If the government of Mexico were threatened by a revolution or civil war	48%
If the Soviet Union tried to overthrow a democratic government in Eastern Europe	44%
If North Korea invaded South Korea	44%
If Arab forces invaded Israel	43%
If Iraq refused to withdraw from Kuwait	42%
If Japan were invaded by the Soviet Union	39%
If the government of El Salvador were about to be defeated by leftist rebels	28%
If the government of the Philippines were threatened by a revolution or civil war	22%

Source: Chicago Council on Foreign Relations, 1990

increasingly frustrated by the failure of the international community to take action, they were still unwilling to support any U.S. military action without European involvement.

Americans persisted in their belief that the United States is under no obligation to intervene. The CBS News poll of May 4–5, 1993, found that 52 percent of Americans did not believe that the United States has a responsibility there, while only 37 percent of Americans thought it does. The same poll found that a solid majority, 77 percent of Americans, felt that the war in Bosnia is the responsibility of the Europeans and that American involvement should follow only after a commitment by the Europeans. Many Americans indeed believe the United States has already done enough to stop the war in Sarajevo and Bosnia; Yankelovich surveys found 49 percent thought so in August 1992, while 59 percent took that position in January 1993.

The CNN/USA Today poll reported that in May 1993 a majority of Americans preferred that the United States not get involved in Bosnia at all. When asked about the possibility of the "United States conduct(ing) air strikes against Serbian military forces," 55 percent were opposed while 36 percent favored such an action. But sentiment has been rising in support of sending U.S. forces as part of a multilateral operation. Indeed, the ABC poll found that a majority, 65 percent of Americans, favored air strikes against Bosnian Serb positions as long as these are carried out in conjunction with our European allies.

Throughout the fall and winter of 1992–93, a majority of Americans (58 percent according to ABC) still firmly opposed the use of U.S. ground forces under any circumstances. Americans were deeply divided on sending U.S. ground troops to the region even as part of a UN peacekeeping force because of the serious risks involved. The CBS poll found that 48 percent favored sending U.S. troops as part of a UN peacekeeping effort, but nearly as many (45 percent) opposed this action. Support went above the 50 percent level only when ground troops were not mentioned specifically and if an in-place peace agreement was posited.

There were many signals that the public was waiting for cues from the president as to the range of possible military options. Given President Clinton's reluctance to make a direct appeal to the American people in support of anything less than multilateral military action in Bosnia, there was mixed evidence relating to a "rallying 'round the president" effect. The May CBS poll found 35 percent approved of Clinton's efforts, 35 percent disapproved, and 30 percent offered no comment. Roughly equivalent CNN/*USA Today* results found 48 percent approved and 35 percent disapproved while ABC reported 54 percent of Americans gave their approval and only 34 percent disapproved. These results seemed most directly influenced by the more general ratings of the president's performance in April and May 1993.

The CNN/*USA Today* poll asked Americans what they considered to be very good, good, or not good reasons for launching U.S. air strikes against Serbian forces. Sixty-three percent of Americans mentioned our "moral obligation" to stop ethnic cleansing; 57 percent cited stopping the spread of ethnic conflict in Europe. Only 49 percent claimed the U.S. "national security interests at stake in Bosnia" as a good or very good reason. Asked to give reasons why the United States should not launch air strikes, 73 percent mentioned avoiding American casualties, while 65 percent questioned their military efficacy. More tellingly, 71 percent sought to prevent the United States from getting drawn into the fighting, and 61 percent cited U.S. economic problems as a good or very good reason for the United States to stay out.

The shadow of Vietnam clearly hung over attitudes on Bosnia as some direct polling dramatically demonstrated. A Gallup poll of January 1993 found that 41 percent of Americans feared that U.S. intervention in Bosnia would end up like the war in Vietnam, while 47 percent saw an outcome more like that of the Gulf War. The CNN/*USA Today* poll of May 6, 1993, found similar responses to the same question: 43 percent feared an outcome more like Vietnam, and 49 percent speculated the war would be more like that in the Gulf. Public opinion remained polarized. Significantly, too, the CNN/*USA Today* poll found in early May that 84 percent of Americans would not approve of Clinton conducting air strikes without the approval of Congress.

Comparison with Attitudes
on the Gulf and on Somalia

Popular reluctance and misgivings over goals and instruments in Bosnia contrast sharply with the pattern of opinion with respect to the use of U.S. military force both in the Gulf and in Somalia. Although the story is far from over, the probable reasons for the differences seem clear and quite compelling.

Both the Gulf and Somalia enjoyed substantial popular support almost from the very first. Shortly after Iraq's brutal invasion of Kuwait, 70 percent of Americans polled by Hart and Teeter supported U.S. military action. As the likelihood of war increased, there were some second thoughts—e.g., by December, a slip to only 63 percent. But as Desert Storm was launched and met with initial success, public support rose further. An ABC/*Washington Post* poll during military action garnered 85 percent approval, while a slightly later Gallup question elicited a remarkable 87 percent.[9]

The humanitarian use of military force in Somalia gained lower levels of support—only 66 percent approved of unilateral U.S. action in the weeks before the mission. Mention of humanitarian purposes or a possible multilateral framework—"a UN effort"— raised figures by another 10 percent. But it was the successful landing in Somalia and the demonstrated lack of risk that made the greatest difference. Subsequent polls showed 80 percent support and more.[10]

What Jentleson describes as the "halo effect" of success is clearly a very powerful factor in opinion trends.[11] Desert Storm's glow lasted almost two years. Five months after its end, 82 percent still declared it not to have been a mistake to send military force there. In the fall of 1991, 84 percent agreed that the U.S. military performance demonstrated that the United States could "still unite and accomplish things." A year after the invasion, 65 percent of Americans supported a potential second use of U.S. military force to compel Iraq's compliance with UN inspections of its military arsenal. In January 1993, 85 percent told ABC News/*Washington Post* interviewers that if Iraq continued to violate the no-fly zone, the United States should be prepared to attack Iraq again.

Unquestionably, public opinion rallied to the symbol of Saddam Hussein as an unscrupulous despot, bent on an anti-American course. The U.S. response to Iraq was also widely perceived as morally just; 56 percent of those interviewed in March 1991 cited moral reasons for the Gulf action, while only 34 percent cited economic factors.[12]

Policy Parameters: Views on the Military

It is important to put these attitudes on the use of force in specific cases into a more future oriented policy context. A critical component is general public attitudes towards the military—as a profession and as an instrument of national action. Americans before World War II had generally held a low opinion of the military, particularly the professional cadre, and often were critical of them as outside the general democratic society. Patriotic feelings fastened rather on conscripts, raised only after a legitimate popular decision to use force and fashioned in the mold of the "citizen soldier."

The postwar period saw a radical change in this opinion profile, especially after the military build-up for Korea and the fixed military deployments in Europe and in Asia. Military forces—professional and conscript—became the embodiment of American values and American commitment against the Communist threat. Approval ratings were high; and the military rose in status vis-à-vis civilian professions for perhaps the first time in peacetime history.

In the Vietnam decade, Americans were deeply divided on how they should now view the military, reflecting their general views on the war itself. Some indeed held the military responsible for both the military defeat and the domestic unrest, and support for the Nixon decision to adopt an all-volunteer force reflected a substantial concern that fewer forces would be available for future interventions.

By the 1980s much of this criticism had waned, and public opinion toward the military was consistently favorable and generally in the 70–75 percent approval range. The end of the cold war reduced this support in the 1990s by only a small fraction. More-

over, favorable opinion increased with evidence of military success; a poll taken during the Gulf War recorded support levels of
85 percent.[13] This paralleled the jump in support (again to 85
percent) recorded after the U.S. bombing of Libya in April 1986 in
retaliation for terrorist activities.

Americans today are prepared to accept a reduction in troop
levels, in response to the reduced overseas threat as well as to
increasing economic constraints on spending. But public opinion
is still divided over what that ideal level should be. In the past,
opinion about the ideal level of U.S. forces was linked to popular
perceptions of the balance between U.S. and Soviet military capability. But this is no longer seen as significant, and, as will be
discussed below, the critical factor appears to be cost and the
trade-off with domestic spending demands.

There are also post–cold war changes not yet clearly crystallized
in American opinion regarding the make-up of military forces and
force structures. The causes seem to be perceptions that the evolving nature of the conflicts for which the U.S. military must be
prepared and the increasingly technical and highly sophisticated
weaponry and equipment employed in combat place new demands on soldiers and open new opportunities for men and
women who do not meet the profile of traditional soldiers.

At this writing, the most contentious issue is President Clinton's
argument that acknowledged homosexuals should be eligible to
serve in the U.S. forces. The public has been quite vocal on this
issue. Those who oppose lifting the ban believe that homosexuality
is incompatible with the rigors and demands of life in the military.
Some object to this legitimation of the gay life style, fearing that it
will be the first step down a slippery slope of specific rights demanded by gays. Those who favor allowing homosexuals in the
military see the ban as blatant and unacceptable discrimination
against individuals, based solely on sexual orientation. They embrace the parallel (readily rejected by the military establishment)
between President Clinton's dilemma and President Truman's
1948 executive order to racially integrate the U.S. military, pointing out that concerns about morale and discipline within the
armed forces echo those objections voiced forty-five years earlier.

A *Newsweek* poll conducted on January 21 and 22, 1993, found that 72 percent of Americans surveyed believe gays can "serve effectively in the military if they keep their sexual orientation private." Only 22 percent of the people surveyed disagreed. When asked if Clinton should "delay his promise to lift restrictions on gays in the military if it will produce morale and readiness problems," 49 percent responded positively. Only 40 percent said that he should not delay his promise. Thus while most Americans are confident about the capabilities of gay soldiers, they are reluctant to force the military to accept homosexuals without proper consideration of the consequences of this decision.

In contrast, public attitudes on the inclusion of women in combat functions within the military have been generally positive throughout the late 1980s. The key issue seems to be the question of equity, and the majority support mirrors the support levels for the equal treatment of women in occupations throughout the society.

Framework Issues:
Opinion on Military Spending

Far more critical in framing the context of intervention is the question of support for military spending, for the continued acquisition of substantial military capability across the spectrum of military needs. It is an issue still in post–cold war definition. The 1992 election campaign saw little mention of the level of defense spending, only somewhat ritualistic affirmations by both Bush and Clinton of the need for a strong defense. In the national campaigns, Democrats smarting from the impact of their proposed defense cuts on the 1988 Dukakis campaign and divided within their own ranks preferred to talk of gradual drawdowns; Republicans mentioned these issues only in general. Yet it is a Washington truism that continuing popular pressure means that defense spending must be reduced, more drastically than any official proposal now contemplates. Cuts were an ever-present issue in a number of key congressional races.

Direct evidence on popular views is somewhat more complex. Public support for defense spending unquestionably increased in the late 1970s and early 1980s. The renewed hostility between the

United States and the USSR fueled a willingness on the part of the American public to rebuild U.S. military power following a period of relative neglect in the early and mid-1970s. The shift in opinion toward increasing the defense budget was quite dramatic, reaching a level of 72 percent at the end of Reagan's first year.[14] Support then fell to 39 percent by December 1982 and declined gradually through the mid-1980s. Many Americans then preferred that the level of military spending be kept the same—a steady 43 percent. By 1987, indeed, a slight majority of Americans surveyed were willing to support substantial cuts in military spending to address the federal budget deficit problem.[15]

The end of the cold war and the emergence of new pressures to lessen the budget deficit through reduced government spending convinced more Americans about defense cuts. A CBS News/*New York Times* poll of February 9–11, 1993, found, for example, that 50 percent of Americans agreed that the "share of tax dollars spent on military and defense programs is too much." By contrast, 6 percent of those surveyed felt that the share spent on military and defense is "too little," and 39 percent said that it is "about right."

This change in attitudes has come relatively quickly, revealing a marked shift from the traditional cautious and careful approach among Americans to defense questions. A Gallup poll, taken between March 30 and April 5, 1992, found that 39 percent of those surveyed "do not favor additional cuts in military spending." Seventeen percent responded that they "favor major cuts," 31 percent said they "favor moderate cuts," and 10 percent "favor minor cuts." Only three months later Gallup results showed 42 percent favored further deep cuts in the military budget beyond those then planned, with only 52 percent opposed to cuts, minor or major.

Conclusions

The sudden dismantling of an international system that had been in place for over forty years, rigidly defining the U.S. military posture and conduct, has left in its wake a nation not yet clear about what role the United States should assume in the post–cold war world. The desire to curtail defense spending and to limit military involvement overseas clashes with the majority's commitment to global leadership and the fulfillment of international obligations. Americans in great numbers feel a moral compulsion to help countries in need and to defend the weak, but they are reluctant to be drawn into unpredictable and open-ended conflicts. They give new recognition to the economic dimensions of security, and they realize the importance of transnational relationships in an increasingly global economy. But they also struggle with how to balance international interests and responsibilities and domestic concerns.

In the abstract, Americans continue to regard the use of military force as a last resort in solving international crises. There is a consistently high level of confidence in the military, especially since the Gulf War of 1991. But much of the public is wary about U.S. involvement in unpredictable overseas ventures, especially without the support and contributions of allies and other countries. The general view is that in most cases, other options must be exhausted before direct military force is used. Even then, victory without exceedingly great sacrifice must be an attainable end. Moreover, Americans are increasingly aware of both the costs and risks involved in any overseas military option, and are increasingly unwilling to give blanket approval for military preparation against a range of unlikely threats.

In specific crises, Americans tend toward more pragmatic judgments about what is to be done, based on increasing attention and a growing fund of real-time information gained through television. They do review past history and are sensitive to earlier parallels, most particularly to continuities with the defining, if not yet resolved, Vietnam experience. They are also subject to halo effects—as approval for the rapid and successful use of force in the Gulf after the fact indicates—when they are convinced that a greater objective has been achieved.

However, on the whole, they look and weigh carefully probable outcomes, foreseeable risks, the projected length of involvement, options for multilateral action, and moral and humanitarian principles. The experience of the 1980s and the early 1990s suggests that within this generally conservative framework, most Americans render a relatively balanced and consistent set of judgments about the use of force in particular, and about the defense policy framework in general. The general expectation now—in contrast to the early cold war period—is that there still is a need for a strong but reduced defense as insurance against uncertainty. But the use of military force is to be the exception in American foreign policy, it is rarely to be unilateral, and it is to involve limited goals and limited means.

The American people also are loyal and patriotic, and they will "rally 'round the flag" when convinced by an effective president that force is to be applied toward a worthy and achievable goal. The mobilization of opinion and support must be against a threat to values, or to the use of military force against an appropriate target of immediate significance. But among the electorate, perhaps even more than within the Congress, this is never an automatic reaction, and much depends on the specifics of the case. An interventionist president is held accountable for the course of the conflict—both directly and at the next election.

Barring a reversal of direction in Russia or an intensified Bosnia-like crisis, these trends will almost certainly continue and grow over the next decade. Memories of the military preparations and deployments judged normal in the cold war era or even in Desert Storm will recede. Echoing earlier American patterns, the almost inevitable push will be for a smaller military at lower cost with fewer overseas deployments. Professionals will almost certainly press for the maintenance of American high-tech advantages, especially for intelligence and early warning of crisis or aggression. If economic conditions and presidential leadership are favorable, they may well win public acceptance.

Future questions about the conditions for the use of American force will very likely be two: what does the public know, and what does the president ask? If in harmony, these factors will allow for slow but sure decision; with even just a significant minority of the public and the Congress at odds with the president, there will be continuing debate and perhaps deadlock. In the end, it may well turn on how quickly the shadow of Vietnam fades for succeeding generations, and the kind of experience—multilateral or unilateral, interventionist or peacekeeping—that defines the post–cold war era.

Polls

A list of polls used follows:

ABC News Polls: Somalia, January 13, 1993; Bosnia, May 7, 1993.

ABC News/*Washington Post* Polls: February 24, 1991; March 1–4, 1991; January 14–17, 1993.

CBS News Poll: The U.S. and Yugoslavia, May 4–5, 1993.

CBS/*New York Times* Polls: October 5–7, 1991; February 9–11, 1993.

CNN/*USA Today* Poll: Bosnia, May 6, 1993.

Chicago Council on Foreign Relations Polls: "American Public Opinion and U.S. Foreign Policy 1991" (ed. John E. Reilly), "Use of U.S. Troops Overseas," 1990 (V-5); "Economic Aid, Military Aid and Arms Sales," 1990 (IV-7); "Preferred U.S. Role in World," 1990 (II-1); "Actual U.S. Role in World," 1990 (II-2); "Vital Interests," 1990, 1986 (III-2).

Communications Consortium Polls: "Public Opinion Polls: Military Spending, An Update" (Dr. Ethel Klein), June 12, June 18, and June 26, 1987.

Gallup Polls: February 28–March 3, 1991; March 30–April 5, 1992; June 12–14, 1992; December 3–4, 1992; January 24, 1993.

Newsweek Polls: January 21–22; April 29–30, 1993.

Hart and Teeter Polls: August 18–19, 1990; December 8–11, 1990.

Los Angeles Times Poll: August 12–14, 1992.

Louis Harris and Associates Poll: July 1980, December 4–8, 1992.

Market Strategies and Greenberg-Lake Poll: June 23–July 1, 1991.

Times Mirror Center for The People & The Press Polls: "The People, The Press & Politics 1990," A Times Mirror Political Typology, October 11, 1990; "The People, The Press & Politics On The

Eve of '92: Fault Lines In The Electorate," December 4, 1991;
"The People, The Press & Politics Campaign '92: 1993—Priorities For The President, Survey XII—Part 2," October 28, 1992.

Yankelovich Polls for *Time*/CNN: (August 1992, January 1993),
January 13–14, 1993.

Notes

[1] See Almond (1960) and Weigley (1973).
[2] See Jentleson (1992), Page and Shapiro (1988), and Reilly (1991).
[3] See Schneider (1992).
[4] Jentleson (1992), p. 50.
[5] Jentleson (1992), p. 53.
[6] See "American Public Opinion and U.S. Foreign Policy 1991" by the Chicago Council on Foreign Relations (ed. John Reilly), March 1991, p. 34.
[7] See "American Public Opinion and U.S. Foreign Policy 1991" (referenced above), p. 29.
[8] See "American Public Opinion and U.S. Foreign Policy 1991" (referenced above), p. 85.
[9] See the Hart and Teeter poll of August 18–19, 1990, the ABC News/*Washington Post* poll of February 24, 1991, and the Gallup poll of February 28–March 3, 1991, on U.S. involvement in the Persian Gulf.
[10] See the Gallup polls of December 3–4, 1992, and December 4–6, and the Louis Harris poll of December 4–8, 1992, on Somalia. Also see the ABC News/*Washington Post* poll of December 11–14, 1992, and the ABC News poll of January 13, 1993.
[11] Jentleson (1992), p. 49.
[12] See the ABC/*Washington Post* poll of March 1–4, 1991, on the Persian Gulf War.
[13] Gergen (1990), p. 79.
[14] Bartels (1991), p. 467.
[15] See the CBS/*New York Times* poll of January 1987, which showed Americans more willing to cut money for defense (54 percent—yes, 40 percent—no) than to cut student loans or aid to farmers.

11

Public Engagement in International Environmental Policy

THOMAS B. STOEL, JR.

Introduction

E nvironmental issues are now established as important subjects of U.S. foreign policy.[1] Problems such as depletion of
the stratospheric ozone layer, global warming of the earth's atmosphere, destruction of wildlife species and ecosystems, ocean pollution, overly rapid population growth, and damage to the environments of developing nations are occupying the attention of policy
makers in this country and around the world.

Unlike many other issues, environmental problems did not

THOMAS B. STOEL, JR. is an environmental attorney and consultant
in Washington, D.C., focusing on issues of international environment and
development. He was a founder of the Natural Resources Defense Council, and from 1974 to 1990 he was director of NRDC's International
Program. He was a lecturer at the Harvard Law School in 1976 and 1977.
From 1980 to 1986 he served as president of the Global Tomorrow Coalition, and from 1982 to 1988 he was a board member of the Environment
Liaison Centre International in Nairobi, Kenya. He has written numerous articles on environmental matters and is the co-author of two books:
Fluorocarbon Regulation and *Aiding the Environment*.

make their way onto the agenda as the result of top-down decisions by a foreign policy elite. Instead, beginning in the early 1970s, they came to the fore because of efforts by environmentalists in and out of government. These efforts were given political force by the strong public concern about the environment that began around the time of Earth Day in 1970 and has continued ever since. That public concern was brought to bear in the political process by environmental organizations, some of which are household names and that collectively have millions of members and thousands of paid professional staff.

The power of the environmental lobby will not be enough to ensure that environmental issues receive the right kind of attention in the future. New approaches will be needed to meet the problems of the 1990s. Single-issue solutions will not suffice for problems like global warming, the environmental impacts of international trade and investment, and ensuring that growth in developing nations is environmentally sound. These issues will require more sophisticated approaches on the part of governmental institutions, interest groups, the media, and the public.

The Environment in U.S. Foreign Policy

The 1970s

Environmental issues first became part of the U.S. foreign policy agenda in the early 1970s. The American public became deeply concerned about environmental protection around the time of Earth Day in 1970. In 1971 and early 1972, Republican and Democratic politicians competed to address environmental problems, as President Nixon sought to equal the environmental record of Democratic presidential contender Edmund Muskie.

The outpouring of public concern gave strength to environmental citizen groups. Older conservation organizations, like the National Audubon Society and National Wildlife Federation, took on new issues of pollution and waste disposal. New organizations like the Environmental Defense Fund and Natural Resources Defense Council used the techniques of science and the law in defense of the environment. These organizations regarded citizen involvement as crucial to their success. Some key organizations, such as the Sierra Club, were passionately democratic, taking their direction from citizen volunteers representing local chapters.

From the beginning, many government officials and citizen groups were global in their outlook. Russell Train, the first chair of the President's Council on Environmental Quality (CEQ) and the former head of the Conservation Foundation, charted an environmental course for the Nixon administration that included international initiatives and made the United States an international environmental leader.[2] When Train became administrator of the Environmental Protection Agency (EPA) in 1973, he was succeeded as CEQ chair and was joined as a leader on international environmental matters by Russell Peterson, who had a scientific background and had been an environmental pioneer as governor of Delaware.

At the popular level, the name "Earth Day" symbolized a global perspective, inspired perhaps by the satellite images of the earth that had entered the public consciousness. Margaret Mead spoke for many when she said at an Earth Day event in 1970:

We have today the knowledge and tools to look at the whole earth. . . . The tenderness that lies in seeing the earth as small and lonely and blue is probably one of the most valuable things that we have now. . . .

Governmental and citizen concern about the environment were not limited to this country. That was made clear when representatives of more than 100 governments gathered in Stockholm, Sweden, in 1972 for the UN Conference on the Human Environment. That conference laid out a remarkably foresighted agenda for intergovernmental action. In an unprecedented phenomenon, thousands of concerned citizens from around the world, including many from the United States, participated in the accompanying Stockholm Environmental Forum.

U.S. actions to protect the international environment during the 1970s included leadership in negotiating the Convention on International Trade in Endangered Species, the World Heritage Convention, the Ocean Dumping Convention, and a treaty banning environmental warfare and unilateral regulation of chemicals thought to deplete the stratospheric ozone layer. The United States provided a disproportionate share of the initial funding for the UN Environment Program, the UN agency that emerged from the Stockholm Conference. We were a leader in providing family planning assistance to slow population growth in developing nations. We played major roles in the other UN "mega-conferences" of the 1970s: those on population, human settlements, water, desertification, and science and technology.

The pace of U.S. actions to protect the international environment slowed during the Carter administration, even though Carter was generally more sympathetic to environmental concerns than Gerald Ford. One reason was that action already had been taken on most of the key issues identified at the 1972 Stockholm Conference. Another was that no officials of the Carter administration played a leadership role comparable to that of Russell Train and Russell Peterson. The public remained concerned about global environmental issues, but environmental organizations may have lessened their pressure because they knew their friends were in power.

The Carter administration did play an important role in negotiating the mammoth Law of the Sea Convention. It sponsored the Global 2000 study, intended to identify global environmental trends to the year 2000 and actions needed to improve them. The Carter administration developed an ambitious action agenda following the appearance of the *Global 2000 Report* in 1980, but the election of Ronald Reagan prevented its implementation.

A break in the string of easy environmental victories came in 1978 when the United States refused to become a party to the Convention on Conservation of Migratory Species of Wild Animals, a treaty intended to protect endangered animals that migrate across international borders. That treaty was perceived by state wildlife agencies as infringing on their power to regulate hunting and trapping, and therefore on U.S. sovereignty. These agencies, allied with hunting interests that were politically powerful and were influential in some U.S. environmental groups, had little difficulty in persuading decision makers in Congress and the executive branch to leave the treaty alone.

The issue of ozone depletion provides an example of how decisions were made during this decade.[3] In 1974 two scientists published an article suggesting that chlorofluorocarbons (CFCs), artificial chemicals used as propellants in aerosol sprays, as refrigerants, and for other purposes, were rising to the stratosphere and depleting the thin layer of stratospheric ozone that protects the earth from harmful ultraviolet radiation. These scientists were so concerned that they quickly became advocates for governmental regulation of the suspect chemicals. An environmental group, the Natural Resources Defense Council, took up the cause and in November 1974 petitioned a federal agency to ban aerosol propellants containing CFCs. A congressional committee held hearings in December 1974. By early 1975 the Ford administration had established an interagency task force to look into the issue. The National Academy of Sciences reported in 1976 that there was reason for concern.

Environmental groups informed the public about the issue and stimulated action at the federal, state, and local levels. Local citizen groups were formed to focus on the issue. The media, fascinated with the possibility that underarm sprays might pose a threat to the global environment, gave the problem much attention. More than twenty states, including the most populous, joined the Natural Resources Defense Council in petitioning federal agencies to regulate CFCs. Several states imposed labeling requirements.

In 1976 the Food and Drug Administration (FDA), acting on the recommendation of the interagency task force, proposed to ban nonessential use of CFCs in aerosol spray propellants, a step that would eliminate 50 percent of U.S. and 25 percent of world use of CFCs. The affected industries argued against a ban, alleging that there would be major economic costs and asserting that the United States should act only in concert with other nations. Nevertheless, final regulations banning nonessential, CFC-propelled aerosol sprays were issued by the Carter EPA and FDA in 1978. Subsequent analyses indicated that the overall costs of switching to alternative aerosol propellants were negligible.

This was a remarkably quick response to a global problem that was totally unknown just four years earlier. It turned out to be too quick for most other nations. The United States shared scientific information with other countries and tried to persuade them to take similar regulatory actions. Canada and Sweden did so. However, U.S. diplomacy failed to convince the European Economic Community (EEC), which accounted for most CFC use outside the United States, to take effective action. There were several reasons for this European reluctance. One was a "not invented here" syndrome: most of the relevant scientific work was done in the United States and the ozone depletion problem was taken less seriously in Europe. A second was that European environmental groups were not as large and influential as those in the United States. They lacked scientific expertise, were denied access to governmental information, and lacked methods, such as lawsuits and petitions to regulatory agencies, of forcing their governments to pay attention. A third reason was the necessity of obtaining agreement among all the major EEC nations.

As illustrated by the ozone depletion issue, a common pattern of U.S. policy making during this period was that scientists identified an apparent environmental problem requiring international action for its solution. Environmental agencies in the executive branch assessed the scientific evidence and spelled out the actions necessary to solve the problem, together with their economic costs. Environmental organizations publicized the issue, and congressional committees held hearings.

Then would come a period of domestic discussion and debate. Environmental groups would advocate governmental action. Elements of the business community often would oppose it. A similar debate would take place within the executive branch and, to some extent, the Congress. Finally, the United States would commit itself to act, usually in concert with other countries.

A notable aspect was that most of these foreign policy initiatives were proposed by officials in the Council on Environmental Quality and the Environmental Protection Agency, in consultation with environmental groups outside government. Despite the creation of the Bureau of Oceans and International Environmental and Scientific Affairs in 1974, the State Department usually implemented environmental policies rather than initiating them. The Congress was supportive but did not play a leadership role. And the foreign policy establishment did not pay much attention.[4]

The business community did not play a major role in international environmental policy making during the 1970s. Some of the issues involved wildlife conservation and were not of great concern to business. Industry was directly affected by the ozone depletion issue but found it hard to participate in the early part of the debate because it had little expertise concerning the key questions of atmospheric science. When regulations were proposed, the executive branch did a good job of analyzing the economic consequences, so business's claims of major adverse impacts were not persuasive.

The Reagan-Bush Years

The Reagan administration's laissez-faire economic doctrines left little room for environmental protection.[5] In the international sphere, Reaganites abandoned U.S. leadership and opposed environmental initiatives. The United States refused to ratify the Law of the Sea Convention despite the fact that the chief U.S. negotiator had been a distinguished Republican, Elliot Richardson; cast the only vote in the UN General Assembly against the UN Charter for Nature; and, almost alone, tried to block international actions to slow population growth at the 1984 UN Population Conference in Mexico City. Antienvironmental ideologues had great influence; for example, Interior Secretary James Watt deleted a commitment to conservation of the earth's biological diversity from the U.S. position statement at an important international meeting because he found the word "conservation" too strong.

This negative approach largely continued during Reagan's second term, with one important exception: U.S. leadership on the issue of ozone depletion.[6] Prodded by scientists and environmentalists and startled by the discovery of the "ozone hole" over Antarctica, the Reagan government pushed for international actions to phase out ozone-depleting chemicals. That policy was opposed by administration hard-liners, mainly in the Office of Management and Budget and the Interior Department, who argued that skin cancer due to excess ultraviolet radiation penetrating a depleted ozone layer could be prevented by wearing broad-brimmed hats and sunglasses. They were subjected to public ridicule after their position was leaked to the media and finally were overruled by President Reagan, who approved a strong U.S. negotiating position proposed by the State Department and EPA. Among other things, the State Department drew attention to the bipartisan support in Congress for a strong treaty and pointed out that in the absence of strong multilateral action the United States might be compelled to act unilaterally as a result of a lawsuit brought by the Natural Resources Defense Council. The administration also was influenced by the fact that U.S. industry preferred an international agreement to the possibility of unilateral action.[7]

Realizing that environmental issues were important to voters, George Bush talked like an environmentalist during the 1988 campaign. But his international policies were much like Reagan's. While providing continued leadership on the ozone depletion issue, the Bush administration tried to block proposals by other nations to deal with problems like global warming of the atmosphere and worldwide loss of biological diversity. These negative policies culminated in President Bush's humiliating appearance at the June 1992 UN Conference on Environment and Development, or "Earth Summit," in Rio de Janeiro, a meeting attended by representatives of more than 150 countries. There, in the media spotlight, the United States stood isolated even from its closest Western allies. The United States was the only major industrialized country that refused to sign the UN Convention on Biological Diversity, and we agreed to the treaty on global warming only after it was greatly weakened to meet our objections.

The global warming issue illustrates the decision-making pattern on many issues under Reagan and Bush. Atmospheric warming due to the presence of carbon dioxide and other gases in the atmosphere is a fact. Without this greenhouse effect, the earth would be some 60 degrees Fahrenheit colder than it is today. Human burning of fossil fuels has caused atmospheric levels of carbon dioxide to increase by 25 percent since the beginning of the industrial era. Scientific models reinforce the common sense conclusion that this CO_2 build-up will exacerbate the greenhouse effect, causing atmospheric temperatures to rise to levels not seen in human history.[8]

The logical conclusion is that humanity either must reduce its emissions of greenhouse gases or subject itself (in the words of one international conference) to "an unintended, uncontrolled, globally pervasive experiment whose ultimate consequences could be second only to a global nuclear war." However, the issue is complicated by scientific uncertainty: because the atmospheric system is so complex, it may be several decades before scientific models are good enough to identify the precise extent of the problem, or before warming becomes apparent in weather patterns. By then, it may be too late to hold the warming to tolerable levels.

When scientists and environmentalists began to air these concerns in the mid-1980s, the reaction of many in the Reagan administration was to downplay the problem and to suggest that the only need was for further study. However, advocacy by scientists and environmentalists, together with the fact that the 1980s were the warmest decade in the past century, aroused public concern. In 1980 the issue of global warming had scarcely been heard of outside the scientific community. By the time of the 1988 presidential campaign, it was so well known that candidate Bush felt compelled to announce that the greenhouse effect would be countered by the "White House effect."

Early statements by Secretary of State James Baker indicated that the Bush administration would agree to some measures to reduce CO_2 emissions, provided that they made economic sense, and would exert leadership in UN sponsored negotiations on climate change. However, Baker soon disqualified himself from working on the issue, citing his investments in energy companies.

From then on, the Bush administration tried to discourage international action. The EPA, which was more action oriented than the rest of the administration, was repeatedly overruled by the White House, where Chief of Staff John Sununu took an interest in the issue and concluded, based on personal examination, that computer based climate models were unreliable. Administration economists alleged that the costs of reducing fossil fuel emissions would put a severe drag on economic growth. The Energy Department's National Energy Strategy, which had the potential to address the issue through a strong emphasis on energy conservation, was reduced to a shadow by the White House.

Congressional committees held hearings at which administration witnesses were urged to act. But the primacy of the executive branch in foreign affairs prevented the Congress from telling the administration what to do.

Environmental groups urged the United States to act domestically by adopting an energy policy featuring energy conservation, but were frustrated by the White House. They dogged the administration at international meetings, where representatives of U.S. nongovernmental organizations (NGOs) routinely participated as observers and held press conferences criticizing the U.S. government position.

U.S. NGOs worked closely with their foreign counterparts. They helped to establish a global Climate Action Network with offices in Africa, South Asia, Southeast Asia, Europe, Latin America, and the United States, and NGO members in scores of countries. NGOs all over the world were able to communicate cheaply and almost instantaneously via electronic mail and interactive electronic "conferences" maintained on sophisticated computer networks, such as EcoNet and GreenNet. These electronic means, together with frequent meetings where attendance by developing-country environmentalists often was subsidized by U.S. foundations or European governments, enabled environmentalists to share information and resources, such as political intelligence and scientific and economic expertise; develop common strategies; and exert coordinated pressure on key governments.

The media played a key role in bringing the global warming issue to prominence, reporting the views of scientists and environmentalists as well as those of governments. Television commentators and the print media became increasingly critical of the Bush administration as it became apparent that the United States was isolated in international negotiations (even Britain's Margaret Thatcher, usually no friend of the environment, believed that something must be done).

Bush faced a dilemma during the 1992 election campaign. The global warming issue could not be avoided: the United States was a party to negotiations aimed at producing an agreement by the time of the June 1992 Earth Summit in Rio, and environmentalists were suggesting that the outcome should be a litmus test of Bush's environmental record. Bush wanted to appear to be an environmentalist, if only because polls indicated that the electorate thought the environment an important issue. Yet his conservative constituency and his advisers, except for EPA Administrator William Reilly, opposed actions to reduce fossil fuel use, and Bush's background in the energy industry may have made him viscerally opposed as well.

By the spring of 1992, the rest of the major industrialized nations had committed themselves to a draft treaty requiring specific reductions in CO_2 emissions by the year 2000. The United States refused to go along, and the treaty signed in Rio was softened so as not to require any specific actions.

Generally speaking, the Reagan-Bush years demonstrated the ability of presidents to prevail on international environmental issues regardless of outside pressures, whether from public opinion, the Congress, or foreign governments. Only in the case of ozone depletion, when there was evidence of an imminent threat to the global environment and environmentalists were able to exert leverage through the courts, did the administration give way.

As in the previous decade, the Congress was usually supportive of international environmental protection, though opposition from conservative Republicans made these issues more partisan than in the 1970s. On budgetary issues, where it could evade a presidential veto, the Congress rejected a number of executive branch proposals to gut international environmental programs. Congressional committees held many hearings on substantive issues. Administration witnesses often were subjected to hostile questioning, but the tradition of executive branch primacy in foreign affairs, together with the threat of a veto, prevented the Congress from requiring international actions to which the administration objected.

Throughout this period, U.S. environmental groups fought to preserve and extend the international gains of the 1970s. In the spring of 1981, they established an umbrella group, the Global Tomorrow Coalition, to coordinate their efforts, engage in public outreach, and strengthen their ties with international population and development organizations (the first chair of the coalition was Russell Peterson, then president of the National Audubon Society). Despite a full plate of domestic environmental problems, the

264   THOMAS B. STOEL, JR.

major environmental groups became increasingly involved in international issues. Almost all of them established international divisions with paid staffs. Their magazines and newsletters, a number of which had circulations in excess of 100,000, became tools for educating and mobilizing the public on these issues.

The environmentalists had allies in the Congress, and they were backed by growing public concern about international environmental issues. They made good use of the media. When the administration in power was willing to act—as in the cases of ozone depletion, U.S. Agency for International Development's environmental efforts in developing countries, and prodding the World Bank to improve its environmental performance—it found partners in the environmental community as well as bipartisan support in the Congress. As described with respect to global warming, U.S. NGOs became increasingly sophisticated in "working" the international system to further their goals.

Despite all of these efforts, the U.S. government generally opposed actions to protect the global environment. As with respect to abortion, the lesson seems to be that on an issue that is not so politically salient as to threaten loss of the presidency or numerous congressional seats, a determined president can have his way.

During the 1980s, the foreign policy establishment largely remained aloof from environmental issues. The considerable literature on these issues was authored mainly by environmentalists. For the most part, foreign policy professionals did not insist on the necessity of continuity in foreign environmental policy. With the exception of the ozone depletion issue, business interests seemed comfortable with U.S. inaction.

Similarly, most of those concerned with international economic issues paid little attention to environmental impacts. The cost of ignoring these connections became apparent in 1991 when major environmental groups announced their opposition to the proposed North American Free Trade Agreement (NAFTA).

Looking Ahead

The Current Situation

The 1992 election brought to power an administration that is more sympathetic to the environment and the need for international environmental protection. Vice President Gore was concerned with international environmental problems in the Senate and is the author of a best-selling book on the subject.[9] In April 1993 President Clinton modified President Bush's policies concerning global warming and loss of biological diversity, by committing the United States to reduce its emissions of greenhouse gases to 1990 levels by the year 2000 and proposing that the United States ratify the UN Convention on Biological Diversity.

As this is written, the Clinton administration is organizing and staffing itself to address these issues. Former Senator Timothy Wirth was appointed State Department counselor for global affairs, with responsibility for oceans, environment, and science; population; and other issues. The administration has announced its intention to reorganize the department and upgrade Wirth's position to under secretary for global affairs. Wirth's newly appointed deputy, Jessica Mathews, dealt with global environmental issues at the World Resources Institute and edited The American Assembly's book on the subject.[10]

Some environmental groups opposed the appointment of Lawrence Summers to be the chair of Clinton's Council of Economic Advisers because of views he expressed on environmental matters when he was chief economist at the World Bank. Summers was not appointed.

The global environment, like most other problems, took a back seat to Clinton's economic plan and health care reform. Since administrations often fail to deal with issues not taken up in the first 100 days, the outlook for major actions on the international environment is uncertain. However, the strong interest of Vice President Gore may well make a difference.

Other factors will make it hard for the Clinton administration to ignore these issues. There is little chance that environmental problems will diminish in importance. These issues emerged in the 1970s because the explosive growth of human population and human economic activity was beginning to have major impacts on the earth's environment. That growth is continuing. The world's population now is about 5.2 billion people and is increasing by about 1 billion people per decade. Economic activity is growing even faster. It is estimated that world economic activity (the equivalent of a nation's gross national product) tripled between 1950 and 1990. It is predicted to triple again between 1990 and 2040, a ninefold increase in less than a century.

The earth's biosphere—the complex web of water, air, land, and living things that supports all life and often is adversely affected by human activities—is finite. It is evident that careful management will be required to sustain economic growth without doing intolerable harm to this life support system. Since the workings of the biosphere do not respect national boundaries, much of that management must occur at the international level. Since some of the most severe environmental damage is occurring in poor developing nations, significant assistance from the wealthier nations will be required to hold the harm to tolerable levels. History indicates that the requisite international action is not likely to occur without U.S. participation and leadership.

Extensive analysis and international consultations to determine the international environmental agenda have already occurred. The UN Conference on Environment and Development reviewed the international environmental situation in exhaustive detail during the period 1990–92. There is wide agreement that the major challenges include:

1. Minimizing global warming by controlling worldwide emissions of greenhouse gases.

2. Conserving an adequate proportion of the earth's biological diversity, primarily by preserving habitats in the tropics.

3. Slowing the rate of population growth.

4. Preventing ocean pollution.

5. Protecting the environments and natural resource base of developing nations, in the face of rapidly increasing populations and the need for economic growth to raise living standards.

6. Protecting the environment while at the same time expanding international trade and investment.

7. Strengthening international institutions so that they will be able to identify emerging problems, coordinate international efforts, enforce international agreements, and help nations that lack the capacity to deal with problems on their own.

There are domestic forces that favor action. The public, according to opinion polls, still thinks that too little is being done to protect the environment and believes that international issues are important. The Congress, like the administration, thinks the economy must be the first priority, but it is likely to be supportive of international environmental initiatives and to urge them on the administration if they are long delayed.

Unlike the situation in some other areas of foreign policy, there is an infrastructure for educating and mobilizing the public about these issues—America's environmental organizations. Some U.S. environmental groups have experienced financial difficulties in the last couple of years, but their total memberships are still in the millions, their credibility with the public is good, they are committed to lobbying on international issues, and they can be a potent political force.

The business community has become more sophisticated about these matters as a result of the analysis and debate that preceded the 1992 UN Conference on Environment and Development.[11] The media are still attentive.

The end of the cold war also has made a difference. The U.S. foreign policy establishment seems more willing to accept environmental issues as part of the "new" foreign policy agenda. And the reduction in defense expenditures may free up some resources.

New Challenges, New Responses

The environmental issues of the 1990s differ significantly from those of the 1970s. One major difference is that the U.S. public has never been asked to pay a significant price to protect the international environment. The energy related actions needed to reduce U.S. CO_2 emissions may impose such costs. The decision not to include a carbon based energy tax in the proposed Clinton economic plan, and the struggle over the BTU tax that was proposed, indicate the kind of resistance that may be encountered. However, the BTU tax was proposed primarily to produce revenue. Environmental groups endorsed it but did not lobby strongly for it.

A second difference is that international environmental problems now are closely linked to basic economic issues. The connection between global warming and energy use is one example. Another is the relationship between environmental protection and trade.

The controversy over NAFTA shows the danger of approaching these issues in a one-sided way. The Bush administration officials who negotiated NAFTA overlooked its failure to address environmental concerns, a defect that was dramatized by poor environmental conditions on the U.S.–Mexico border. On the other hand, some major environmental groups announced their fundamental opposition to NAFTA and allied themselves with protectionist interests. In so doing, they ignored the benefits of free trade, Mexico's need for economic growth, and the environmental advantages of the increased scrutiny of Mexican environmental practices that NAFTA would bring. Environmental issues also have arisen in connection with the General Agreement on Tariffs and Trade (GATT), most notably when a GATT panel ruled that national regulation of tuna harvesting in order to prevent the incidental killing of dolphins was an illegal restraint on international trade.

A third difference is that one important set of international environmental problems, those centering in developing countries, will require substantial amounts of foreign aid. Poor countries need help in such areas as protecting biological diversity, slowing population growth, and adopting energy technologies that minimize greenhouse gas emissions. If the United States is to do its part in providing this assistance, the U.S. public must support the needed expenditures.

This is likely to be a tough sell. Foreign aid has been highly unpopular, due in part to doubts about its effectiveness; the budget crunch makes resources for any federal program harder to obtain; and many domestic programs, backed by public constituencies, are competing for scarce dollars. The problem is complicated by the fact that the countries of Eastern Europe and the former Soviet Union also require assistance, at least in the short term.

These differences will require a new understanding on the part of the public and new roles for the institutions that influence public attitudes and give them political force. *Environmental groups* have played a crucial role in shaping both public opinion and governmental policies. They are still strong, their members appear to be concerned about global issues, and polls indicate that they remain credible with the public. But they face a different task than they did in the 1970s and 1980s. Then they had clear opponents to fight against—polluting corporations and other despoilers of the environment, antienvironmental officials in the Reagan and Bush administrations, and so on. But solving the problems listed above will require positive, cooperative actions, not merely "stopping the bad guys." The UN Conference on Environment and Development suggested that environmental protection and economic development must be regarded not as conflicting goals but as complementary parts of a single process of environmentally sound economic growth, which has come to be known as "sustainable development."

Most U.S. environmental groups now pay lip service to the concept of sustainable development, but in practice many of them are reluctant to concede the need for economic improvement (even today, some environmental groups have no economists on their staffs). When they have done so in specific cases, they often have been criticized by other groups and by some of their own members.

If we are to meet the challenges of the 1990s, environmental organizations must remain true to their environmental vision while at the same time recognizing the validity of economic goals. This will not be easy for a movement that for many has the quality of a secular religion. But if environmentalists do not broaden their horizons, they may, as in the case of NAFTA, ignore the best ways of protecting the environment in the long run. And they may lose public support because they are perceived as zealots.

U.S. environmental organizations also must broaden their scope to appeal to a U.S. population that is increasingly diverse. A movement that has been predominantly white and middle class must reach out to the poor and to minorities.

The *business community* traditionally has been on the opposite side from the environmentalists, arguing that we need to go slow on environmental protection or do nothing at all. The number of U.S. business leaders who are willing to acknowledge the reality of environmental problems and the need to address them is still disappointingly small. Polls indicate that business has little credibility with the public on environmental issues.

If business continues to play this adversarial role, we may repeat the pattern of the 1970s, when distrust of business led to suboptimal solutions (mainly in the domestic sphere) that business had little part in designing. This would be especially unfortunate in the 1990s, when economic incentives and new technologies should play major parts in achieving sustainable development.

The *academic community and think tanks* should be active in analyzing these complex issues. Universities—including schools of business, international affairs, economics, and environmental affairs—need to be involved. So do a variety of think tanks: efforts to think and educate about environmentally sustainable development cannot be left to the World Resources Institute and Resources for the Future. It is troubling that many economic and foreign policy think tanks have no staff members with environmental expertise and pay little attention to the environmental dimensions of the issues they address.

The *media* tend to feature dramatic confrontations of opposing views rather than thoughtful discussions. This encourages interest groups, politicians, and the public to look at choices in "either-or" terms instead of looking for "win-win" solutions. This is the opposite of what is needed: once conflicting positions have been staked out, solutions are likely to be hammered out in adversarial forums rather than by consensus. The kind of sophisticated media efforts that taught the public to understand the ecological wonders and values of tropical forests should be applied to the connections between environment and development.

The Congress must play a very large role. On many international environmental issues, ranging from trade agreements to the actions required to combat global warming to foreign aid, the Congress, not the president, has the power to make the final decision.

And on virtually every issue, congressional committees and arms of the Congress like the Office of Technology Assessment have the ability to explore problems and encourage the development of answers that accommodate environmental and economic needs. The Congress will be most effective if the partisan approach that characterized these issues in the 1980's gives way to a genuine search for solutions, and if congressional committees are reorganized to take into account the connections between economic and environmental matters.

The *president* must lead. A problem like global warming, which goes to the core of U.S. energy policy, cannot be resolved without strong presidential leadership. Only the president can bring the public to understand the need for long-range investments like those in foreign aid (a point proved by President Clinton in the spring of 1993 when he supported aid to Russia).[12] And presidential leadership is required to help the public sort out complex issues like NAFTA.

The president's team in the executive branch must recognize the crosscutting nature of these issues. The environment should not be treated as an isolated issue to be handled by specialists. Seasoned economic and foreign policy professionals should work on these matters side by side with environmental experts.

The proposed creation of an under secretary for global affairs at the State Department elevates environmental matters to a higher level but does not ensure that the connections between environmental and economic issues will be fully recognized.[13] And the Clinton reorganization of the Executive Office may have missed an opportunity to integrate environmental and economic issues. As this author has suggested elsewhere, instead of creating a National Economic Council, President Clinton might have been better advised to establish a Council on the Economy and the Environment.[14]

The Clinton administration understood the need for crosscutting institutions when it established in June 1993 the President's Council on Sustainable Development. The council will bring together business leaders, environmentalists, and public officials to explore ways of combining economic growth and environmental protection.

Executive branch procedures should be revised to facilitate public involvement in environmental foreign policy. Government officials should be required to provide effective opportunities for public participation through such mechanisms as environmental impact statements, prompt responses to Freedom of Information Act requests, national and regional hearings, and structured negotiations between conflicting interests.

As always in our democracy, *"the public"* plays many parts on environmental issues: as voters and subjects of opinion polls, as members of environmental organizations, as consumers who influence the world by their habits and choices. The theme of this book is "engaging the public," but this chapter has made it clear that public opinion has been engaged in the making of international environmental policy for the past two decades. The challenge in the 1990s is not so much to engage the public as to make sure that the public understands the need for new approaches.

Recent opinion polls indicate that the public is willing to pay, and even make life style changes, in order to protect the environment. But the kind of public support that will be needed if the United States is to play a leadership role on the issues of the 1990s—including support for traditionally unpopular measures like increases in taxes and foreign assistance—will not come easily. All of the institutions discussed above will have to participate in the right way.

There is also a need for public education. Schools, network and public television, popular books, and efforts by civic and environmental groups have made the public broadly aware of many environmental problems. But it will take additional efforts to create understanding of the need for sustainable development and the actions required to bring it about.

Notes

[1] See, for example, Carnegie (1992a) and Mathews (1991).
[2] See Council on Environmental Quality (1971) and (1972).
[3] See Stoel, Miller, and Milroy (1980).
[4] It is noteworthy that Henry Kissinger's extensive memoirs mention only one environmental initiative: the treaty banning environmental warfare.
[5] Richard Benedick, the State Department diplomat who led U.S. efforts to secure a treaty preventing ozone depletion, refers to "senior officials who would

normally as a matter of principle [oppose] environmental regulations" and for whom "no persuasion seemed possible." Benedick (1991), pp. 58–59.

[6] See Benedick (1991) for an overview of the decision-making process on this issue from a governmental perspective.

[7] See Benedick (1991), pp. 59–66.

[8] See, for example, Schneider (1989).

[9] Gore (1992).

[10] Mathews (1991).

[11] See, for example, Schmidheiny (1992).

[12] Experience suggests that the public will be more supportive of multilateral or bilateral aid if it is designated specifically for environmental protection. The multilateral fund that is part of the Montreal Protocol for protection of the ozone layer provides one example of how to do this.

[13] In deciding on this organizational structure, the Clinton administration accepted the recommendation of the Carnegie Endowment/Institute for International Economics Commission on Government Renewal. An internal State Department study recommended that State have an under secretary for economics and the environment. See Carnegie (1992b), pp. 15–16, and U.S. Dept. of State (1992), organization chart.

[14] See Stoel (1992), p. 469.

Bibliography

Allison, Graham, and Gregory F. Treverton. 1992. *Rethinking America's Security: Beyond Cold War to New World Order.* New York: W.W. Norton.

Almond, Gabriel A. 1960. *The American People and Foreign Policy.* New York: Praeger.

Ambrose, Stephen E. 1991–92. "The Presidency and Foreign Policy." *Foreign Affairs* 70: 120–137.

Bartels, Larry M. 1991. "Constituency Opinion and Congressional Policy Making: The Reagan Defense Buildup." *The American Political Science Review* 85: 457–474.

Benedick, Richard. 1991. *Ozone Diplomacy.* Cambridge: Harvard University Press.

Bob, Daniel, and SRI International. 1990. *Japanese Companies in American Communities.* New York: Japan Society.

Bock, Joseph G., and Duncan L. Clarke. 1986. "The National Security Assistant and the White House Staff: National Security Policy Decisionmaking and Domestic Political Considerations, 1947–1984." *Presidential Studies Quarterly* 16: 258–279.

Burtless, Gary. 1990. *A Future of Lousy Jobs.* Washington, D.C.: The Brookings Institution.

Carnegie Endowment for Peace National Commission on America and the New World. 1992a. *Changing Our Ways: America and the New World*. Washington, D.C.: The Brookings Institution.

Carnegie Endowment and Institute for International Economics Commission on Government Renewal. 1992b. *Memorandum to the President-Elect: Harnessing Process to Purpose*. Washington, D.C.: Carnegie Endowment for International Peace.

Cotton, Timothy Y.C. 1986. "War and American Democracy: Electoral Costs of the Last Five Wars." *Journal of Conflict Resolution* 30: 616–635.

Council on Environmental Quality. 1971. *Environmental Quality: Second Annual Report*. Washington, D.C.: U.S. Government Printing Office.

———. 1972. *Environmental Quality: Third Annual Report*. Washington, D.C.: U.S. Government Printing Office.

Destler, I.M. 1992. *American Trade Politics*. New York: Institute for International Economics/Twentieth Century Fund. 2nd ed.

Destler, I.M., Leslie H. Gelb, and Anthony Lake. 1984. *Our Own Worst Enemy: The Unmaking of American Foreign Policy*. New York: Simon and Schuster.

Friedman, George, and Meredith LeBard. 1991. *The Coming War with Japan*. New York: St. Martin's Press.

Gergen, David. 1991. "America's New Heroes." *U.S. News & World Report*, February 11, 1991.

Goldsborough, James. 1993. "California's Foreign Policy." *Foreign Affairs* 72:2.

Gore, Albert. 1992. *Earth in the Balance*. Boston: Houghton Mifflin.

Green, Mark. ed. 1992. *Changing America: Blueprints for the New Administration*. New York: Newmarket Press.

Hansen, Carol Rae. ed. 1992. *The New World Order: Rethinking America's Global Role*. Flagstaff: Arizona Honors Academy Press.

Hyland, William. 1990. "America's New Course." *Foreign Affairs* 69:2.

Jentleson, Bruce W. 1992. "The Pretty Prudent Public: Post-Vietnam American Opinion on the Use of Military Force." *International Studies Quarterly* 36: 49–74.

Kennedy, Paul. 1987. *The Rise and Fall of the Great Powers*. New York: Vintage.

Krugman, Paul. 1992. *The Age of Diminished Expectations: U.S. Economic Policy in the 1990s*. Cambridge: Massachusetts Institute of Technology Press.

Mann, Thomas E. ed. 1992. *A Question of Balance*. Washington, D.C.: The Brookings Institution.

Mann, Thomas E., and Norman J. Ornstein. 1992. *Renewing Congress: A First Report*. Washington, D.C.: The Brookings Institution/American Enterprise Institute.

Mathews, Jessica Tuchman. ed. 1991. *Preserving the Global Environment: The Challenge of Shared Leadership*. New York: W.W. Norton.

Mathias, Charles McC. 1992. "Limits of Leadership: The United States." In Muller and Schweigler 1992.

Mayhew, David. 1992. *Divided We Govern*. New Haven: Yale University Press.

McCombs, Maxwell E., and Donald L. Shaw. 1976. "Structuring the Unseen Environment." *Journal of Communication* 26:2.

Moran, Theodore H. 1993. *American Economic Policy and National Security*. New York: Council on Foreign Relations Press.

Mueller, John E. 1971. "Trends in Popular Support for the Wars in Korea and Vietnam." *The American Political Science Review* 65: 358–375.

Mulcahy, Kevin. 1986. "The Secretary of State and the National Security Adviser: Foreign Policymaking in the Carter and Reagan Administrations." *Presidential Studies Quarterly* 16: 280–299.

Muller, Steven, and Gebhard Schweigler. eds. 1992. *From Occupation to Cooperation: The United States and United Germany in a Changing World Order*. New York: W.W. Norton.

National Security Strategy of the United States. 1991. Washington, D.C.: U.S. Government Printing Office.

Page, Benjamin I., and Robert J. Shapiro. 1988. "Foreign Policy and the Rational Public." *Journal of Conflict Resolution* 32: 211–247.

Prestowitz, Clyde. 1988. *Trading Places: How We Allowed Japan to Take the Lead*. New York: Basic Books.

Reich, Robert B. 1992. *The Work of Nations: Preparing Ourselves for 21st-Century Capitalism*. New York: Vintage Books.

Reilly, John. 1991. "Public Opinion: The Pulse of the '90s." *Foreign Policy* 82: 79–96.

Rowley, Anthony. "Ease Up Japan." *Far Eastern Economic Review*, August 6, 1992.

Schneider, William. 1992. "The Old Politics and the New World Order." In Hansen 1992.

Schlesinger, Arthur Jr. 1992. *The Disuniting of America*. New York: W.W. Norton.

Schlesinger, James. 1993. "Quest for a Post–Cold War Foreign Policy." *Foreign Affairs* 72:1.

Schmidheiny, Stephan. 1992. *Changing Course: A Global Business Perspective on Development and the Environment.* Cambridge: Massachusetts Institute of Technology Press.

Schneider, Stephen. 1989. *Global Warming: Are We Entering the Greenhouse Century?* San Francisco: Sierra Club Books.

Shapiro, R., and B. Page. 1988. "Foreign Policy and the National Public." *Journal of Conflict Resolution* 32: 211–247.

Stoel, Thomas. 1992. "Overview: Environmental Policy." In Green 1992.

Stoel, Thomas, Alan Miller, and Breck Milroy. 1980. *Fluorocarbon Regulation.* Lexington: Lexington Books.

U.S. Department of State Management Task Force. 1992. *State 2000: A New Model for Managing Foreign Affairs.* Washington, D.C.: U.S. Department of State.

Weigley, Russel F. 1973. *The American Way of War.* Bloomington: Indiana University Press.

Wright, John W. 1990. *The Universal Almanac.* Kansas City: Andrews and McMeel.

Yankelovich, Daniel. 1991. *Coming to Public Judgment: Making Democracy Work in a Complex World.* Syracuse: Syracuse University Press.

———. 1992. "A New Vision for U.S.–Japan Relations." Japan Society, *Business Luncheon Notes,* May 13, 1992.

Final Report of the Eighty-Third American Assembly

A t the close of their discussions, the participants in the Eighty-third American Assembly, on "Public Engagement in U.S. Foreign Policy After the Cold War," at Arden House, Harriman, New York, June 3–6, 1993, reviewed as a group the following statement. This statement represents general agreement; however, no one was asked to sign it. Furthermore, it should be understood that not everyone agreed with all of it.

When the cold war ended a new world began. Many Americans imagined that the United States could turn away from foreign affairs and finally concentrate attention on domestic problems—the budget deficit, the loss of jobs, decaying cities, polarized race relations, spiralling health care costs, the scourge of drugs, nonperforming schools. But reality soon intervened. There is a growing awareness that such problems have now spread across borders, and that the fate of the United States and its people is tied to actions in other countries, as well as what we do here at home.

The line separating "foreign" policy from "domestic" has become so blurred that much of our domestic success now rides on international affairs. Under these circumstances, genuine public participation in setting our new international agenda is both a growing reality and an increasing necessity. Yet a rigid distinction between foreign and domestic policies still dominates our institutions, habits, and practices. It underlies the notion that we can somehow shift our attention from "foreign policy" to "domestic priorities," when in fact the two are inextricably intertwined. But while this merging of two policy arenas and the public's need to be involved undeniably complicate matters, they also offer opportunities to advance the quality of our democracy.

During the cold war, the world was seemingly a more dangerous but a simpler place. We had an enemy, and our policy was to contain that enemy. That enemy has collapsed, and we have lost the unifying framework on which U.S. foreign policy was based. Now there is only a vacuum. Americans must forge a new framework that addresses the question of why and how much they want to be involved in trying to shape the larger world order.

The end of the cold war has also changed the main concerns of our policy: before 1990, they were largely political and military; in the future, they also include economic, humanitarian, and environmental concerns.

Since the late 1940s, our foreign policy has been formulated and executed from the top down by a foreign policy elite that functioned largely independently of the concerns and opinions of the public. Today, foreign policy is more influenced than ever before by the spontaneous and uncoordinated actions of citizen groups. If foreign policy could ever have been insulated from the hurly-burly of normal domestic politics, it cannot any longer. The defense budget, for example, now faces new competition for money for everything from social services to deficit reduction.

But it is not only the collapse of the Soviet Union that has put Americans in a new world. The United States has become an integral part of a new global economy. There is an international quest for investment, for jobs, and for new markets for goods and services. In this more competitive world, unskilled and semiskilled workers are especially vulnerable, and the widening gap between rich and poor has placed stress on our sense of community.

American society also faces other challenges.

• Demographic changes have brought about a diversity that is both a source of divisiveness and a valuable resource. Immigration from Asia and Latin America continues to change the nature and expectations of the public, with many Americans finding new ways to pursue their ethnic identities and interests in the political arena.

• Mistrust has grown. Citizens have diminished faith in the press, Congress, business, the major political parties, and many other institutions whose role is to mediate between citizens and their government. Instead, the public seeks out groups or individuals who claim to be independent of vested interests.

• Technology has drastically increased the ability of citizens to reach and organize others of like mind. Interactive television, 900 numbers, faxes, computer bulletin boards, modems, cable television, talk shows—all these and more offer opportunities for direct action and communication. But this new technology also presents risks. For example, instant polling can distort and trivialize public opinion, undermining serious deliberation.

We can address these challenges only if citizens from all regions, sectors, and groups participate in defining a new and sustainable national consensus. This must be grounded not only in people's self-interest and personal values, but linked also to a broader conception of the nation's interests. People must accept that with active participation in the national dialogue comes grave individual responsibilities: to pay taxes for the common good, and, if need be, to take up arms or support those who do.

Our hopes rest not in a new "foreign" policy devised by a few "wise men" meeting in their own private councils or the inner circles of government, but in public deliberation, communication, and consultation among broad groups of interested and informed citizens. Sustainable solutions on the most critical issues will depend on engaging the public in decision making at all levels.

Engaging the public in this manner can strengthen our democracy, but will be far from easy to accomplish. How can a genuine dialogue be initiated between leaders and citizens under conditions of inattention, mistrust, and fragmented interests? How can we raise the level of public attention to complex foreign policy subjects and information about them? These are hard questions, but they must be answered by a public whose voice is sober, thoughtful, and responsible—the voice of a considered public judgment. Failure will result in a public voice that is angry, resentful, impulsive, and irresponsible, one that will impede the country's ability to cope with today's international complexities.

In a sense we need to return to 1946, when we engaged in a nationwide consensus-building discussion about the basic framework of U.S. foreign policy. Then we defined the world in terms of a struggle between democracy and communism, a moral framework that guided specific policies. In 1990 this framework collapsed. We now require a grand dialogue as to what the new value-driven framework ought to be for the U.S. role in the post–cold war era. However, it now must engage a much broader group of Americans.

Moving Toward Serious Public Dialogue

How should Americans respond? First, we need to rethink how we develop policy and how the government can invite the public to participate in shaping it. The issues are complex, involving competing interests and strongly held values. Policy choices must reflect these. Leaders and citizens need to engage in a two-way process of sorting out the nation's choices, so that all involved can understand and confront their real costs and benefits.

Unfortunately, the government continues to operate in the cold war mode. When national security considerations were the prime determinant of foreign policy, this may have been a viable model. However, now that other concerns—economic, humanitarian, environmental—take an increasing share of the national agenda, other actors such as private citizen groups both initiate and carry out policies that are truly international in scope, sometimes in competition with national organizations and leaders.

The timing and nature of public involvement will differ from issue to issue. The decision-making process on Bosnia will be different from that on the North American Free Trade Agreement (NAFTA) or on global warming, and so will the process of public engagement. But a broad range of institutions will be engaged. To these we now turn.

The Presidency

The challenge begins with the president. We have inherited a conception of the "man in the Oval Office" hearing all the evidence, making lonely decisions, and then persuading the nation. This role is appropriate for many issues. The president must make hard decisions on complex matters, particularly in the national security sphere. However, foreign policy making increasingly resembles the process by which domestic policies are made, and the president must be prepared to build mutually supportive coalitions at home and abroad that will give authority and legitimacy to his/her decisions. Therefore, there are important occasions when the president needs to adopt a more collegial form of leadership: as leader and *energizer* of the process by which the nation comes to resolution of difficult issues.

The goal of this process is to lead other citizens and institutions to confront controversial issues and make durable policy choices. This involves listening, drawing out people's interests, and values, crafting policy proposals that respond creatively to these, re-exploring and readjusting them, and then presenting a well-reasoned choice. The president needs to be a leader in touch with the people, interacting with them and responsive to their wishes, but also articulating their stakes in seemingly distant international issues.

There are several methods available to a president as he/she plays this role.

- Regular press conferences are helpful, but means should be sought to bring in more questions that reflect broad public concerns, not the latest hot-button issue inside the beltway. More frequent meetings might also mitigate this tendency. The president should also experiment with press conferences outside of Washington, D.C. to give resonance to issues that are important beyond the beltway.
- "Town hall" meetings *can* provide good face-to-face communication between presidents and citizens, but mainly if they address issues that are still in the deliberative phase so there can be a genuine exchange of ideas. Members of the president's cabinet and staff should regularly hold such meetings as well.

• The Little Rock economic forum of December 1992 was a useful educational tool, because it exposed a broad audience to an assortment of expert presentations, underscoring the complexity of issues and choices. But future forums of this type should involve a broader spectrum of Americans.

Through these and other approaches, the president can work with Americans in shaping the policy goals that will guide them into the next century.

This role is not without risk. By consulting and deliberating with the nation, its friends and allies, rather than simply deciding and informing them, the president may sometimes be criticized for weakness or vacillation. However, if presidents persist in this approach on selected issues, and if the nation is responsive to it, the resulting policies will ultimately be more sustainable, for they will better reflect a shared vision that unites the citizenry.

The Executive Branch

Reform of the Department of State, the U.S. Agency for International Development, intelligence gathering, and other foreign policy entities should reflect the growing interdependence of foreign and domestic affairs. Expanded public affairs and intergovernmental exchange programs can connect the nation's diplomats more directly to state and local issues, giving practical meaning to Secretary of State Warren Christopher's concept of an American desk at the Department of State. Foreign assistance can build transnational, grassroots partnerships between our civil society and those of emerging democracies and market economies abroad.

The Congress

In the vision of our Constitution's framers, Congress was to be *the* institution linking citizens with their government. Yet public respect for Congress has rarely been lower. Its members are increasingly seen as careerists linked more to Washington than to the communities that sent them. Despite continual communications with constituents and near-weekly flights to members' home districts, Congress is seen as being out of touch with the people.

Seldom are members seen as acting in the national interest rather than in some special interest. Yet they, like citizens at large, are caught in webs not of their own making. Driven by the need to raise campaign money, locked into narrow committee jurisdictions and roles, victims of increasingly frenetic schedules, members of Congress find it ever more difficult to play *the* deliberative role so central to a strong legislature and its public reputation. The public, in turn, looks toward term limits and other changes that address symptoms of the problem rather than root causes.

The Gulf debate of January 1991 was a glowing exception: members were seen not as representing special interests but as representing the public as they deliberated seriously and responsibly about whether to go to war, and moving to individual judgment. The public watched, and when the vote was taken to use force, there was a sense that the issue had been fairly joined and a legitimate decision reached. Congress rose sharply—albeit temporarily—in public esteem.

Many specific procedural changes could improve Congress's functioning; these are beyond our capacity to consider here in detail. So is campaign finance reform, which may well be the heart of the matter. Pending basic structural change, Congress should look for ways to replicate the Gulf experience—to engage in serious dialogue with each other before a national audience on important national issues. At the committee level, genuine issue fora cannot replace the typical, sparsely attended hearings, but they could offer a supplement, and C-SPAN can bring them to a small but influential national audience. Issue fora at home can enrich ties with constituents. In these ways, members of Congress will be seen and heard going about the nation's business.

More broadly, Congress should consider organizational reforms that enable members and committees to take broader views of issues—cutting the number of subcommittees, and members' assignments to them; employing ad hoc, temporary panels for issues that cut across current jurisdictions; and revising the jurisdictions of committees to improve their focus on the increasingly economic substance of "foreign" policy issues.

The Media

The breakdown of the sharp distinction between "foreign" and "domestic" policy creates new roles and opportunities for the media, but we should keep in mind that the media are no longer simply the traditional press, consisting of establishment journals, newspapers, and networks. They now include a vast array of alternative communications vehicles, such as public access cable television, call-in talk shows, "infotainment," specialty media, computer and telecommunications networks, and in the near future, interactive television. We are only just beginning to grasp the implications of these rapidly multiplying sources of information and opinion, but it is already clear that they will be central to engaging the public in the formulation of national policy. They offer many avenues for communicating with both the general public and particular segments of the population, and, increasingly, ways of engaging the public in two-way conversations.

The media also have a critical role in making more explicit the links between events in distant lands and their repercussions for average Americans. Local newspapers and television stations, in particular, need to illuminate the fact that foreign affairs has become a local story. To make this vital connection, media leaders need to enlarge their own understanding of our interdependent world through, for instance, career education, seminars, trade publications, and foreign fellowships. We urge national news organizations to enlarge their coverage of international economics, which has such direct impact on the U.S. workforce.

Nongovernmental Groups

Between the centers of foreign policy making and the general public is a growing number of intermediary groups: nongovernmental organizations (NGOs), labor and business (including multinational corporations), and grassroots citizen movements. They play three distinct roles: as actors independent of Washington, as influences on Washington, and as implementers of government programs ranging from promoting democracy in Russia to combatting hunger in Somalia. In all three roles, such associations and advocacy groups bring both exposure and intensity of view to the process of defining policy options and determining the policies themselves. Furthermore, they seek to engage their constituents on issues and choices with specific transnational implications, without necessarily considering consultation at the national level. But if those often competing and narrow based interests are not properly balanced, there is a risk of paralysis in policy, or government-by-interest-group. Neither contributes to building broad based, post-cold war public support for far-sighted policies.

One key to the role of private, issue-focused groups lies in the marketplace of broader public opinion. The debate over the relative merits of NAFTA, for example, has served as a catalyst for an extraordinary level of transnational networking and coalition building among heretofore unconnected individuals and interest groups throughout North America, involving both supporters and opponents of the agreement. This activity has extended not just to those with commercial interests, but to groups deeply concerned with matters of values ranging from protection of the environment to immigration issues. Potentially, these activities can invite the general public to consider the merits of NAFTA and similar policies in a more knowledgeable light.

Thus, in a variety of ways and at numerous levels, nongovernmental actors are fully engaged. Indeed, on issues like the environment, they are sometimes in the lead.

It is important to balance a vision of these groups as basically destabilizing in nature with the recognition that these networks of domestic interest groups and crossborder coalitions also weave together the interests of the citizenry across borders and across interest groups, contributing to the formation of an evolving notion of societal independence.

State and Local Governments

States and localities are also assuming an increasingly active role on the foreign policy scene. Many have established direct economic, cultural, and humanitarian relationships with their foreign counterparts, and are now asserting the interests of their constituencies with the federal government on a broad range of trade and other economic issues. They have also taken action on more traditional foreign policy matters, most notably in the context of relations with South Africa, which has had a direct impact on the national foreign policy.

The General Public

The institutional changes we have discussed are not enough in themselves to forge a better connection between the public and policy making. They need to be part of a broader strategy for public deliberation. Without such a strategy, the institutions, no matter how thoroughly they are revised, are likely to revert to old patterns. Just as the foreign policy/domestic policy dichotomy is enshrined in our understanding, so, too, is there an enshrined model of communicating with the public. This is based on an increasingly outmoded model of "public education," where leaders impart some of their greater knowledge to the masses and the public is expected to climb on board.

Changing realities force us to rethink how various publics can participate in the policy process. We need to recognize that although there is incredible diversity in our society, there are also certain shared core values. We need to build on and encourage the nascent shift in moral attitudes, away from an almost exclusive emphasis on rights and entitlements toward a more balanced view wherein responsibilities are as important as rights, and where reciprocity plays a central role. For instance, some domestic sacrifice from the public will be necessary to strengthen our economy in the race for a fair share of the global marketplace.

An effective strategy must start with a new understanding of who the public is and how people think. Public deliberation is not just a matter of absorbing facts. From the public's point of view, most of the issues we are talking about—immigration, economic competition, diversity, military intervention—also evoke passion, emotion, and values. The emotional nature of these issues creates fierce resistance, causing the public to seek either superficial and painless solutions or one-sided ones. Until and unless these value questions are directly addressed, the public will not give its government lasting support for carrying out any solution.

What is required is a new way of thinking about the public and public opinion, one that recognizes that deliberation is an ongoing process. It moves through a series of stages, from the first awareness that an issue is important, through the painful task of wrestling with the pros and cons of various solutions, to a final consensus or compromise, itself subject to reconsideration. This journey cannot be carried out by the public alone. Leaders in government, business, labor, the universities, and the media have to present a broader range of choices to the public in a timely fashion and create mechanisms that will allow the various publics to debate and discuss those choices.

Greater public engagement in foreign policy must also be accompanied by heightened support for education in world affairs. Abundant survey data attest to widespread public ignorance of basic geography, and to lack of knowledge and understanding of other languages and cultures. Efforts underway across the nation to strengthen elementary and secondary curricula must urgently address these needs. Moreover, the nation's colleges and universities should be urged not only to change their curricula and increase opportunities for exchange programs, but also to serve their communities as lively centers of public information and discussion on international issues and how they affect the daily lives of citizens. Through strengthening the role of international education, we can equip the next generation to be active participants in the public dialogue because they will understand the global dimension of policy decisions.

While leaders can facilitate the process, the public itself must be ready to do the hard work of sorting out the pros and cons, working through its own resistances and value conflicts, and coming to see the necessity of hard choices and difficult trade-offs. Only then can leaders take responsibility for fashioning and implementing policy with confidence that it can be sustained.

Participants
The Eighty-Third American Assembly

H. BRANDT AYERS
Editor and Publisher
The Anniston Star
Anniston, AL

DOUGLAS J. BENNET, JR.
Assistant Secretary of State for
    International Organizations
U.S. Department of State
Washington, DC

LEO BOGART
New York, NY

FRANCES J. BRACKETT
Executive Director
Charlotte World Affairs
    Council
Office of International
    Programs
University of North
    Carolina—Charlotte
Charlotte, NC

SAM BROWNBACK
Secretary of Agriculture
Kansas State Board of
    Agriculture
Topeka, KS

*FRANCES G. BURWELL
Executive Director
Center for International and
    Security Studies at
    Maryland
School of Public Affairs
University of Maryland
College Park, MD

JOHN H. COSTELLO
President
The Citizens Network for
    Foreign Affairs
Washington, DC

†LESTER M. CRYSTAL
Executive Producer
MacNeil/Lehrer Newshour
New York, NY

*GREGORY CURTIS
Editor
Texas Monthly
Austin, TX

I. M. DESTLER
Director
Center for International and
    Security Studies at
    Maryland
School of Public Affairs
University of Maryland
College Park, MD

†ROBERT H. DONALDSON
President
The University of Tulsa
Tulsa, OK

†AMITAI ETZIONI
University Professor
George Washington University
Washington, DC

PAUL FORD
Chairman-elect
Foreign Policy Association
Partner
Simpson Thacher & Bartlett
New York, NY

CAROL L. GARNER
Executive Director
Columbus Council on World
    Affairs
Columbus, OH

*JAMES O.
    GOLDSBOROUGH
Foreign Affairs Columnist
San Diego Union-Tribune
San Diego, CA

RITA E. HAUSER
President
The Hauser Foundation
Chair of the Board
International Peace Academy
New York, NY

‡JAMES F. HOGE, JR.
Editor
Foreign Affairs
New York, NY

JOHN IMMERWAHR
Senior Research Fellow
Public Agenda Foundation
Chair
Department of Philosophy
Villanova University
Villanova, PA

‡B. R. INMAN
Chairman of the Executive
    Committee
Science Applications
    International Corporation
Austin, TX

STEVEN L. ISENBERG
Deputy Publisher
Newsday/New York Newsday
Long Island and New York
    City, NY

MAHNAZ ISPAHANI
Program Officer, U.S. Foreign
    Policy
The Ford Foundation
New York, NY

ARNOLD L. KANTER
Senior Fellow
The RAND Corporation
Washington, DC

ROBERT A. KAPP
President
Washington Council on
    International Trade
Seattle, WA

ADRIAN KARATNYCKY
Assistant to the President
AFL-CIO
Washington, DC

RONALD S. KATZ
Coudert Brothers
San Francisco, CA

CATHERINE McARDLE
    KELLEHER
Senior Fellow, Foreign Policy
    Studies
The Brookings Institution
Washington, DC

ALAN R. KEMPER
Former Chairman
National Corn Growers
    Association
Lafayette, IN

CHARLOTTE KENNEDY
Executive Director
World Affairs Council of
    Oregon
Portland, OR

STEVEN KULL
Director
Program on International
    Policy Attitudes
Center for International and
    Security Studies at
    Maryland
School of Public Affairs
University of Maryland
College Park, MD

**GEORGE LATIMER
Former Mayor of St. Paul,
    Minnesota
Dean, School of Law
Hamline University
Minneapolis, MN

HUGH J. LAWSON
Program Assistant
Office of the President
Rockefeller Brothers Fund
New York, NY

SALLY LILIENTHAL
President
The Ploughshares Fund
San Francisco, CA

FRANKLIN A. LINDSAY
Chairman (retired)
Itek Corporation
Associate
Center for International Affairs
Harvard University
Cambridge, MA

**ABRAHAM F.
    LOWENTHAL
Director
Center of International Studies
University of Southern
    California
Los Angeles, CA

RICHARD W. LYMAN
President Emeritus
Stanford University
Palo Alto, CA

LAWRENCE MALKIN
Chief U.S. Correspondent
International Herald Tribune
New York, NY

KAY J. MAXWELL
President
League of Women Voters of
    Connecticut
Greenwich, CT

†DONALD F. McHENRY
University Research
    Professor of Diplomacy &
    International Affairs
School of Foreign Service
Georgetown University
Washington, DC

JAMES MOODY
Professor, Health Policy
Medical College of
    Wisconsin
Milwaukee, WI

NORMAN J. ORNSTEIN
Resident Scholar
American Enterprise
    Institute for Public Policy
    Research
Washington, DC

ALVIN H. PERLMUTTER
President
Alvin H. Perlmutter, Inc.
New York, NY

DON REEVES
Director
Trade & Development
  Program
Bread for the World
Institute on Hunger &
  Development
Washington, DC

WILLIAM A. REINSCH
Legislative Assistant
Office of Senator John D.
  Rockefeller IV
United States Senate
Washington, DC

ROBERT L. RINNE
Senior Adviser for National
  Security
Sandia National Laboratories
Livermore, CA

MEREDITH REID
  SARKEES
Department of Political
  Science
Niagara University
Niagara, NY

THEODORE SCHELL
Senior Vice President
Strategic Planning and
  Corporate Development
Sprint Corporation
Kansas City, MO

ENID C. B. SCHOETTLE
Senior Fellow
Director, Project on
  International Organizations
  & Law
Council on Foreign Relations
New York, NY

SUSAN C. SCHWAB
Former Assistant Secretary and
  Director General
U.S. and Foreign Commercial
  Service
U.S. Department of
  Commerce
Washington, DC

JOHN W. SEWELL
President
Overseas Development
  Council
Washington, DC

SUSAN L. SHIRK
Director
Institute on Global Conflict &
  Cooperation
University of California, San
  Diego
La Jolla, CA

PETER J. SPIRO
Shea & Gardner
Washington, DC

THOMAS B. STOEL, JR.
Environmental Attorney &
  Consultant
Washington, DC

JOHN STREMLAU
Deputy Director
Policy Planning Staff
U.S. Department of State
Washington, DC

CATHRYN L. THORUP
Acting Director
Center for U.S.-Mexican
  Studies
University of California, San
  Diego
La Jolla, CA

ROBERT C. TOTH
Former National Security and
   Foreign Correspondent of
   Los Angeles Times
Times Mirror Center for the
   People & the Press
Washington, DC

ROBERT J. WHITE
Associate Editor
Editorial Department
Star Tribune
Minneapolis, MN

**DOUGLAS C. WORTH
Vice President
Governmental Programs
International Business
   Machines Corporation
Washington, DC

BERNELL WRIGHT
Vice President, Strategic
   Alliance
Citibank Corporate
   Technology Office, Inc.
New York, NY

DANIEL YANKELOVICH
Chairman
DYG, Inc.
President
Public Agenda Foundation
New York, NY

GORDON B. ZACKS
Chairman & Chief Executive
   Officer
R. G. Barry Corporation
Pickerington, OH

**Discussion Leader
*Rapporteur
‡Delivered Formal Address
†Panelist

STEERING COMMITTEE AND ADVISERS

for International Series of American Assemblies

Michael H. Armacost
George W. Ball
C. Fred Bergsten
Zbigniew Brzezinski
William P. Bundy
Richard N. Cooper
Kenneth W. Dam
Jan V. Dauman
Edwin A. Deagle, Jr.
*Lawrence S. Eagleburger
Geza Feketekuty
Harry L. Freeman
Alton Frye
Richard N. Gardner
George J.W. Goodman
Robert D. Hormats
Robert H. Legvold
Roger E. Levien
William H. Luers

Jessica Tuchman Mathews
Charles McC. Mathias, Jr.
Donald F. McHenry
Martha T. Muse
Joseph S. Nye, Jr.
Robert Oxnam
Victor H. Palmieri
Hugh T. Patrick
William D. Rogers
John G. Ruggie
Enid Schoettle
*Brent Scowcroft
John W. Sewell
Jack Sheinkman
Alfred C. Stepan
**Peter Tarnoff
Cyrus R. Vance
Marina v. N. Whitman

*Resigned to join the Bush administration
**Resigned to join the Clinton administration

The American Assembly

The American Assembly was established by Dwight D. Eisenhower at Columbia University in 1950. It holds nonpartisan meetings and publishes authoritative books to illuminate issues of United States policy.

An affiliate of Columbia, the Assembly is a national, educational institution incorporated in the state of New York. The Assembly seeks to provide information, stimulate discussion, and evoke independent conclusions on matters of vital public interest.

American Assembly Sessions

At least two national programs are initiated each year. Authorities are retained to write background papers presenting essential data and defining the main issues of each subject.

A group of men and women representing a broad range of experience, competence, and American leadership meet for several days to discuss the Assembly topic and consider alternatives for national policy.

All Assemblies follow the same procedure. The background papers are sent to participants in advance of the Assembly. The Assembly meets in small groups for four lengthy periods. All groups use the same agenda. At the close of these informal sessions participants adopt in plenary session a final report of findings and recommendations.

Regional, state, and local Assemblies are held following the national session at Arden House. Assemblies have also been held in England, Switzerland, Malaysia, Canada, the Caribbean, South America, Central America, the Philippines, and Japan. Over one hundred sixty institutions have cosponsored one or more Assemblies.

Arden House

The home of The American Assembly and the scene of the national sessions is Arden House, which was given to Columbia University in 1950 by W. Averell Harriman. E. Roland Harriman joined his brother in contributing toward adaptation of the property for conference purposes. The buildings and surrounding land, known as the Harriman Campus of Columbia University, are fifty miles north of New York City.

THE AMERICAN ASSEMBLY

Columbia University

CLIFFORD M. HARDIN	Missouri
J. ERIK JONSSON	Texas
KATHLEEN H. MORTIMER	New York
CLARENCE C. WALTON	Pennsylvania

Index